FENTON ART GLASS

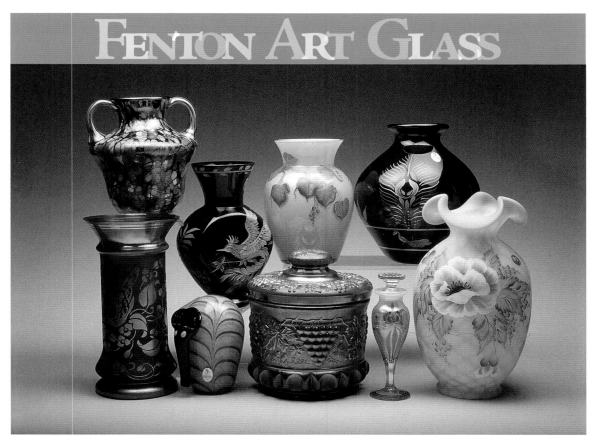

A Centennial of Glass Making
1907 to 2007 and Beyond

Revised and Expanded Second Edition

Debbie and Randy Coe

Schiffer Publishing Ltd

4880 Lower Valley Road • Atglen, PA 19310

Other Schiffer Books By The Author:
Animal Pitchers. ISBN: 0764323857. $19.95
Avon's 1876 Cape Cod Collection: Glass Dinnerware.
    ISBN: 9780764336799. $19.99
The Colors of Heisey Glass. ISBN: 0764325078. $35.00
Corning Pyroceram® Cookware. ISBN: 9780764331398. $29.99
Elegant Glass: Early, Depression and Beyond.
    ISBN: 9780764327759. $29.95
Fenton Basket Patterns: Acanthus to Hummingbird.
    ISBN: 0764322729. $29.95
Fenton Basket Patterns: Innovation to Wisteria & Numbers.
    ISBN: 0764322907. $29.95
Fenton Burmese Glass. ISBN: 076431968X. $29.95
Glass Animals & Figurines. ISBN: 0764317075. $29.95
Liberty Blue Dinnerware. ISBN: 0764324713. $14.95

Other Schiffer Books on Related Subjects:
The Big Book of Fenton Milk Glass, 1940-1985. John Walk.
    ISBN: 076431596X. $29.95
Early Fenton Rarities: 1907-1938. Thomas K. Smith.
    ISBN: 0764322877. $29.95
Fenton Glass Cats & Dogs. Tara Coe-McRitchie.
    ISBN: 0764314890. $19.95
Fenton Glass Compendium: 1940-1970. John Walk.
    ISBN: 0764314084. $29.95
Fenton Glass Compendium: 1970-1985. John Walk.
    ISBN: 0764313444. $29.95
Fenton Rarities, 1940-1985. John Walk.
    ISBN: 0764315951. $29.95
Glass Elephants. Myra Coe-Hixson.
    ISBN: 0764319353. $24.95

Schiffer Books are available at special discounts for bulk purchases for sales promotions or premiums. Special editions, including personalized covers, corporate imprints, and excerpts can be created in large quantities for special needs. For more information contact the publisher:

Published by Schiffer Publishing, Ltd.
4880 Lower Valley Road
Atglen, PA 19310
Phone: (610) 593-1777; Fax: (610) 593-2002
E-mail: Info@schifferbooks.com

For the largest selection of fine reference books on this and related subjects, please visit our website at **www.schifferbooks.com**
We are always looking for people to write books on new and related subjects. If you have an idea for a book, please contact us at proposals@schifferbooks.com

This book may be purchased from the publisher.
Please try your bookstore first.
You may write for a free catalog.

In Europe, Schiffer books are distributed by
Bushwood Books
6 Marksbury Ave.
Kew Gardens
Surrey TW9 4JF England
Phone: 44 (0) 20 8392 8585; Fax: 44 (0) 20 8392 9876
E-mail: info@bushwoodbooks.co.uk
Website: www.bushwoodbooks.co.uk

Copyright © 2012 by Debbie & Randy Coe
Library of Congress Control Number: 2012939777

Type set in Adobe Jenson/Souvenir Lt BT

ISBN: 978-0-7643-3680-5
Printed in China

A view of factory under construction in 1906
Archival photo used with permission from the Fenton Art Glass Company

Contents

A view of the bay window inside the Fenton Art Glass Museum

A view inside
the Collectors
Showcase shop

ACKNOWLEDGMENTS

Both our daughters along with their husbands, Tara & Jeff McRitchie and Myra & Stephen Hixson, have shared some of their own collections with us for this publication. We really appreciate their generosity. They are the love of our life and we feel truly blessed to have them enrich our lives. Our first grand child, Amelia Hixson, was born in October 2006 and we have already given her some Fenton animals. Since our last edition, we have been blessed with two more granddaughters, Avery Hixson in November 2008 and Faith McRitchie in January 2010. As we were completing this edition, Tara and Jeff have announced they are expecting our next grandchild in July 2012. It is never too early to get a person started on collecting. We feel a collecting family stays in closer touch with each other. Even with our busy lives, we need to take time to do things with the ones we love. We also have an additional thank you to Tara and Jeff for their assistance in proofing our information and assisting with the book format.

All of the following people either brought glass to our house to photograph, allowed us to come to their home to photograph or allowed us to photograph their Fenton at a show or at the Pacific Northwest Fenton Association (PNWFA) annual convention. Because of these people's generosity, this book contains a vast assortment of beautiful glass. We are deeply indebted to all of you. A giant thank you goes out to: Darlene & Gordon Cochran; Ckris & Judy Cord; John Fallahee; Dovie & John Fields; Dan & Delene Haake, Bill Harmon, Debbie & Ed Lane; Donna & Ron Miller; Jackie Shirley; Dean Six; Jack & Jackie Skaw; Les & Jackie Stewart; Francis & Gretchen Thompson; Juanita Williams & Jean Word.

Marian Thornton and her daughter Jenni Halverson own a huge Fenton shop called Collectors Showcase in Snohomish, Washington. We were allowed access to the entire shop to photograph any of the glass we needed. We had so many beautiful pieces of glass, both old and new, to photograph. It was such a great advantage to have so many pieces in one place that we felt like we were in glass heaven. In the upper right corner is a photo of her shop so you can see how much is packed into one place. If you see a piece pictured in this book that you would like to buy, feel free to contact Marian or Jenni, since it may have come out of their shop. Their phone number is: 360-568-1339 or email at: collectorsshowcase@verizon.net

John Walk is another generous person who supplied us with some glass patterns that we were not able to find in our area. This sharing of information between authors helps all of our jobs go so much easier. We really appreciate all of his help.

We greatly appreciate all of the information that Nancy and George Fenton provided us about themselves and about the company. Their assistance was a terrific asset to this book. George and Nancy have spent many hours studying marketing trends to see that their products have an appeal to the current decorating theme and collecting market. Their insight was greatly appreciated and we thank them for providing the Foreword. We also appreciate the effort they spent reviewing our material.

Howard Seufer formerly worked for Fenton in quality control. Even though he is now retired from Fenton, he is very enthusiastic about helping whenever the need arises. He frequently is called upon to take photos for different events at Fenton. Once again he came to our assistance by photographing various family members, decorators and designers along with some scenes from the factory. These photos would not have been possible without his help. He is one super guy with a great love and devotion for Fenton.

There are some terrific people at Fenton who were very valuable to us when trying to get things accomplished clear across the country. Jennifer Maston was a huge help to Howard Seufer when he was in the museum photographing various pieces for us. James Measell furnished us information about the pieces in the museum. Chris Benson provided us some detailed information.

We were very fortunate in September 2011 to add a great many photographs while we were in Colorado doing the Pike's Peak Glass Show in Castle Rock. While there, Marcee Becker also provided us with some great hospitality and we were able to photograph so many different examples in her home. She is one awesome lady along with her family who we really appreciate for all the sharing they provided to us.

A huge thank you to all of you. This book was only made possible because of the generous sharing from everyone.

George Fenton, President of Fenton Art Glass Company

FOREWORD

Fenton Art Glass is now over 105 years old. The world and we have gone through vast changes since those first days of decorating functional pitcher sets in Martins Ferry, Ohio. The constant through it all has been a Fenton passion for producing fine quality colored glass.

During these 105 years we paid homage to the "art" in Fenton Art Glass by redeveloping lost colors from the nineteenth century, inventing new ones and seeking out exceptional artists to push the envelope in glass decoration. Glass baskets are another area of artistic craftsmanship in continuous development at Fenton. We have produced more basket shapes and handle styles than any company in the world. Visitors to our studio delight in watching fiery liquid ribbons turn into perfectly arched handles within seconds.

Fenton handlers are proud of their skills. The finishing touch to a Fenton basket is the handler's "mark." The mark is earned only after a long period of training and apprenticeship. When finally reaching the status of handler, the craftsman designs a personal stamp that becomes his mark, or signature, to complete each basket he makes.

Interest in handcrafted glass has ebbed and flowed throughout our long history. We would like to thank Debbie and Randy Coe for their work in supporting glass art, and specifically Fenton, as they educate new readers about the hand craftsmanship of glass.

George and Nancy Fenton
March 2011
Note: This foreword was sent to us before the factory announcement was made in July 2011.

Nancy Fenton, Director of Design

INTRODUCTION

Our goal in doing this book is to leave a lasting testament of all the many beautiful different types of glass that Fenton produced in the last 100 years. We wanted to provide a wide range of glass examples that were first produced when the factory opened and continue through all of the decades up to the present. We felt a true presentation of beautiful Fenton glass under one cover for the first time would truly delight all types of collectors.

How often do you get to witness two monumental events of one glass company? In the last couple of years, Fenton family, employees and collectors have had a chance to celebrate the impact that the Fenton Art Glass Company has had on the collecting community. In 2005, Fenton marked their 100 years of being in business. This is quite an accomplishment when you consider how many glass companies never made it to this point.

The start of 2011 for Fenton was one of hope that they could see their way through their economic problems. By June, that hope had diminished and was replaced with despair. On July 6th, George Fenton made the very sad announcement that they were ceasing glass production. He stated that the company would begin liquidating glass and would be looking at different options to keep the company afloat. See the full announcement in the last chapter.

Through the eleven decades at Fenton, numerous changes have taken place at the factory. Technological updates have been made throughout the factory. Yet, when you step into the glass factory itself, some things remain the same. The glass is still mixed in batches with the color formulas carefully guarded. The workers handle the molten glass and either blow or press it into a mould. The piece can be flared or crimped into a special shape. The decorators all hand-apply the paint. The term "hand made" is an accurate description of all of the gorgeous glass that is produced at Fenton.

Both the beginning and advanced collector will find this book a necessary and convenient reference source to stimulate their enjoyment of beautiful Fenton Glass.

The front of the factory that serves as the entrance to the gift shop.

MEASUREMENTS

Like all hand made glass, some variations will exist in size from one piece to the next. Catalog listings will show a size from the mould. Actual height and width measurements were taken off each piece of glass as it was photographed. As the glass worker handles each piece, the size can change. The vase could be swung out more or the handle could be pulled more. Then again, if the handle is taller, the width might be smaller. If the handle is shorter, then the width would be wider. When the shape was irregular, the larger measurement was used. Hand made means each piece is special and unique.

VALUE GUIDE

All the values shown in this book are for glassware in **mint condition only**. Any type of damage will diminish the value of the piece. The discounted value should be reflected on the extent of the damage and whether it hurts the appearance of the piece. An air bubble in the glass would be considered minimum as compared to a huge crack. Pieces that have been repaired also should reflect a value far below normal, depending on their appearance.

Both collectors and dealers were consulted to contribute values so we could obtain a true reflection of the current market. The listed values have been derived from actual dealer sales, what collectors have paid, prices seen at shows, auction results and national publications. Some of the pieces were not found on the secondary market prices, so the value listed here was based upon the original selling price. As with any type of collectible glass, there are some regional differences in supply and demand.

Ultimately, the collector needs to decide what they would be willing pay for a specific item. The authors have tried to list sustainable values and not ones for an isolated piece selling for a record amount. Their job was to report the prices that were found, not to set values based on their opinions. This book is to be used only as a guide when determining what an item is worth, based on available information. Many older items have appreciated in value because of the cost of a similar new item. Other times prices do go down based on the supply and demand for the piece. This fact is not popular, but one that has became a reality for most dealers and collectors.

Some pieces are so rare—or even unique—that it is impossible to give a fair evaluation of the price. For this situation we have used the following: **Value Not Established**.

Neither the author nor publishers assume any responsibility for transactions that may occur because of this book.

1907 TO 1909
THE BEGINNING YEARS

After several years of working for someone else, Frank and his brother John decided to establish their own company in 1905. At that time they were actually just a decorating company. They bought glass from several different companies and then decorated it in their own fashion. This continued to work well for some time until these glass companies realized how much Fenton was making off their glass and decided to taper off how much glass they sold Fenton. One way of not being dependent on someone else is to develop your own source. That is exactly what the Fenton brothers decided to do. They proceeded to build their own factory.

The transition from only decorating glass from other companies to actually making their own must have been a triumphant one for Fenton and because of this, we consider the year of 1907 to be very monumental. The goal of making their first piece of glass before New Years day of 1907 was only missed by two days. Fenton's first actual piece of glass was produced on January 2, 1907. The Fenton family and all their workers were now on their way to establishing themselves in the glass industry. They must have felt such a joy and a sense of pride to see the very first piece of glass made at the new Fenton factory. A crystal cream pitcher in the Water Lily and Cattails pattern was that special first piece. Factory photos from 1907 also show decorated water sets and opalescent glass being made that first year.

John Fenton was president, his brother Frank L. held the position of secretary & general manager, and their brother Charles was vice-president. It soon became apparent that John and Frank could not work together. John left to found the Millersburg Glass Company in 1909. Frank assumed the presidency and two other brothers, Robert and James, joined the company.

One of the first types of glass that Fenton produced was an iridescent style of glass that had a rainbow sheen to it. Metallic salts were sprayed on a pressed pattern while it is still hot to develop a beautiful hue on the surface. This glass would set the Fentons off to an early successful start. In the October 24, 1907 *Crockery and Glass Journal*, this new glass was called Iridill and proclaimed as having a metallic luster finish just like the Favrile glass being made at Tiffany. These wonderful names gave the air of fine elegance to the relatively inexpensive new type of glassware. The journal described this new glass as being made by the Fenton Art Glass Company and was listed as being reasonably priced. As this decade was ending, Carnival glass became a prime leader in Fenton's sales.

Chocolate, 1907 to 1910
Left: Waterlily and Cattail #8, Butter, **$125; Right:** Orange Tree #1902, Hat pin holder, **$98**

Founding family photo in 1907
*Archival photo used with permission
from the Fenton Art Glass Company*

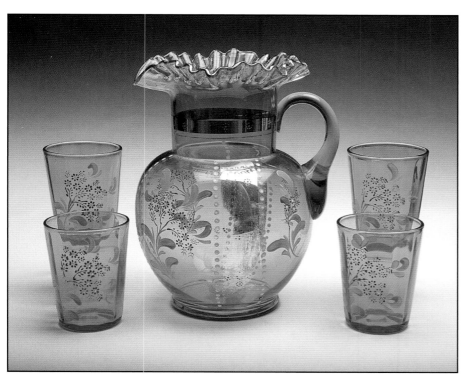

Enameled #628 Water set, Blue, 1907
Left and Right: tumblers, 4" tall, **$20** each;
Center: water pitcher, 9.75" tall, **$125**

THE FENTON ART GLASS PLANT
WILLIAMSTOWN W. VA.

Diamond Point Columns vase, 13.75" tall,
Blue Opalescent, 1907, **$48**

A view of the original 1907 factory
*Archival photo used with permission from
the Fenton Art Glass Company*

Women in the
decorating department
*Archival photo used
with permission from
the Fenton Art Glass
Company*

Water Lily and Cattail open sugar,
3.75" tall, French Opalescent,
1908, **$25**

Blue Opalescent, 1908 to 1912
Left: Waterlily and Cattails #8
bowl, 11" wide, square crimp, **$45**;
Right: Honeycomb and Clover
bowl, 8.5" wide, **$85**; **Front:**
Beaded Stars bonbon, 6.25" long,
$30
Note: In photographing, we found
a distinct difference in the Blue
Opalescent colors. It would appear
that during the production times, a
change occurred in the opalescent
formula.

Amethyst Opalescent, 1908 to 1912
Left: Waterlily and Cattails #8 bowl, 9"
wide, **$60**
Front: Blackberry Spray bowl, 5.25"
wide, **$18**; **Right:** Blackberry Spray plate,
6" wide, **$25**
Note: Both pieces of Blackberry Spray
were made from the same mould.

Rose #2, Mug, 4" tall, Amethyst Opalescent, 1908 to 1912, **$35**

Boggy Bayou (Reverse Drapery), Swung vases, 1908
Left: Green Opalescent, **$75**; **Right:** Amethyst
Opalescent, **$85**

Drapery, 1908
Left: Plate, 9" wide, Blue Opalescent, **$65**; **Right:**
Bowl, 9", Amethyst Opalescent, crimped, **$68**

1910 TO 1919
CARNIVAL AND STRETCH YEARS

Carnival glass continued to produce strong sales at Fenton. Early *Butler Bros.* advertisements called it "Wonder" or "Venetian Art Iridescent" glass. It was also described as a "poor man's Tiffany." *Butler Bros.* was a trade publication that listed a wide range of merchandise from which retailers could place orders for their stores. Sales kept improving in some years growing faster than others. The company soon became very affluent.

The Fenton Art Glass Company produced a huge range of patterns of carnival glass until the 1920s. Different shapes were a major part of carnival production. A few of today's favorite pieces include bowls, compotes, plates, and vases. Berry sets and water sets are some examples of the other pieces that can be found. A few of the shapes that get special attention are ice cream bowl, epergne, hand grip plate, and funeral vase. Colors highly desired among Fenton collectors are Aqua Opalescent, Celeste Blue, Cobalt, Ice Blue, Ice Green, Red, Topaz, and White. Pastel colors are always a favorite of collectors. A few of the desirable patterns to find include Basket weave with open edge, Dragon (several styles), Goddess of Harvest, Kittens, Lion, Milady, Orange Tree, Peacock & Urn, Persian Medallion, Peter Rabbit, Plaid, Stag & Holly, and Two Flowers. Advertising pieces are also among favorites of collectors to obtain. Count yourself lucky to have any piece of advertising in your collection. A few examples include Brazier's Candies, Central Shoe Store, Elks commemorative, Exchange Bank, Getts Pianos, Gevurtz Bros. Furniture, Illinois Soldiers & Sailors Home, and Paradise Sodas.

During War World I there was such a severe shortage of labor that Fenton had to work hard to obtain men to work in their factory. In fact, for the first time Fenton resorted to hiring women to work in hot metal. It was such a hot and unpleasant place to work and not many women lasted very long. Fenton worked hard to make sure all the male workers treated the women fairly.

The popularity of Carnival Glass started to decline during the last of the teens but Fenton continued producing this glass into the 1920s. Fenton again tried to capture the public's attention with an introduction of plain iridized glassware referred to now as Stretch Glass. This exciting new glassware helped keep Fenton on the road to prosperity.

Plate, 11" wide, Crystal, Hand cut floral design by James Fenton, 1912 to 1917, **$250**
Note: James was the foreman of the cutting shop

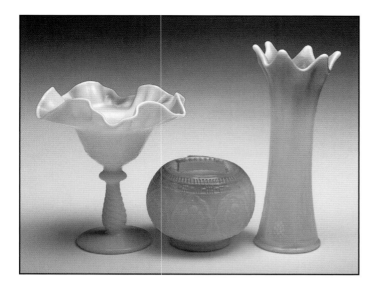

Custard with Green stain, originally called Peach
Blow, 1915
Left: Sailboats #1802 compote, 6" tall, **$30**;
Center: Persian Medallion rose bowl, 3.5" tall, **$40**;
Right: Butterfly and Berry #1124 vase, 8" tall, **$25**

Persian Blue, 1915
Top Left: #546 creamer, 3" tall, white enamel decoration, **$25**
Left: #546 sugar, 2.5" tall, white enamel decoration, **$25**; **Center:**
Banded Laurel #599 vase, 8.5" tall, **$35**; **Right:** #598 rose bowl,
3.5" tall, embossed floral with white enamel decoration, **$35**

Carnival vases, 1911 to 1919
Left: Rustic, 19" tall, funeral, Marigold, **$450**;
Center: Diamond and Rib, 11" tall, Green,
$65; **Right:** Rustic, 17.25" tall, Cobalt, **$175**

Young workers outside factory
*Archival photo used with permission from the Fenton
Art Glass Company*

Zigzag with Morning Glory decoration, Marigold Carnival, 1910
Left: Pitcher #1015, **$295; Right:** Tumbler, **$35**

Decorated Enamel on Ruby, 1910
Left: Cannonball #821, Pitcher, **$350; Right:** Tumbler, **$48**

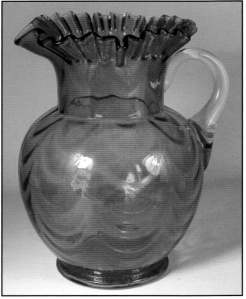

Drapery Optic, Pitcher, Blue Opalescent, 1910, **$295**

Drapery Optic, Pitcher, Amberina, 1910, **$500**

#165 ½, Crystal, wheel cut, 1912
Left: creamer, 3" tall, flat, **$8; Right:** sugar, 2.5" tall, flat, **$8**

Cherries and Scales #1134, Nutmeg stain on Custard, 1915
Left: Covered butter, **$145**; **Center:** Master berry bowl, footed, **$85**;
Right: Berry bowl, footed, **$35**

Lion, Plate, 7" wide, Green
stain on Custard, 1915, **$75**

Wine and Roses #922, Marigold Carnival, 1915
Left: Pitcher 64 ounces, **$375**; **Right:** Wine goblet, footed, **$60**

Orange Tree and Scroll, Tankard pitcher, Cobalt Blue, 1914,
$750

Laurel #599, Persian Blue, 1915
Left: Covered Butter, **$85**; **Center:** Covered Sugar, **$35**;
Right: Puff Box, **$38**

Marigold Carnival, 1911 to 1919
Left: Panther interior/ Butterfly and Berry exterior 3 footed bowl, 5.5" wide, **$65**; **Center**: Holly plate, 9.5" wide, **$195**; **Right:** Horse Medallion interior/berry exterior plate, 7.5" wide, **$250**

Cobalt Carnival, 1911 to 1919
Top Left: Orange Tree creamer, 3.25" tall, **$75**; **Top Center**: Persian Medallion #1044 plate, 6.25" wide, **$135**; **Top Right:** Orange Tree sugar, 3" tall, **$75**
Bottom Left: Orange Tree interior/ Bearded Berry exterior bowl, 8" wide, **$150**; **Bottom Right:** Plaid bowl, 9.25" wide, **$450**

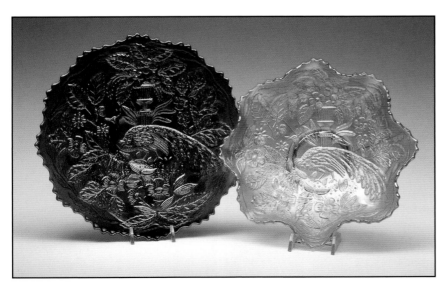

Peacock at the Urn, Carnival, 1915 to 1919
Left: plate, 9.5" wide, Cobalt, **$495**;
Right: bowl, 9" wide, Marigold, **$350**

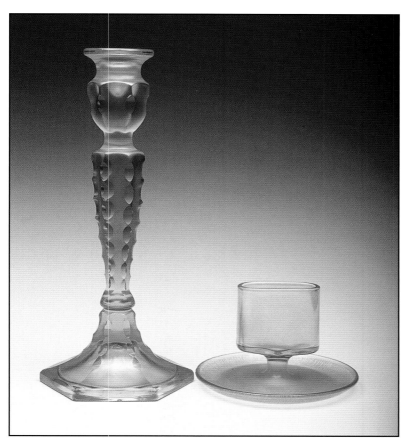

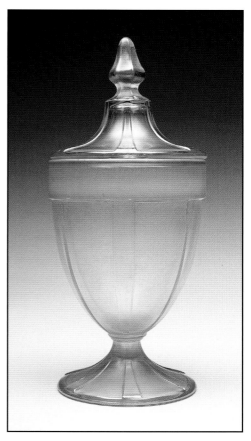

Florentine Green Stretch, 1917 to late 1928
Left: #349 candlestick, 10.5" tall, with cutting, **$95**; **Right:** #556 card/cigarette holder, 3.5" tall, ash receiver foot, **$60**

#636 candy jar, 1 pound, 10" tall, Florentine Green Stretch, 1917 to 1928, **$60**

Florentine Green Stretch, 1917 to 1928
Left: #9 candy dish, 8.75" tall, **$45**; **Center:** #545 bowl, 6.25" wide, **$24**; **Right:** #401 night set, 6.75" tall, **$98**

Store display dealer sign, 3" tall, 5" wide,
Celeste Blue stretch, 1917 to 1928, **$2000**

Celeste Blue Stretch, 1917 to 1920s
Back Left: #9 candy jar, 9" tall, grape wheel cut, **$95**; **Back Center:** #9 candy jar, 8" tall, **$35**; #643 covered bonbon, 6.25" tall, **$35**; **Back Right:** #401 night set, 6.75" tall, **$98**
Front Left: #202 small round, stacking ashtray, 2.25" wide; **Front Center:** #202 medium round, stacking ashtray, 2.85" wide; **Front Right:** # 202 large round, stacking ashtray, 3.15" wide, **$65 set**

Celeste Blue, 1917 to 1920s
Left: #9 candy jar, 9" tall, grape wheel cut, Stretch, **$95**; **Center:** Rib Optic #222 lemonade pitcher with Royal Blue handle, footed, 10" tall, 62oz., 1920s, **$245**; jug coaster, 5.25" wide, Royal Blue, **$45**; **Right:** Rib Optic #1352 ice tea tumbler with Royal Blue handle, 5" tall, 12oz., 1920s, **$45**; #220 coaster, 3.25" wide, Royal Blue, **$35**

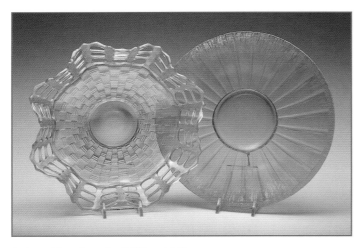

Celeste Blue Stretch, 1917 to 1920s
Left: Open Edge Basket #1092 bowl, 9" wide, **$295**; **Right:** #631 Paneled cake plate, 9.5" wide, **$85**

Celeste Blue Stretch, 1917 to 1920s
Left: #55 ½ flower stopper cologne, 7" tall, **$295**; **Center:** #401 night set, 6.5" tall, **$98**; **Right:** #549 candlestick with black base, 8" tall, **$150**

Frank Sr. taking Frank Jr. to the factory, 1918
Archival photo used with permission from the Fenton Art Glass Company

Carnival
Back: Orange Tree interior/Bearded Berry exterior plate, 9.25" wide, White, 1919, **$195**
Front: Persian Medallion #1044 rose bowl, 3.25" tall, Pastel Marigold, 1919, **$145**

Kittens #299, Marigold Carnival, 1918
Left: bowl, 4.5" wide, **$125**; **Right:** cup, 2" tall, **$75**

Carnival Grouping
Top: Captive Rose, Plate, 9" wide, Marigold, **$450**
Bottom Left: Dragon and Strawberry, Bowl, 9" wide, Amethyst, **$950**; **Bottom Right:** Basketweave with Open Edge #1092, Bowl, 9" wide, Ice Blue, 1911 to 1925, **$600**

1920 TO 1929
THE AGE OF COLOR

As carnival sales slowed down, they were replaced with Stretch Glass. The rainbow colors of Stretch included Aquamarine, Florentine Green, Grecian Gold, Persian Pearl, Tangerine, Celeste Blue, Topaz, Red, Velva Rose, and Wisteria. These colors were also offered in non-iridized versions.

By the middle 1920s, the net worth of Fenton was over a quarter of a million dollars. Quite an accomplishment considering how little the brothers had in 1905, when the company was started with less than $300 between them.

A bold experiment was tried in 1925 when Fenton hired a group of European glass workers to develop a line of art glass for them. The idea was to make some similar types of glass to compete with what Tiffany and Steuben were making at the time. While the glass was absolutely wonderful, the cost of producing it was very high and was not feasible for production. These workers left when their year was over.

Also during this time period, the new opaque colors of Black, Chinese Yellow, and Jade were introduced. Fenton's first dinnerware patterns of Diamond Optic and Lincoln debuted in the late 1920s.

In the late 1920s, sales began declining and for the first time Fenton lost money for several years. The stock market crash in 1929 signaled a massive slow down in many industries. This was a trying time for all of the glass companies, including Fenton. Money was short at Fenton and was borrowed from every source that could be found. The main concern was to keep the factory open even with sales being drastically reduced. All workers were given shortened shifts until sales improved. Everyone was willing to make the sacrifice to hold on to their job.

Red Carnival, 1920s
Left: Acorn #835 bowl, 7.5" wide, **$395**; **Center**: Open Edge Basket #1092 bowl, 5.5" wide, **$195**; **Right:** Sailboats #1774 bowl 6.5" wide, **$395**

Carnival, 1920s
Top: Cherry Circles handled bowl, 7.5" wide, Cobalt, **$75**
Bottom Left: Captive Rose bowl, 8" wide, Amethyst, **$85**; **Bottom Right:** Two Flowers bowl, 7.75" wide, Cobalt, **$225**

Dragon and Lotus #1656 bowl, 8.5" wide, Green Carnival, 1920s, **$225**

Amethyst Carnival, 1920s
Left: Dragon and Strawberry bowl, 9" wide, **$950**; **Right:** Vintage #469 two piece epergne, 5" tall, **$145**

Carnival, 1920s
Left: Heart and Vine bowl, 8.5" wide, Amethyst, **$120**; **Center:** Persian Medallion plate, 10.5" wide, Cobalt, **$950**; **Right:** Little Flowers bowl, 5.75" wide, Green, **$65**

Red Stretch, 1920s
Left and Right: #449 candlestick, 8.75" tall, **$395**; **Center:** #9 Candy jar, 8.75" tall, **$350**

Dragon and Lotus #1656 bowl, 9" wide, Red Carnival, 1920s, **$1,800**

Grecian Gold #621 vase, 7.85" tall, Deco cutting, early 1920s, **$75**

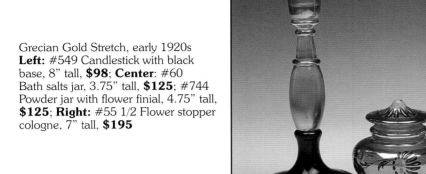

Grecian Gold Stretch, early 1920s
Left: #549 Candlestick with black base, 8" tall, **$98**; **Center**: #60 Bath salts jar, 3.75" tall, **$125**; #744 Powder jar with flower finial, 4.75" tall, **$125**; **Right:** #55 1/2 Flower stopper cologne, 7" tall, **$195**

#549 two tone candlesticks, 8.5" tall, 1924 to 1928
Top Left: Grecian Gold/Persian Pearl, **$125**; **Top Right:** Grecian Gold/ Black, **$98**
Bottom Left: Ruby/Black, **$150**; **Bottom Center:** Celeste Blue Stretch/ Black, **$150**; **Bottom Right:** Ruby with Sterling Overlay, **$95**

Young Frank holding a dog toy about 1922 *Archival photo used with permission from the Fenton Art Glass Company*

Ruby, 1921 to 1935
Top Left: Plymouth #1620 tumbler, 4" tall, **$24**; **Top Center:** September Morn #1645 nymph, 7" tall, **$250**; **Top Right:** Sheffield #1800 vase, 6" tall, **$35**
Center Left: Plymouth #1620 ice bucket, 6" tall, **$95**; **Center:** Georgian #1611 shaker, 4.25" tall, **$25**; Open Edge Basket #1091 candleholder, 2.25" tall, **$45**; **Center Right:** Dancing Lady #901 vase, 8.5" tall, **$600**
Bottom Left: #1934 decanter with flower stopper, 9.5" tall, **$185**; #1934 goblet, 2.5" tall, **$16**; **Bottom Center:** #1672 candleholder, 2.25" tall, **$35**; **Bottom Right:** Diamond Optic #1502 lamp base, 8" tall, **$175**; Georgian #1611 wine, 3.5" tall, **$18**

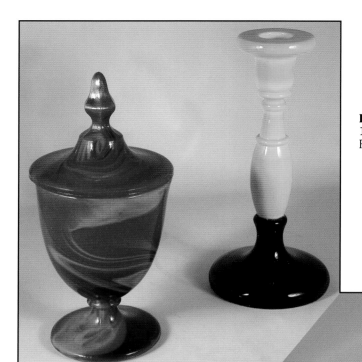

Left: Half pound candy jar #8, Mandarin Red, 1924, **$295**; **Right:** Two tone candlestick, Flame and Royal Blue, 8.5" tall, **$495 rare**

Wisteria Stretch, 1921 to 1928
Left: Vase #612, flared, 6.5" tall, **$85**; **Center:** Covered #9 candy, 3/4 lb., **$125**; **Right:** Candlestick #749, Two tone, Crystal base, 12" tall, **$250**

Grape and Cable #920, Footed bowl, Venetian Red, 1925, **Value Not Established**

Jade, 1921 to 1930s
Top: Vase #847, 5.5" tall, melon style, **$45**
Bottom Left: Bud vase #251, tulip shape, 11.75" tall, **$75**; **Center:** Vase, square top, 8" tall, **$85**; **Right:** Vase #1530, 17" tall, **$195**

Jade, 1921 to 1930s
Back: Leaf #175 **Left:** 8" tall, 8" wide, **$35**; **Right:** 10" tall, 11.25" wide, **$45**
Front Left: Candlestick, 3.75" tall, **$30**; **Center:** Georgian #1611, tumbler, 2.5" tall, **$18**; Candlestick, 8" tall, **$40**; **Right:** Bath salts jar #16, 4.5" tall, **$50**

Jade, 1921 to 1930s
Flared vase grouping, 1921 to 1930s
Left: 8.25" tall, **$65**; **Center:** 6" tall, black five legged base, **$145**; **Right:** Flip, 8" tall, **$125**

Jade, Dolphin handled #1533, 1921 to 1930s
Top: Comport, 4" tall, 6.5" wide, **$35**
Bottom Left: Comport, 4.5" tall, 7" wide, **$45**; **Bottom Right:** Vase, 4.25" tall, 6.5" wide, black five legged base, **$145**

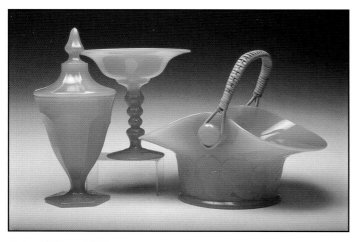

Jade, 1921 to 1930s
Left: Covered candy #835, 9.5" tall, 4.5" wide, **$80**; **Center:** Comport #260, 6" tall, 6.5" wide, **$48**; **Right:** Big Cookies #1681, basket, 5" tall, 10.25" long, 7.5" wide, **$125**

Lincoln Inn #1700, Jade, 1921 to 1930s, **$24 each**
Left: Sherbet; **Right:** Plate, 8" wide

Topaz Stretch, 1921 to 1930
Far Left: #401 night set, 6.5" tall, **$145**; **Left:** #220 ice tea tumbler with Cobalt handle, 4.5" tall, coaster, Cobalt, **$95**; **Center:** #220 covered pitcher with Cobalt handle, 10" tall, **$350**; coaster tray, Cobalt, **$95**; **Right:** ice tea tumbler with cobalt handle, 4.5" tall, coaster, **$95**

Jade, 1921 to 1930s
Top Left: #1608 dolphin handled bowl, 6.15" tall, **$150**; **Top Center:** Diamond Optic #1616 ice bucket, 6.25" tall, **$60**; **Bottom Center Top:** #1562 bowl, 13.75" long, **$60**; **Bottom Center:** #1562 bowl, 15" long, **$75**; **Right:** #1530 vase, 11.75" tall, **$98**

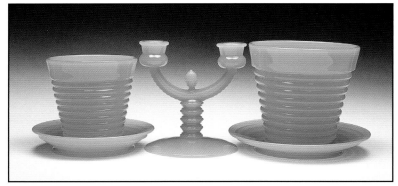

Jade, 1921 to 1930s
Left: #1554 flower pot 4.6" tall with liner 6.25" wide, **$175**; **Center:** #2318 duo candlestick, 5.75" tall, **$95**; **Right:** #1555 flower pot 5.5" tall with liner 7.4" wide, **$195**

Jade, 1921 to 1930s
Top Left: Dancing Lady #900 bowl, 10.5" long, **$350**; **Top Right:** #847 fan vase, 5.5" tall, **$48**
Bottom Left: #844 candy box with flower finial, 6.25" tall, **$350**; **Bottom Center:** Diamond Optic #1502 dolphin fan vase, 6" tall, **$48**; **Bottom Right:** #857 fan vase, 8" tall, **$75**; novelty dog #307, 2.5" tall, **$45**

Royal Blue, 1924 to 1930s
Left: #107 vase, 6" tall, footed, **$60**;
Center: Georgian #1611 nut cup, 2"
tall, **$20**; **Right**: Lincoln Inn #1700
water goblet, 5.8" tall, **$35**

Chinese Yellow, 1924 to 1930s
Left: jug, 6" tall, footed, **$295**; **Center:**
#621 flared vase on five legged black base,
8.5" tall, **$195**; **Right:** Big Cookies #1681
basket, 10.5" long, **$250**

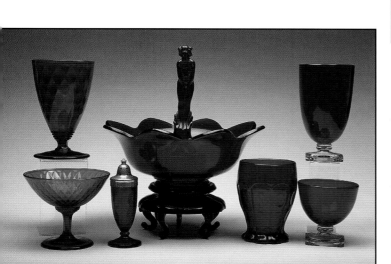

Royal Blue, 1924 to 1930s
Top Left: Diamond Optic #1502 tumbler, 5.25" tall,
footed, **$28**; **Top Right:** Elizabeth #1639 tumbler, 5.25"
tall, **$45**; **Bottom Left:** Diamond Optic #1502 sherbet,
3.5" tall, **$16**; Diamond Optic #1502 shaker, 4.5" tall,
$45; **Bottom Center:** #848 flared petal bowl, 8.75"
wide with September Morn #1645 nymph and Black
5 legged base, **$425**; **Bottom Right:** #1933 tumbler,
4.25" tall, **$18**; Elizabeth #1639 cupped sherbet, **$30**

Chinese Yellow, 1924 to 1930s
Left and Right: #848 candlestick three
legged, 4.5" wide, **$75** pair; **Center:**
#846 cupped bowl with 5 legged Black
base, 6.5" wide, **$165**

#1562-2, Oval bowl, 14" long,
Chinese Yellow, Black decorated,
1925, **Value Not Established**

Chinese Yellow, 1924 to
1930s
Left: Vase #894, 10"
tall, **$145**; **Center:**
Bowl #846, 8" wide,
flared, three tab black
base, **$145**; **Right:**
Candleholder #315,
3.5" wide, **$50**

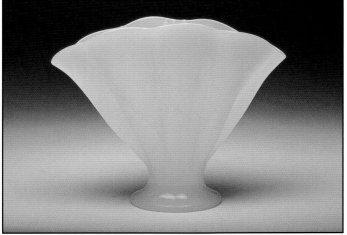

Chinese Yellow, 1924 to 1930s
Left: Big Cookies #1681, Covered Macaroon Jar, **$350**; **Center:**
Three footed candleholder #848, **$40**; **Right:** September Morn
Nymph #1645, Bowl #848, Black five legged base, **$950 set**

Fan vase #857, 8" tall, Chinese Yellow, 1924 to 1930s, **$250**

Diamond Optic #1502, Leaf cutting,
basket, 6" tall, 7" wide, Green, 1927 to
1938, missing chrome plated handle, **$60**

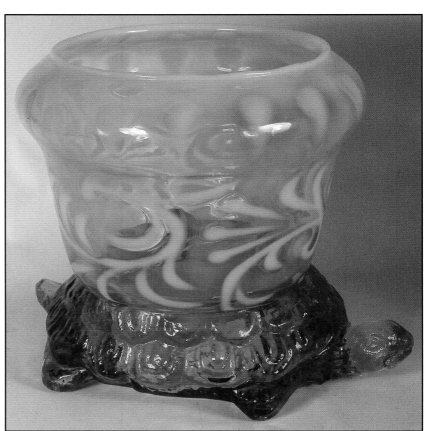

Buttons and Braids, Aquarium bowl, Green
Opalescent; Turtle base, Green, 1929, **$1250**

Green Transparent, 1920s and 1930s
Left and Right: Petal #1234 candleholders, 4.25" wide, **$20** pair; **Center:** Rib and Holly Sprig #231 compote, 4.25" tall, **$22**

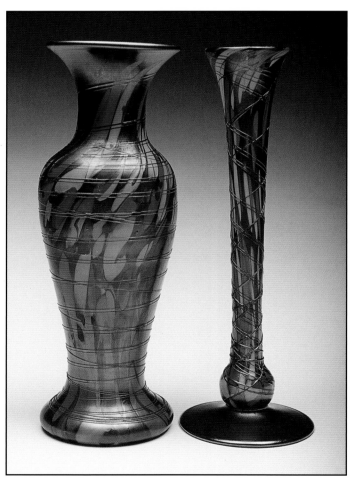

Free Hand Art Glass, Mosaic, 1925 to 1926
Left: #3008 vase, 11" tall, **$1,450**;
Right: #3021 vase, 11" tall, **$1,200**

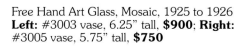

Free Hand Art Glass, Mosaic, 1925 to 1926
Left: #3003 vase, 6.25" tall, **$900**; **Right:** #3005 vase, 5.75" tall, **$750**

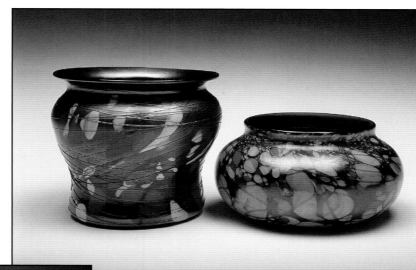

Free Hand Art Glass, Mosaic,
1925 to 1926
Left: #3014 vase, 4.65" tall,
$600; **Right:** #3049 vase,
3.15" tall, **$500**

Free Hand Art Glass, Mosaic,
1925 to 1926, #3003 vase,
6.25" tall, footed, **$800**

Free hand Art Glass, Mosaic,
1925 & 1926
Left: #3029 vase, 8" tall,
$1,150; **Right:** #3039 three
footed vase, 7" tall, **$1,450**

Free Hand Art Glass, Hanging Vine #3026 bowl, 9" wide, Turquoise Blue with Royal Blue foot, 1925 to 1926, **$1,800**

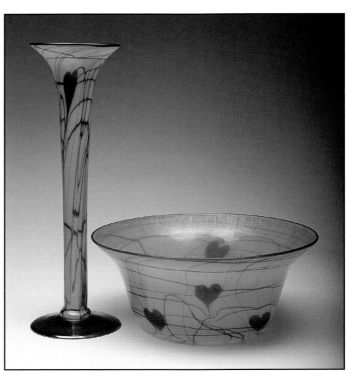

Free Hand Art Glass, Antique Green, 1925 & 1926
Left: Hanging Heart #3020 bud vase with Royal Blue base, 12" tall, **$950**; **Right:** Hanging Heart #3017 bowl, 8.5" wide, **$1,200**

Free Hand Art Glass, Mosaic #3035 high footed bonbon, 9"tall, 1925 to 1926, **$2,900**

Hanging Vine, free hand Art Glass, #3024 Vase, 10" tall, Turquoise Blue with Royal Blue base, 1926, **Value Not Established**

Free hand Art Glass vase, Black handles and threading, 10" tall, Antique Green, 1926, **Value Not Established**
Note: This vase sat in the library of Frank L. Fenton for many years

Free Hand Art Glass, Antique
Green, 1925 to 1926
Left: Pulled Feather #3017 bowl,
8.25" wide, **$1,000**; **Center:**
Hanging Heart #3012 vase, 4.35"
tall, **$1,500**; **Right:** Hanging Heart
#3005 vase, 7.25" tall, **$2,000**

Free hand Art Glass, Karnak Red, 1925 to 1926
Left: Hanging Heart #3026 footed bowl, 8.65"
wide, **$4,000**; **Right:** Hanging Vine #3002
vase, 6.75" tall, **$4,500**

Hanging Hearts, free hand Art Glass,
#3024 Egyptian Vase, 21" tall, Karnak
Red, 1925, **Value Not Established**

Free hand Art Glass #3006 vase,
10.5" tall, Karnak Red, 1925 to
1926, **$4,500**

Rib Optic, Amberina, 1920s
Left: Ice tea tumbler, Royal Blue coaster, **$175**; **Right:** Ice tea pitcher #222, **$700**

Ringed Panels, Cameo Opalescent, 1926
Left: Creamer pitcher, **$95**; **Right:** Open sugar bowl, **$95**

Spiral Optic, Cameo Opalescent, 1926
Left: Pitcher #1636, **$295**; **Right:** Tumbler, **$60**

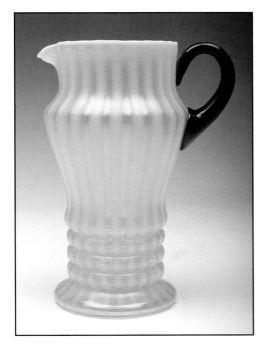

Rib Optic pitcher with Royal Blue handle, 8.25" tall, four rib base, Victoria Topaz, 1926, **$995**

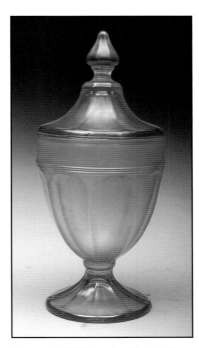

Covered #636 candy, 9" tall, 4" wide, Paneled, Footed, Velva Rose, 1926 to 1928, **$48**

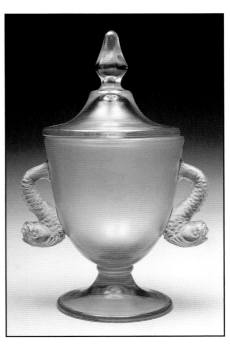

Dolphin #1532 handled covered candy, 8.75" tall, Velva Rose Stretch, 1926 to 1928, **$85**

Cameo Opalescent, 1926 to 1927
Top Left: #923 mayonnaise, 3.75" tall, **$60**; **Top Center:** #231 Ribbed bowl with rolled edge, 9.5" wide, **$48**; **Top Right:** Dolphin #1533 fan vase, 5.25" tall, **$75**; **Bottom Left:** Dolphin #1533 compote, 5" tall, **$85**; **Bottom Center:** #318 candlestick, 2.75" tall, **$25**; #735 cone candy jar, 8.5" tall, **$95**; **Bottom Right:** #643 covered bonbon, 5.75" tall, **$85**

Velva Rose Stretch, 1926 to 1928
Left: #59 cologne, 4" tall, **$165**; **Right:** Diamond Optic #53 cologne, 5" tall, **$175**

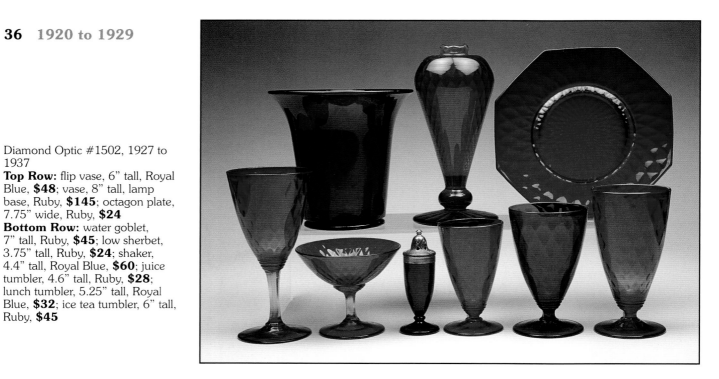

Diamond Optic #1502, 1927 to 1937
Top Row: flip vase, 6" tall, Royal Blue, **$48**; vase, 8" tall, lamp base, Ruby, **$145**; octagon plate, 7.75" wide, Ruby, **$24**
Bottom Row: water goblet, 7" tall, Ruby, **$45**; low sherbet, 3.75" tall, Ruby, **$24**; shaker, 4.4" tall, Royal Blue, **$60**; juice tumbler, 4.6" tall, Ruby, **$28**; lunch tumbler, 5.25" tall, Royal Blue, **$32**; ice tea tumbler, 6" tall, Ruby, **$45**

Diamond Optic #1502, 1927 to 1937
Top: bonbon basket, 5.5" wide, Aquamarine, **$50**
Center Left: basket, 7" wide, Ruby, **$95**; **Center:** basket, 7" wide, Black, **$65**; **Center Right:** creamer, 3.5" tall, Green, **$18**
Bottom Left: tumbler, 6" tall, ice tea, footed, Orchid, **$50**; **Bottom Center:** basket, 8" wide, Jade Green, **$65**; **Bottom Right:** sugar, 3.5" tall, Green, **$18**

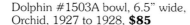

Dolphin #1503A bowl, 6.5" wide, Orchid, 1927 to 1928, **$85**

Diamond Optic #1502, Orchid, 1927 to 1928
Left: ice tea tumbler, 6" tall, **$38**; **Right:** compote, dolphin handle, smooth top, 4.5" tall, **$48**

Aquamarine, 1927 to 1933
Left: row boat ashtray, 5.25" long, **$45**; **Right:** Dolphin #1600 rolled edge bowl, 9.5" wide, **$125**

Diamond Optic #1502, Aquamarine, 1927 to 1930s
Top Left: creamer, 3.35" tall, **$28**; **Center:** swung vase, 17.75" tall, **$125**; **Bottom Left:** sugar, 3.35" tall, **$28**; **Right:** vase, 6" tall, **$75**

Diamond Optic #1634-1702, Wheel cut design, Rose, 1928
Left: Pitcher, **$225**; **Right:** Tumbler, **$30**

Stretch Fan vases
Top: #857 vases: 8" tall: **Left:** Velva Rose, 1926 to 1928, **$75**, **Center:** Tangerine, 1927 to 1929, **$98**; **Right:** Persian Pearl, 1920s, **$60**
Center: #847 vase, 6.5" tall, Topaz, 1921 to 1930, **$60**
Bottom: #857 vases, 8" tall: **Left:** Aquamarine, late 1920s to 1930s, **$60**; **Center:** Florentine Green, 1920 to 1928, **$75**; **Right:** Celeste Blue, 1918 to 1920s, **$85**

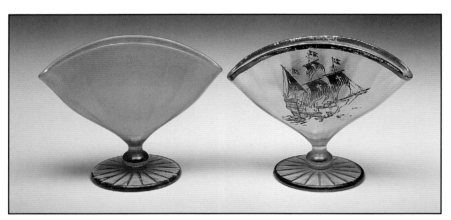

#570 fan vase, 5.15" tall
Left: Tangerine Stretch, 1927, **$65**;
Right: Florentine Green Stretch, silver overlay ship decoration, 1926, **$95**

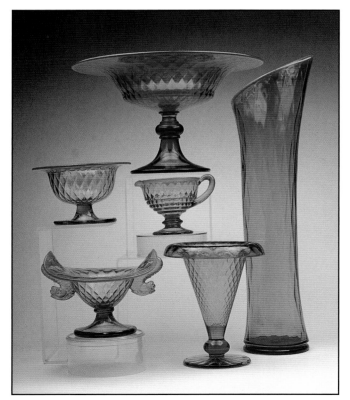

Tangerine Stretch, 1927 to 1929
Top: Laurel Leaf plate, 13" wide, octagonal shape, **$145**
Bottom Left: #847 vase, 6" tall, fan shape, **$65**; **Center:** #10 candy dish, 6.5" tall, **$245**; **Right:** #857 vase, 8" tall, fan shape, **$95**

Diamond Optic #1502, Tangerine, 1927 to 1929
Top: comport, 7" tall, high standard, **$245**; **Center Left:** mayonnaise bowl, 5.75" wide, **$125**; **Center:** creamer, 3.5" tall, **$45**
Front Left: comport, 5" tall, dolphin handled, **$95**; **Front Center:** vase, 7" tall, rolled edge, **$125**; **Front Right:** vase, 18.25" tall, swung, **$195**

Rib Optic, Guest or night set #200, Tangerine stretch, 1927, **Note:** opaque handle, **$650**

Flared vases, Tangerine stretch, 1927 to 1929
Left: #621, 6.25" tall, **$75**; **Right:** Diamond Optic #1502, 8.25" tall, **$350 rare**

Tangerine Stretch, 1927 to 1929
Back: Vase #835, unusual six sided top, 5.75" tall, **$65**
Left Front: Covered #835 candy, 9.5" tall, 4.25" wide, **$95**; **Front Center:** Center handle tray #317, 10.25" wide, **$85**; **Front Right:** Interior Panel Optic, fan vase #572, 8.75" tall, 6.25" wide, **$75**

Tangerine Stretch, Dolphin handled, #1533, 1927 to 1929
Top: Comport, 4.25" tall, 5.5" wide, **$65**
Bottom Left: Fan vase, 5.25" tall, 6" wide, **$65**; **Bottom Right:** Fan vase, 6.25" tall, 6.75" wide, **$75**

Black, 1928 to 1933
Top Left: Fan vase #857, 5.25" tall, 8.5" wide, **$35**
Left: #857 Fan vase, 7.75" tall, 10" wide, **$48**; **Right:**
Vase #1531, swung 14" tall, **$85**

Bowl #1600, dolphin handled, 8.5" wide, 5.75"
tall, footed, Black, 1928 to 1933, **$85**

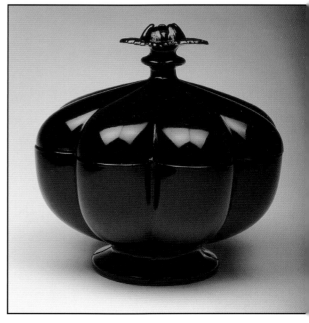

Wide Rib #100, Black, 1928 to 1933
Left: Tumbler, 4.25" tall, **$24**; **Center:** Pitcher, 7.75" tall, **$125**; **Top**
Right: Creamer, 4" tall, **$18**; **Bottom Right:** Sugar, 3.75" tall, **$18**

Covered #844 candy with flower finial, 6.5" tall,
6.5" wide, Black, 1928 to 1933, **$275**

Elephant Flower #1618 bowl, "Jumbo", 7" tall, 8.5" long, 1928
Top: Crystal, **$350**; **Bottom Left:** Black Satin, **$600**; **Bottom Right:** Amethyst, **$450**

Black, 1928 to 1933
Left: #1684 macaroon jar, 6.5" tall, **$100**; **Center:** Elizabeth #1639 syrup jug, 4.85" tall, **$135**; **Right:** Elizabeth #1639 batter jug, 8" tall, **$225**

Wide Rib #100, Black, 1928 to 1933
Left: sugar, 4" tall, **$18**; **Right:** creamer, 4" tall, **$18**

Lincoln Inn #1700 shakers on tray: shakers, 4.4" tall, Jade; tray, 5.5" tall, Black, 1928 to mid 1930s, **$200**

Plymouth #1620, Cocktail shaker, 8" tall, 3.75" wide at top, 2.85" wide at base, Ruby, 1921 to 1935, **$125**

Lincoln Inn #1700, Ruby, 1928 to 1935
Top Left: goblet, 7" tall, dinner, **$45**; **Top Center:** goblet, 4" tall, wine, **$36**; **Top Right:** plate, 8" wide, salad, **$25**
Bottom Left: tumbler, 5.25" tall, juice, **$36**; **Bottom Center:** finger bowl 5" wide and liner 6.6" wide, **$48**; **Bottom Right:** goblet, 5.75" tall, sherbet, **$30**

1930 TO 1939
The Time of Struggle

Even with the slow economy, Fenton was looking to the future to offer new types of glass. New dinnerware lines, Georgian, Plymouth and Sheffield, were offered. New opaque colors of Mandarin Red, Moonstone and Pekin Blue debuted in 1932. Two years later Mongolian Green appeared and was soon followed by Periwinkle Blue. These colors were inspired by the Asian colors called Peking Glass. Unique satin etchings also enhanced the lines. Opalescent glass was also reintroduced. Several transparent colors also helped to increase sales. Kresge and Woolworth accounts also accounted for a large portion of sales.

There were two special incidents that propelled Fenton out of the Depression and back on the road to prosperity. The Dormeyer Company of Chicago needed someone to make mixing bowls for their electric mixers. Fenton was approached about making these bowls. The first recorded sales of about $4500 came in 1933 and increased a year later by four times. It is amazing to note that, by the end of this decade, sales from this arrangement had been pushed up to $35,000. This was a surprising turn-around for Fenton.

Another special arrangement would seal their financial future. This one involved the Wrisley Company. They were looking for a unique style of bottle in which to sell their perfume. Modifications were made to a Hobnail barber bottle to adapt it into a perfume bottle. The bottles were sent to Wrisley to be filled with colored cologne. To accent the bottle, a pretty bow was attached to it. The perfume bottles were an amazing success with the public. Sales were huge and more bottles were ordered. Soon a matching puff box was made, along with a bath salt jar. Sales to Wrisley amounted to over a quarter of a million dollars in 1939. This was a huge financial success to Fenton. Even after Wrisley moved his account over to Hocking, Fenton was developing other Hobnail pieces to place in their line.

Another new idea for Fenton was inspired by the central European glass artisans of the 1920s. The art of applying a thin stream of molten glass to the edge of a piece is known as ringing. Glass with this applied ribbon was known to be crested or petticoat glass. Crests have become a trademark of Fenton, with many different colors being used. Fenton employee Pete Raymond first learned this ringing skill in the 1930s, based on the European style. He wondered if a colored glass could be applied to a French Opalescent piece. Cobalt glass was spun on French Opalescent and Blue Ridge, Fenton's first crest line, which was introduced in 1939.

Coin Spot, 1930s
Left: miniature lamp, 11" tall, Cranberry Opalescent, **$395**;
Right: mug, 4.5" tall, Green Opalescent with black handle, **$95**

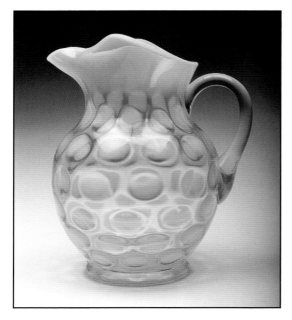

Coin Spot #1353 pitcher, 9.75"tall, Green Opalescent, 1930s, **$195**

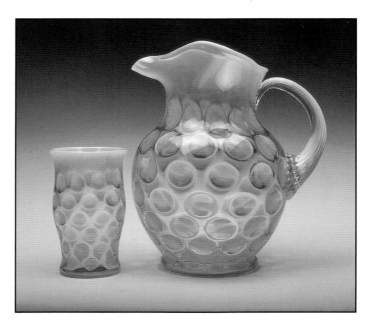

Coin Spot #1352, Blue Opalescent, 1930s
Left: Tumbler, 5.25" tall, 12 ounces, **$25**; **Right:** Pitcher, 9.75" tall, 6" wide, ice lip, Crystal ribbed handle, **$145**

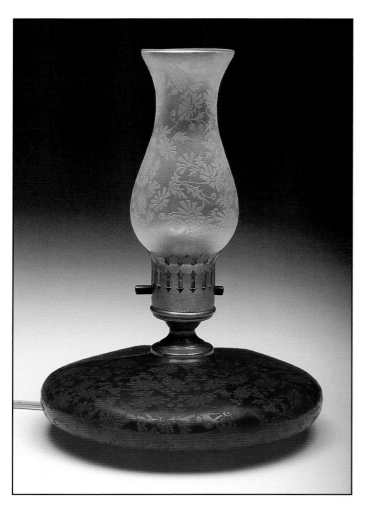

Boudoir #G-70 lamp, 10" tall, Ruby with Crystal shade, etched, 1930s, **$295**

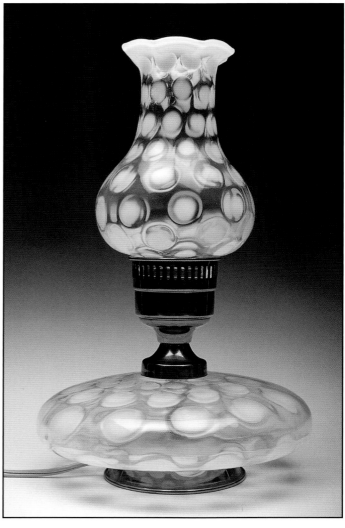

Coin Spot #G-70 electric lamp, 13" tall, French Opalescent, 1931 to 1932, **$145**

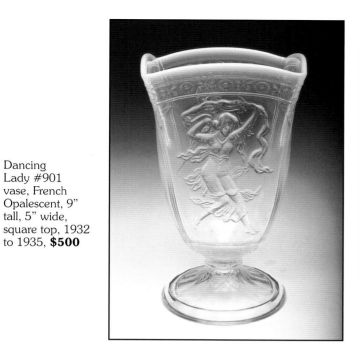

Dancing Lady #901 vase, French Opalescent, 9" tall, 5" wide, square top, 1932 to 1935, **$500**

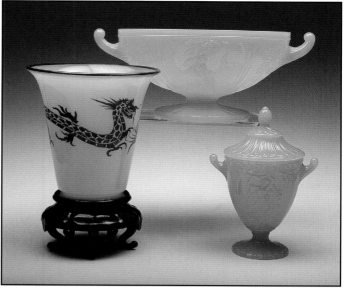

Pekin Blue, 1932 to 1933
Left: #621 flared vase, 6" tall, black dragon decoration with Black five legged base, **$595**; **Center:** Dancing Lady #900 oval bowl, 10.75" long, **$450**; **Right:** Dancing Lady #901 urn, 7" tall, **$950**

Dancing Lady, Crystal, 1932 to 1935
Top: #900 basket bonbon, satin accents, 8" long, handled, **$145**
Bottom Left: #901 vase, 8.75" tall, satin accents, flared, **$295**; **Bottom Center:** #900 oval bowl, 11.75" wide, handled, **$195**; **Bottom Right:** #901 vase, 8.75" tall, **$275**

Dancing Lady #901, Crystal, satin accents, 1932 to 1935
Top: vase, 4.25" tall, **$95**
Bottom Left: vase, oval, 4.25" tall, **$95**; **Bottom Right:** vase, 4.25" tall, **$125**

Top: Elizabeth #1639 tumbler, 5.15" tall, Black with Jade foot, 1930 to 1933, **$65**
Bottom Left: #848 cupped bowl, 6" wide, September Morn #1645 nymph and Black 5 legged base, 7" tall, Jade, 1933, **$375**;
Bottom Center: Elizabeth #1639 sugar, 3.25" tall, Jade with Black foot, 1930 to 1933, **$45**; **Bottom Right:** #848 flared bowl, 9" wide, Jade with Black September Morn #1645 nymph and Black 5 legged base, 7" tall, 1933, **$425**

Elizabeth #1639 mint jar, 7.25" tall, Black top and Jade foot, 1930 to 1933, **$250**

#1645 September Morn nymph, 7" tall, 1933 to 1936
Left to Right: Rose, **$185**; Dark Green, **$225**; Black, **$250**; Jade, **$200**; Ivory, **$225**; Light Green, **$195**; Royal Blue, **$275**

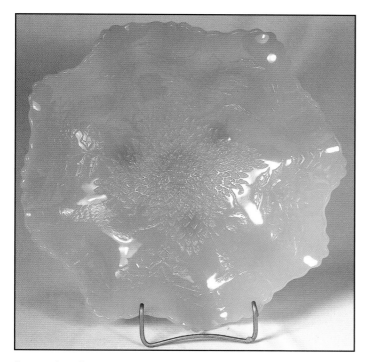

Stag and Holly, three toed bowl #1608, Jade, 10" wide, 1930, **Value Not Established**

Bath set #1617-54, Jade with black star decal, six piece set, 1930, **$500**

Jade, 1931 to 1932
Left: Georgian jug, 64 ounces, **$195**; **Right:** Strawberry jar, **Value Not Established**

Table lamp, cut floral pattern, Jade, 1931, **$450**

#1645 September Morn nymph, 7" tall, 1933 to 1936
Top: Milk Glass in cupped bowl, 6" wide, Black 5 legged base, **$345**
Bottom Left: Cobalt in flared bowl, 8" wide, Black 5 legged base, **$450**; **Bottom Center:** Crystal in Hobnail #1932 legged bowl, 7" wide, **$195**; **Bottom Right:** Ruby in cupped bowl, 6" wide, Black 5 legged base, **$425**

Georgian #1611, Amber, 1931 to 1939
Back Row: dinner plate, 10" wide, **$12**; lunch plate, 8" wide, **$5**
Front Row: sugar, 3.5" tall, **$7**; cup and saucer, **$8**; creamer 3.5" tall, **$7**

Big Cookies #1681 macaroon jar, 7" tall, 1933 to 1934
Left: Black, **$145**; **Center:** Jade, **$145**; **Right:** Amber, **$195**

#893 lamp, Ginger Jar shape, 7.5" tall, Moonstone, flower etching, 1932 to 1934, **$295**

#893 ginger jar, 8.25" tall, dragon decoration, Moonstone with Black lid and base, 1932 to 1934, **$600**

Elizabeth #1639 covered syrup jug, 4.85" tall, Lilac, 1933, **$250**

Plymouth #1620, Stiegel Green, 1933 to 1937
Left: tumbler, 4" tall, flat, **$20**; **Right:** sherbet, 4.1" tall, **$12**

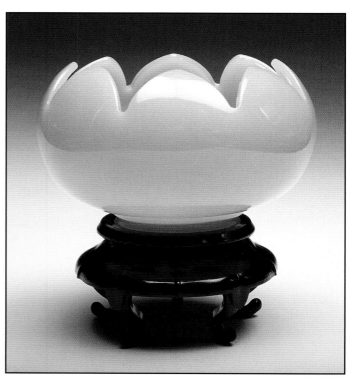

#848 cupped bowl, 6.5"wide, on Black 5 legged base, Lilac, 1933, **$175**

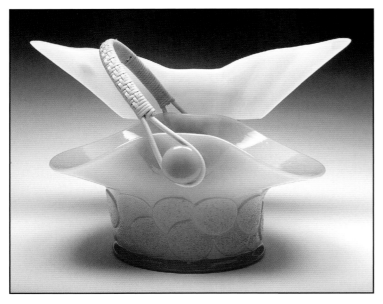

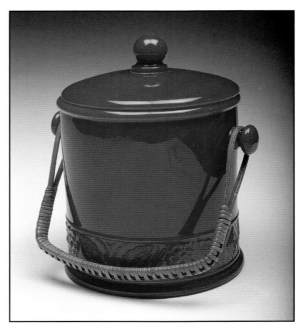

Lilac, 1933
Top: #1562 oval bowl, 13.5" long, **$95**; **Right:** Big Cookies #1681 basket, 10" long, **$275**

#1684 macaroon jar, 7" tall, Mandarin, 1933 to 1935, **$250**

Lilac, 1933
Left: Flower pot and liner #1554, **$198**; **Right:** Bowl #1608, dolphin handled, 10" long, **$245**

Diamond Optic #53 puff box, 4.5" wide, Lilac top, Jade bottom, 1933, **$85**

Mandarin Red, 1933 to 1935
Left: Dancing Lady #901 vase, 8.75" tall, **$595**; **Center:** #893 ginger jar with gold decoration, 8.5" tall, Black lid and base, **$295**; **Right:** Peacock #791 vase, 7.5" tall, **$225**

Mandarin Red, 1933 to 1935
Top: #846 bowl, 9.25" wide, **$125**; **Bottom Left:** 1684 basket 9" long; **$135**; **Bottom Right:** #847 fan vase 6" tall, **$68**

#308 ashtray, 4" wide, Mandarin, intaglio, 1933 to 1935, **$48**

Fan vases
Top: #857, 8" tall, Crystal, Silvertone etching, 1937 to 1938, **$48**
Center Left: #857, 8" tall, Mandarin Red with gold decoration, 1933 to 1935, **$98**; **Center:** #847, 6" tall, Black with silver overlay, 1928 to 1933, **$65**; **Center Right:** Jade with silver overlay, 1933 to 1935, **$85**
Bottom Left: #857, 8" tall, Ruby, 1933 to 1935, **$65**; **Bottom Center:** #847, 6" tall, Lilac, 1933, **$95**; **Bottom Right:** #857, 8" tall, Moonstone, 1932 to 1934, **$85**

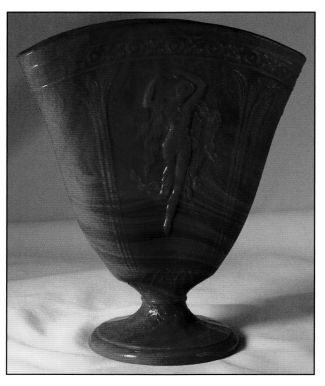

Vases, Mandarin Red, 1934
Left: Basketweave #1093 vase, 5.5" tall, **Value Not Established**
Right: #888 vase, 10" tall, **$400** very rare

Dancing Lady #901, fan vase, Mandarin Red, 9" tall, 1933 to 1935, **$850**

Mandarin Red, 1933 to 1935
Top Left: Bowl #950, 10.5" long, **$95**
Bottom: Bowl #847, 6.5" wide, **$50**; **Center:** Vase #847, 5" tall, **$60**; **Right:** Flip vase #1668, 8" tall, **$350**, Candlestick #318, 2.5" tall, **$35**

Sung Ko vases, 1935
Left: #200 vase 7" tall, **Value Not Established**;
Right: #1935 vase 8" tall, **Value Not Established**

Sung Ko, #893 Ginger Jar, 8.5" tall, with
original black lid and base, 1935, **Value Not
Established**

Mongolian Green, 1934
to 1935
Top Center: #621 flared
vase, 6.25" tall, **$65**
Bottom Left: Dancing
Lady #901 vase, 8.5" tall,
$450; **Bottom Center**:
#1684 Macaroon Jar, 6.5"
tall, **$250 Bottom Right:**
Dancing Lady #901 vase,
9" tall, cupped, **$495**

Periiwinkle Blue, 1935
Back: Bowl #847, 10.75" wide, **$85**
Front Left: Flared vase #621, 6" tall, black base, **$95**; **Front Right:** Cupped bowl #847, 4" tall, 6" wide, black five legged base, **$125**

Periwinkle Blue, 1934 to 1935
Top: #847 fan vase, 5" tall, **$65**; **Top Center:** #1504 clover bowl with dolphin handles, 10" wide, **$495**; **Top Right:** Peacock #791 vase, 7.5" tall, **$245**
Bottom Left: #1684 macaroon jar, 6.5" tall, **$295**; **Bottom Center:** #847 rose bowl, 4" tall, **$48**; **Bottom Right:** #1684 basket, 9" long, **$225**

Dancing Lady #901, Periwinkle Blue, 1934 to 1935
Left: vase, 9" tall, cupped, **$595**; **Right:** vase, 8.5" tall, flared, **$500**

Elephant whiskey bottle, 8.1" tall, Periwinkle blue, 1933 to 1935, **Value Not Established**

Open Edge Basket #1092, 1930s
Top Left: plate, 7.5" wide, Green Opalescent, **$40**; **Top Right:** bowl, 8" wide, Ruby, **$60**
Bottom Left: bowl, 9" wide, Black, **$60**; **Bottom Right:** plate, 9" wide, Royal Blue, **$75**
Front: bowl, 5" wide, French Opalescent bowl, **$30**

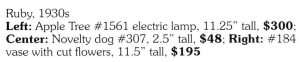

Ruby, 1930s
Left: Apple Tree #1561 electric lamp, 11.25" tall, **$300**;
Center: Novelty dog #307, 2.5" tall, **$48**; **Right:** #184 vase with cut flowers, 11.5" tall, **$195**

Amber, platinum trim, 1935
Left: #1934 whiskey tumbler, 2.4" tall, **$15**; **Right:** #1934 decanter with flower stopper, 9" tall, **$98**

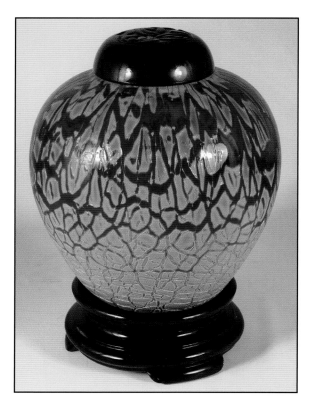

Ginger Jar #893, Experimental, Periwinkle Blue, 1935, **Value Not Established**
Note: Black lid and base are not original

Vase #898, Cameo acid cutback floral pattern, experimental, Royal Blue, 1934, **Value Not Established**

Georgian #1611, Ruby, 1931 to 1942
Left: Comport, cupped in and flared top, **$75**; **Center:** Covered candy, **$65**; **Right:** Comport, flared, **$38**

Ming #750, Dolphin handled bonbon, 1935 to 1936
Left: Rose, 2" tall, 5.5" wide, **$24**; **Right:** Crystal, 2.5" tall, 6.5" long, **$16**

Left: Pineapple #2000, Bowl, 12.75" wide, Rose, 1938, **$85**; **Right:** Apple Tree #1561, Electric Lamp, Ming Etching #846, 11.25" tall, Crystal, 1935 to 1936, **$250**

Velvatone, Crystal, 1935 to 1937
Left: Vase #200, 7" tall, flared,
$150; **Right:** Covered bonbon
#846, **$185**

Ming, Crystal, 1935 to 1936
Left: Stacking refrigerator set,
four piece, **$225**; **Center:**
Liquor tumbler, **$24**; **Right:**
Decanter #1934, flower
stopper, **$125**

Plymouth #1620 with Ming Etching, Crystal, 1936
Back Left and Right: Tumbler, Old Fashion, **$20**; **Back Center:** Ice Bucket, **$95**; **Front:** Covered box, **$95**

Wild Rose, Hurricane lamp, Crystal, 1935, **Value Not Established**

Crystal Satin Etching, 1935 to 1939
Top Left: Big Cookies #1681 basket with Poinsettia etching #43, 11" long, **$150**; **Top Center:** Leaf Tier #1790 plate, 6.5" wide, **$35**; **Top Right:** #857 vase with Silvertone etching, 8" tall, **$60**
Bottom Left: #893 ginger jar with Wistaria etching, 8.25" tall, **$195**; **Bottom Center:** #844 covered bonbon flower finial with San Toy etching, 6" tall, **$250**; novelty sunfish #306, 2.75" tall, **$45**; **Bottom Right:** #893 ginger jar with Ming etching, 8.5" tall, **$145**

Green Ming, 1935 to 1936
Top: #950 cornucopia candlesticks, 5.75" tall, **$85 pair**
Bottom Left: #950 bowl, 10.5" long, **$75**; **Bottom Right:** #893 ginger jar, 7.5" tall, Black lid and base, **$250**

Ming satin etching, Crystal, 1935 to 1936
Left: ball ashtray/cigarette holder, 3.25" tall, **$45**; **Right:** bowl, 12.75" wide, intaglio, **$95**

Intaglio Fruit, Coaster, 4" wide, Crystal, 1930s, **$38**

Rose, 1931 to 1936
Left: Big Cookies #1681, Macaroon Jar, **$195**; **Right:** Ashtray, Wheel cut floral design by James Fenton, **$50**
Note: James was foreman of the cutting shop.

Rose, 1935 to 1936
Left: Ming #846 ginger jar with metal ormolu, **$350**; **Top Center:** Diamond Optic #1502 water goblet, 6.75" tall, **$45**; **Bottom Center:** Peacock #711 bookend, 6" tall, **$250**; **Right:** Ming #846 cupped bowl with September Morn #1645 nymph and Black 5 legged base, **$375**

Satin etching, 1935 to 1936
Left: #1684 Ming basket, 9" long, Crystal, **$48**; **Center:** #1684 Ming basket, 9" long, Green, **$75**; **Right:** #1616 Wistaria basket, 9.75" long, Crystal, **$85**

Wistaria etching, Crystal, 1937 to 1938
Left: #249 cake plate, 11.75" wide, footed, **$48**; **Center:** #33 tumbler, 3.85" tall, **$18**; **Right:** #33 cocktail shaker, 10" tall, **$85**

Wistaria, #200 guest set (shown apart), 8" tall overall, Crystal, 1937 to 1938
Left: tumbler, 3.75" tall; **Right:** pitcher, 7.25"tall, **$225 set**

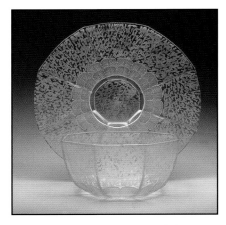

Ming #750, Crystal, octagonal shape, layered embossed leaves at base, 1935 to 1936
Punch set: bowl, 9" wide, 4.75" tall; plate, 14.75" wide, **$85 set**

Wistaria satin etching, Crystal, 1937 to 1938
Left and Right: #604 punch cups, 2" tall, paneled, **$20 each**; **Center:** punch bowl, 12.75" wide, paneled, **$225**

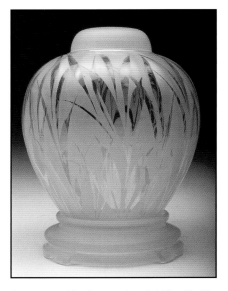

San Toy #33, Ginger Jar, 8.25" tall, 6" wide, Crystal, 1936, **$145**

Crystal, 1937 to 1938
Top: Wistaria satin etching, #33 liquor tray, 12.75" long, intaglio, **$95**
Bottom: celery relish tray, 12.75" long, 3 part, intaglio, **$75**

Poinsettia #43 satin etching, vase #183, 6.75" tall, 1938 to 1939, **$95**

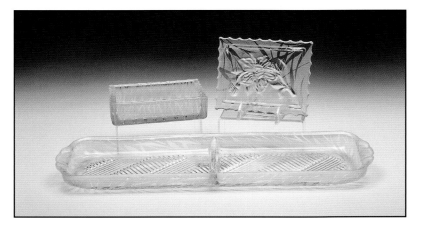

San Toy #33 etching, Crystal, 1936
Top: #5889 cigarette box, 4.5" long, **$95**
Bottom: #12 relish tray, divided, 14.25" long, **$95**

Scenic #1562-2 oval bowl, 13.5" long, Crystal, 1938, **$95**

Satin etching (name to this etching has not been identified), Crystal, 1935 to 1939
Left and Right: #950 cornucopia candlesticks, 6" tall, **$65 pair**;
Center: #950 bowl, 11" long, **$55**

Twin Ivy satin etching, 1939, detail of etching

Close up of above etching

Sheffield #1800 vase, 8.25" tall, Silvertone etching, Amber, 1937 to 1938, **$75**

Sheffield #1800, Rose Bowl, 3.75" tall, 5.5" wide, Amber, 1937 to 1938, **$15**

Silvertone satin etching #184, vase, 9.85" tall, Crystal, 1937 to 1938, **$60**

Sheffield #1800, Mermaid Blue, 1936 to 1938
Back: bowl, 12.5" wide, Silvertone etching, **$60**
Front Left: vase, 6" tall, footed, **$35**; **Center:** bowl, 6.5" wide, 3 footed, **$28**; **Right:** tulip vase, 6.25" tall, **$45**

Left: #1621 etching dolphin handled bowl, 9.5" wide, Crystal, 1937 to 1938, **$40**; **Right:** Silvertone, 3 footed bowl, 9.5" wide, Amber, 1934 to 1938, **$20**

Silvertone Etching, bowl #950, 5.5" tall, 10" long, 8.5" wide, Mermaid Blue,1937 to 1938, **$65**

Left: Pineapple #2000, Bowl, 12" wide, Amber, three footed, 1938, **$24**; **Right:** Silvertone #1000, Bonbon, 6.5" wide, Amethyst, three footed, 1934 to 1938, **$24**

Pineapple #2000, duo candlestick, 5.5" tall, 6" spread across top, 5.25" wide round base, pineapple finial in center, Crystal, 1938, **$35**

Pineapple #2000 satin etching, Crystal, 1938
Left: covered bonbon, 5.25" tall, flat, **$40**; **Right:** covered bonbon, 6.25" tall, footed, **$48**

Historic America, Crystal, Special Order for Macy's, 1937
Left: plate, 7.75" wide, Niagara Falls scene, **$48**; **Right:** goblet, 6" tall, Capitol at Washington scene, **$60**

Historic America, Crystal, special order for Macy's department store, 1937
Left: Tumbler, 6" tall, Broadway scene from New York, **$48**; **Center:** Cup plate, Mount Vernon scene, 4" wide, **$48**; **Right:** Finger bowl, 4" wide, Prairie Schooner scene and liner, 6" wide, Rocky Mountains scene, **$75**
Note: Scenes were based on the Johnson Bros. dinnerware pattern of the same name.

Opaque Colors, Special Order for Edward P. Paul, 1930s
Left: lamp, 10.25" tall, Opaque Blue, **$65**; **Center:** #848 candlesticks, 1.75" tall, Kitchen Green, **$60 pair**; **Right:** lamp, 10.25" tall, Kitchen Green, **$75**

Spiral Optic, 1939
Left: #1920 top hat vase, 12" wide, Green Opalescent, **$250**; **Right:** #170 hurricane lamp, 10.75" tall, French Opalescent, **$85**

Spiral Optic, Blue Opalescent, late 1930s
Left: #893 ginger jar with Black lid and base, 8.5" tall, **$300**; **Center:** Black base, 5" wide, **$35**; **Right:** #186 vase, 8" tall, **$60**

Rib Optic, Blue Opalescent, 1939
Left: #220 covered pitcher with Royal Blue handle, 9.75" tall, **$350**; Royal Blue coaster tray, 6.5" wide, **$95**; **Right:** #222 tumbler with Royal Blue handle, 5.25" tall, **$60**; Royal Blue coaster, 3.25" wide, **$25**

Spiral Optic #16 perfume, 5.5" tall, Blue Opalescent with black flower stopper, late 1930s, **$250**

Rib Optic, Green Opalescent, 1938
Left: #1352 tumbler with Royal Blue handle, 4.6" tall, **$45**; with Royal Blue coaster, 3.25" wide, **$25**; **Center:** #220 covered pitcher with Royal Blue handle, 10" tall, **$300**; with Royal Blue tray, 6.4" wide, **$95**; **Right:** #3 sugar, 3.15" tall, **$85**

Ring Optic, 1939
Left: lamp base, 8" tall, French Opalescent, **$48**; **Center:** lamp base, 8" tall, Cranberry Opalescent, **$98**; **Right:** lamp base, 6" tall, **$85**

Blue Ridge, 1939 to 1940
Top: vase #188, 6.5" tall, flared, **$375**
Bottom Left: basket #1921, 13" tall, **$350**;
Bottom Center: hat vase #1924, 4" tall, **$75**; **Bottom Right:** hat vase #1923, 6" tall, **$250**

Blue Ridge, 1939 to 1940
Top Left: vase #186, 8" tall, **$98**
Left and Right: candleholder #1523, 4.25" tall, **$165 pair**; **Center:** bowl #1522, 10.25" wide, September Morn nymph, Royal Blue base, **$375 set**; **Far Right:** hurricane #170, 9.75" tall, **$245**

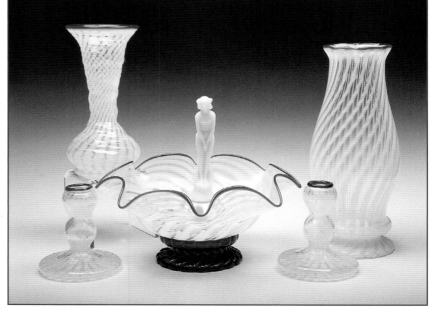

Daisy and Button #1900, duo candlestick, 4.25" tall, 7.5" wide, Crystal, 1937 to 1938, **$20**

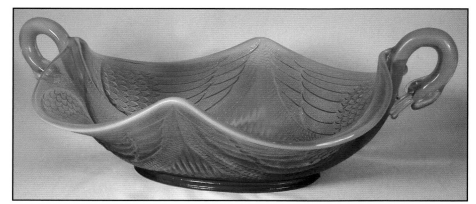

Dancing Lady vase #901, cupped and flared, Topaz Opalescent, 1938, **$750**

Swan #6, console bowl, 11.5" long, Blue Opalescent, 1938, **$125**

Apple Tree vase #1561TO, Topaz Opalescent, 1938, **$198**

Spiral Optic, Cranberry
Opalescent, 1939
Left: Pitcher 64 ounce, Bulbous,
$350; **Right:** Tumbler, 10
ounce, **$50**

Hobnail, Barber Bottle, 7.5" tall,
Cranberry Opalescent, Made
for LG Wright, missing chrome
plated drip top, 1939, **$200**

1940 TO 1949
THE WAR YEARS

During the American Great Depression, Fenton had put off doing repairs to save money. It became apparent they had been delayed too long on June 29, 1940, when the smoke stack collapsed. Part of the factory was destroyed along with several of the glory hole furnaces. Built of bricks, the stack had weighed over 250 tons and was part of the original building. Under normal circumstances, the stack should be repaired every seven years. The whole factory was quickly shut down and repairs were started a few days later. While the repairs were being done, glass was made in day tanks outside and then taken to the lehrs or glory holes if additional work needed to be done. As a result of this catastrophe, a new factory was redesigned, updated and fire proofed.

The opalescent colors of Blue, Cranberry, French and Topaz increased the public interest in the Hobnail pattern. In the 1940s, the following crests were introduced: Ivory, Peach, Aqua, Crystal, Silver, Gold and Rose.

With the outbreak of World War II, needed chemicals were in short supply and production was altered on some of the glass until the war ended. Opalescent glass was eliminated for awhile in favor of plain, transparent colors. Crystal was substituted for some colors.

With European products being cut off during the war, several importers came to Fenton to find new products to sell. AA Importing, Abels, Wasserburg & Company (Charleton line), DeVilbiss, Edward P. Paul, Jay Willfred, and Weil Ceramics all purchased glass from Fenton during the war years. The new pattern of opalescent, Coin Dot, debuted in 1947 with the colors of Blue, Cranberry, French, and Honeysuckle.

A very sad day in Fenton's history occurred on May 18, 1948, when Frank L. died of a heart attack. Suddenly his young, inexperienced sons, Frank M. and Bill, were thrust into the company leadership roles. Frank took over as president and Bill took on sales presentations. While Frank M. did not have the same skill as his father in designing patterns, he frequented antique shops in search of attractive pieces to use as an inspiration for new moulds at Fenton.

Hobnail, baskets, Topaz Opalescent, 1941 to 1944
Top Left: #389 fan cone footed, 8" wide, **$165**; **Top Right:** #3830TO, flat, 10" wide, **$150**
Center: #389 deep hat, 13.5" wide, **$475**
Front Left: #3837TO deep crimped, 7" wide, **$78**; **Front Right:** #3834TO, 4.5" wide, **$58**

Ivory Crest, 1940 to 1941
Top Left: #201 vase, 5.5" tall, **$48**; **Top Right:** vase #201, 5.25" tall, **$45**
Bottom Left: #201 rose vase, 4.75" tall, **$48**; **Center:** #186 tulip vase, 8.25" tall, **$60**; #951 cornucopia candleholder, 5.75" tall, **$65**

Left: Frank M. Fenton; **Center:** Frank L. Fenton; **Right:** Jake Rosenthal at the factory in 1940
Archival photo reprinted with permission from the Fenton Art Glass Company

Hobnail, Green Opalescent, 1940 to 1941
Left: #389 bonbon candleholder, 6.5" wide, **$48**; **Right:** #389, rose bowl, 5" tall, **$75**

Hobnail lamp, 6.5" tall, Green Opalescent, Special Order for Edward P. Paul & Company, 1940 to 1941, **$100**

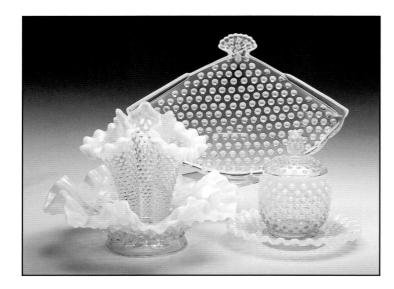

Hobnail, French Opalescent, 1940 to mid 1950s
Back: #389 fan tray, 10.5" long, **$24**
Front Left: #3801FO petite epergne, 6.5" tall, 3 horn **$78**; **Right:** #3903FO jam set, 5.5" tall, 3 piece, **$48**

Hobnail, French Opalescent, 1940 to mid 1950s
Left: #389 rose bowl, 4.5" tall, flared, **$25**; **Top Center:** #3885FO powder box, 3.5" tall, wood lid, **$28**; **Bottom Center:** #389 bonbon, 4" wide, **$14**; **Right:** #389 cone fan vase, 6" tall, **$28**

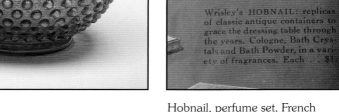

Hobnail, Cranberry Opalescent, 1940 to 1967
Top Left: #3901CR creamer, 3.75" tall, **$70**
Bottom Left: #389 candy box, 5.5" tall, 6.5" wide, **$495**;
Right: #3967CR pitcher, 7.75" tall, **$295**

Hobnail, perfume set, French Opalescent, Original Wrisley advertisement, 1940s

Hobnail, Blue Opalescent, 1940 to 1954
Top Center: #3901BO creamer, 3.25" tall, **$20**
Bottom Left: #3956BO vase, 6" tall, cupped, **$42**; **Center:** #3901BO sugar, 3.25" tall, **$20**; **Right:** #3958BO vase, 8" tall, **$55**

Hobnail #3977BO butter, Blue Opalescent, .25 pound, 1940 to 1954, **$300**

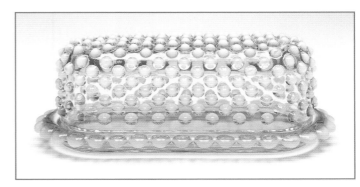

Hobnail, Blue Opalescent, 1940 to 1954
Left: #3803BO mayonnaise bowl, 4.5" wide with liner, 6" wide, **$85**; **Center:** #3222BO punch bowl and base, 1.75 gallons, **$260**; **Right:** 33847BO punch cup, 4.5oz., **$24**

Hobnail #389 fan vases, 1940s to mid 1950s
Top: French Opalescent, 7.5" tall, **$38**; French Opalescent, 5.5" tall, **$28**; Topaz Opalescent, 5.5" tall, **$54**
Bottom: Blue Opalescent, 7.5" tall, **$60**; Blue Opalescent, 5.5" tall, **$48**; Topaz Opalescent, 7.5" tall, **$85**

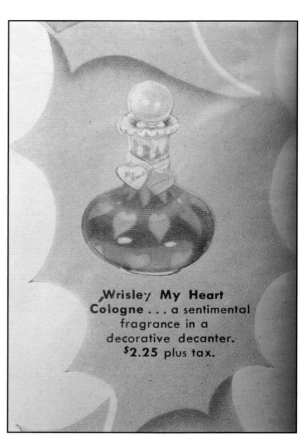

Heart Optic vase, 4.75" tall, French Opalescent, single crimp top, twist neck, special order for Wrisley, 1940s, **$38**

Heart Optic, Perfume bottle, French Opalescent, Original Wrisley advertisement, 1940s

Hobnail #389, Epergne, 9" wide, Blue Opalescent, 1941 to 1943, **$250**

Blue Opalescent, 1941 to 1943
Left: Hobnail #389, cookie jar, **$350**;
Right: Hobnail vase #3855, **$18**

Hobnail, Cranberry Opalescent
Left: Vase #3858, 8" tall, double crimp top, 1941 to 1969, **$98**; **Center:** Fan vase (card holder) #389, 3.75" tall, 3.5" wide, 1940 to 1951, **$45**; **Right:** Student Lamp #389, 18" tall, 8.5" wide, 1941, **$125**

Hobnail vase #3859CR, Cranberry Opalescent, 1941 to 1945, **$225**

Hobnail, jam set #3903, 4.75" tall, 6" wide, Cranberry Opalescent, 1948 to 1957, **$125 set**

Ruby Silver Crest, Special Order for Jay-Willfred Company, 1940
Top: #835 vase, 6" tall, **$95**; **Right:** #1522 bowl, 9.5" long, **$175**
Bottom: #835 vase, 5.5" tall, **$95**; **Center:** #680 cornucopia candleholder, 6" tall, **$95**; **Right:** #184 vase, 8.5" tall, **$160**

Hobnail, pitchers, Topaz Opalescent, 1941 to 1944
Top: #3964TO squat, 4.5" tall, **$75**
Left: #3762TO syrup, 5.75" tall, crimped top, **$75**; **Right:** #389, high tankard, 8.25" tall, **$450**
Center: #3965TO flat squat, 5.25" tall, **$85**; **Front Right:** #3366TO syrup, 5.5" tall, **$75**

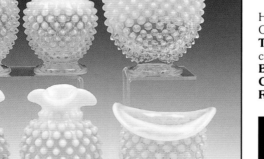

Hobnail, #3855 vases, 4" tall, Topaz Opalescent, 1941 to 1944
Top Left: flared top, **$25**; **Top Center:** cupped flared, **$25**; **Top Right:** fan, **$48**
Bottom Left: crimped, **$24**; **Bottom Center:** triangle crimp, **$28**; **Bottom Right:** two sides rolled over, **$35**

Hobnail, Topaz Opalescent, 1941 to 1944
Back: #389 fan tray, 10.5" wide, **$38**
Bottom Left: #389 shakers, 4.5" tall, footed, **$85** pair;
Bottom Center: #389 mustard, 3.5" tall, **$48**; **Bottom Right:** #3869TO cruet, 4.75" tall, **$75**

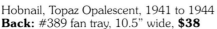

Hobnail, vanity items, 1940 to 1950s
Left: #3865 cologne bottles, 4.5"
tall, Topaz Opalescent, **$85**, French
Opalescent, **$32**; **Center:** #3885BO
puff box, 3.5" tall, Blue Opalescent,
$45; **Right:** #3865 cologne bottles,
4.5" tall, Cranberry Opalescent, **$85**,
Blue Opalescent, **$48**

Worker flaring out the top of a vase
*Archival photo reprinted with
permission from the Fenton Art
Glass Company*

Daisy and Button #1900, Vanity
set – perfume (two) bottles 4"
tall, covered puff box 3" wide,
fan shaped tray 10.5" wide,
Topaz, 1948, **$350**

Back: #920 shell bowl, 10.5"
wide, Peach Crest, 1940 to 1949,
$100
Front Left: #1925 basket, 12"
tall, Peach Crest, 1940 to 1949,
$145; **Front Center:** #201,
vase, 4" tall, Peach Blow, 1939
to 1940, **$40**; **Front Right:**
#194 vase, 11.5" tall, Peach
Crest, 1940 to 1949, **$85**

Left: Peach Crest #187 vase, 5.25" tall, 1940 to 1949, **$38**;
Center: #192 vase, 4.5" tall, Peach Blow, 1939 to 1940, **$30**;
Right: Peach Crest #192 vase, 6.5" tall, 1940 to 1949, **$35**

Little Flowers atomizers, 4.24" tall, Special Order for
DeVilbiss, 1941
Top: #CS100-8, French Opalescent, **$68**
Bottom Left: #CS100-10, Green Opalescent, **$98**;
Bottom Right: #CS100-9, Blue Opalescent, **$85**

Dot Optic, Melon #711 ewer,
6" tall, Crystal with Topaz
handle, 1941 to 1945, **$65**

Plume, Special Order for DeVilbiss, 1941
Top Left: #D100-41 cologne, 4.5" tall, French
Opalescent, **$65**; **Top Right:** #S100-307
atomizer, 4" tall, French, **$60**
Bottom Left: #D100- 43 cologne, 4.5"
tall, Topaz Opalescent, **$80** and #S100-309
atomizer, 4" tall, Topaz, **$85**; **Bottom Right:**
#D100- 42 cologne, 4.5" tall, Blue Opalescent,
$70 and #S100-308 atomizer, Blue, 4" tall, **$75**

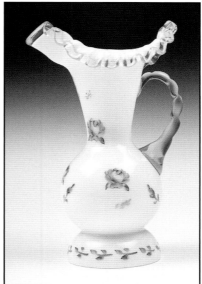

#7264AC jug, 9" tall, Aqua Crest, Charleton decoration, 1941 to 1943, **$100**

Scroll atomizers, 6.5" tall, Opalescent, Special Order for DeVilbiss, 1941
Top: #CS250-1, French, **$125**
Bottom Left: #CS250-3, Topaz, **$195**; **Bottom Right:** #CS250-2, Blue, **$165**

Aqua Crest, #37 Miniatures, 1942
Left: Vase, 2.5" tall, **$38**; **Center:** Basket, 4" tall, **$60**; **Right:** Pitcher, 2.5" tall, **$45**

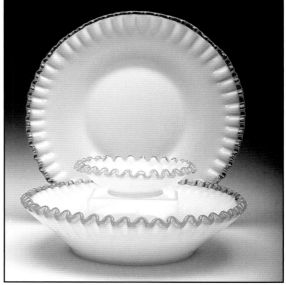

Aqua Crest, 1941 to 1943
Top Left: #187 vase, 5" tall, **$45**; **Top Right:** #835 vase, 6"tall, **$60**
Bottom Left: #4517 vase, 6.75" tall, **$60**; **Bottom Center:** #36 vase, 4.25" tall, **$28**; Melon #192 candleholder, 3.75" tall, **$40**; **Bottom Right:** #1925 basket, 11.25" tall, **$195**

Aqua Crest, 1941 to 1943
Back: #7210AC plate, 11.5" wide, **$58**; **Top Center:** #7222AC dessert bowl, 5.5" wide, **$18**; **Bottom Center:** #7220AC salad bowl, 10.25" wide, **$58**

Diamond Optic, Ruby Overlay, 1942 to 1948
Left: #1924 basket 4.75" tall, **$48**; **Center:** #192 vase, 7.75" tall, **$68**; **Right:** #1924 creamer, 4" tall, **$38**

Diamond Optic #192 vases, Melon, Ruby Overlay, single crimp, 1942 to 1949
Left: 5" tall, **$24**; **Center:** 6" tall, **$29**; **Right:** 6" tall, **Note:** the bottom half is only crystal, **$38**

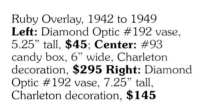

Ruby Overlay, 1942 to 1949
Left: Diamond Optic #192 vase, 5.25" tall, **$45**; **Center:** #93 candy box, 6" wide, Charleton decoration, **$295 Right:** Diamond Optic #192 vase, 7.25" tall, Charleton decoration, **$145**

Diamond Optic, Ruby Overlay, Huntington Art Works, 1942 to 1945
Left and Right: Melon #192 cologne bottle, 4.5" tall; **Center:** #192 powder box, 3.75" tall, **$295 set**

Diamond Optic, Mulberry, 1942
Top Left: #192 vase, 5" tall,
$85; **Top Right:** #192 jug, 6"
tall, **$125**
Bottom Left: #1924 hat
vase, 3.25" tall, **$75**; **Bottom
Center:** #192 vase, 7.5" tall,
$175; **Bottom Right:** #1924
creamer, 3.75" tall, **$95**

Diamond Optic #1353, Mulberry,
1942
Left: Water pitcher, 70 ounce,
$495; **Right:** Tumbler, 4" tall, **$100**

Melon #192 Crystal Crest vase, 6.5" tall, Charleton decoration,
1942, **$125**

Crystal Crest, 1942
Back: #1522 bowl, 11.25"wide, **$85**;
Front: #1924 hat vase, 3.5" tall, **$60**

Vase grouping, Crystal Crest, 1942
Top Left: #36, 4" tall, tri corner, **$45**; **Top Right:** #1924 Jack in Pulpit hat, 3.75" tall, **$50**
Bottom Left: #36, 4" tall, double crimp, **$45**; **Bottom Center:** #36 vase, 4" tall, square top, **$50**; **Bottom Right:** #1924, 3.75" tall, double crimp, **$45**

Left: Rose Crest, candlestick #1523, 4.75" tall, 1944 to 1947, **$38**; **Right**: Crystal Crest, cologne bottle #192, 8.75" tall, 1942, **$175**

Charleton, 1940s
Top Left: Silver Crest, fan vase #7357, 6.5" tall, **$30**; **Bottom Left:** Peach Crest, Melon vase #192, 6" tall, **$50**; **Center:** Silver Crest, three tier tray #7295, 15" tall, 12" wide, **$125**; **Top Right:** Silver Crest, plate #7217, 8.5" wide **$38**; **Bottom Right:** Silver Crest, comport #7228, 3.75" tall, 7" wide, **$30**

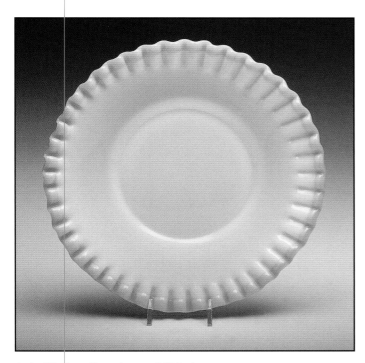

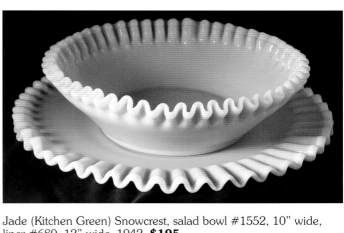

Jade (Kitchen Green) Snowcrest, salad bowl #1552, 10" wide, liner #680, 12" wide, 1942, **$195**

Jade (Kitchen Green) crest #680 plate, 8.5" wide, 1942, **$65**

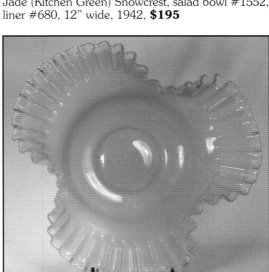

Jade (Kitchen Green) with clear crest, #1522 bowl, 10" wide, 1942, **$98**

Jade (Kitchen Green) Snowcrest, 1942
Left: Cornucopia candleholder #957, **$95**;
Right: Dessert bowl and liner #680, **$98**

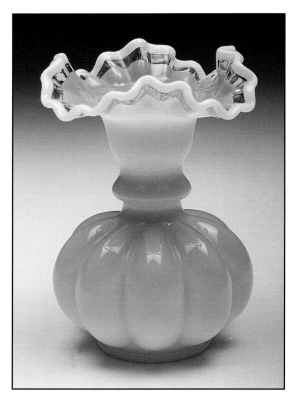

Melon #192 Crystal Peach Crest vase,
6.5" tall, 1942, **$145**
Note: This is a variation of the regular
Peach Crest since it has a Milk Glass
crest just like Crystal Crest.

Silver Crest, 1942 to 1950s
Far Left: #7262SC vase, 12.75" tall, **$145**;
Top Center: #7237SC basket, 7.5" tall, **$45**;
Top Right: #7280SC candy box, 9.5" tall, **$65**
Bottom Left: #37 miniature vase, 2.15" tall, **$85**;
Bottom Center: #1924SC hat basket, 7" tall, **$48**;
Bottom Right: #7206SC shaker, 4.85" tall, **$40**

Melon # 192 vanity set, Silver
Crest, Charleton decoration,
1942 to 1950s
Left and Right: perfume
bottle, 5" tall; **Center:** powder
box, 4.5" tall, **$185 set**

Blue Overlay, 1943
Top Center: Melon #216 jug, 6" tall, **$38**
Left: #203 basket, 7.5" tall, **$48**;
Center: Melon #216 candleholder, 3" tall, **$28**;
Right: Melon #192A jug, 8.25" tall, **$58**

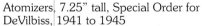

Atomizers, 7.25" tall, Special Order for
DeVilbiss, 1941 to 1945
Top: Ivory Crest, #CS750-1, **$125**
Bottom Left: Blue Overlay, #CS750-3, **$85**;
Bottom Right: Peach Crest, #CS750-2, **$95**

Gold Crest, 1943 to 1944
Top Center: #1924 hat basket, 7" tall, **$40**
Bottom Left: #186 vase, 8.25" tall, **$28**;
Center: #7474 candlestick, 6" tall, **$24**;
Right: Melon #192 vase, 8.25" tall, **$32**

Left: Melon Vase, 5.5" tall, Blue Overlay, double crimp, Gold encrusted etching, attributed to Lotus, **$75**; **Right:** Lotus Store Display Sign, 3" tall, 4.5" wide, red and gold plastic, **$100**
Note: We have not been able to verify that this vase was decorated by Lotus at this time. In talking with Dean Six, who authored the Lotus book, he thinks that it is a strong possibility that Lotus did the decoration but at this time we have not found any proof.

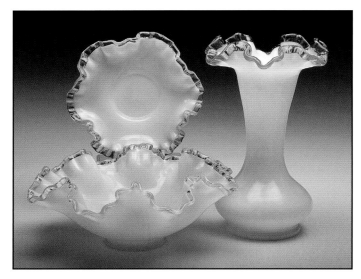

Rose Crest, 1944 to 1947
Top: #36 bonbon, 6" wide, **$15**;
Front Left: #205 bowl, 8.5" wide, **$35**
Right: #186 vase, 8.25" tall, **$38**

Coin Dot, French Opalescent, 1947 to early 1950s
Left: #1467FO pitcher, 9.5" tall, **$195**;
Center: #208 vase, 5.5" tall, **$40**;
Right: #1925FO basket, 10.5" tall, **$125**

Epergne, four horn, 16" tall, special order
for LG Wright, 1944 to 1947
Left: Rose Crest, **$350**;
Right: Aqua Crest, **$375**

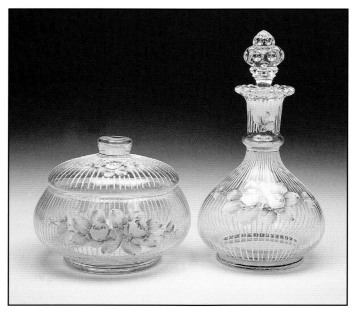

Crystal, Charleton decoration, mid 1940s
Left: #93 candy box, 6" wide, **$75**;
Right: #814 cologne, 9.5" tall, **$75**

Coin Dot, Blue Opalescent, 1947 to 1955
Top: #208 vase, 5.5" tall, **$65**
Left: #914 vase, 11" tall, handled, **$195**;
Center: #1353 tumbler, 4" tall, **$40**;
Right: #1553 pitcher, 9.5" tall, **$245**

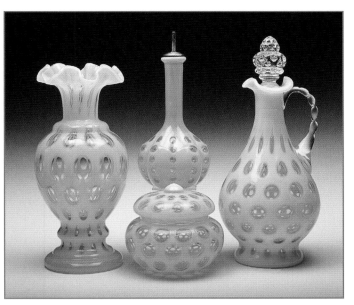

Coin Dot, Blue Opalescent, 1947 to 1955
Top Center: #1471BO barber bottle, tall, 7.5" tall, **$150**;
Left: #194BO vase, 10.75"tall, **$195**;
Bottom Center: #91 candy jar, 4.5" tall, **$95**;
Right: #894 decanter, 12.5" tall, **$395**

Coin Dot, Blue Opalescent, 1947 to 1955
Left: #1437BO basket, 7" tall, 7" wide; **$85**;
Right: #1430BO basket, 8.5" tall, 10" long, **$275**

Leaf #175, plate, 8.5" long, 8" wide, Blue Opalescent,
1941 to 1943, **$30**

Glass blower in the factory
*Archival photo reprinted with permission
from the Fenton Art Glass Company*

Coin Spot atomizer, 3.25" tall, Blue Opalescent, Special Order for DeVilbiss, 1947, **$60**

Beaded Melon atomizers, 6.25" tall, Special Order for DeVilbiss, late 1940s
Top: Milk Glass, #S350-22, **$65**
Bottom Left: Rose Overlay, #S350-24, **$95**;
Bottom Right: Blue Overlay, #S350-23, **$85**

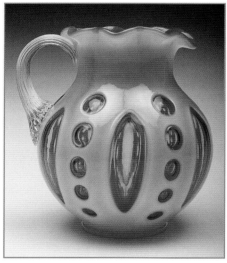

Dot and Miter pitcher, 6" tall, Cranberry Opalescent, Special Order for LG Wright, 1947 to 1949, **$400**

Coin Dot, #S5100-1 dresser set, Cranberry Opalescent, Special Order for DeVilbiss, late 1940s, **$395 set**
Top: atomizer, 4.75" tall
Bottom Left: powder box, 4.75" tall; **Bottom Right:** ashtray, 2" tall

Coin Dot, Cranberry Opalescent, 1947 to 1948
Left: Hat basket #1435, **$75**; **Center:** Vase #189, double crimp, **$125**; **Right:** Cruet #1469, 8", **$135**

Coin Dot, Cranberry Opalescent, 1947 to 1964
Left: #208 cruet, 7" tall, **$250**; **Center:** #1456CR, vase, 8.25" tall, **$125**; **Right:** #1441CR vase, 7" tall, **$95**

Beaded Curtain and Diamond Optic miniature kerosene lamp, 9" tall, Cranberry Opalescent Satin, 1947 to 1949, **$450**

Plymouth #1620 covered cigarette box, 4" wide, Crystal, chrome tray, Special Order for Farber Bros, 7" wide, 1948 to 1950, **$45**

Ivy Overlay, 1949 to 1952
Top Left: Beaded Melon #711 tulip vase, 4.75" tall, **$25**; **Top Right:** #1925 vase, 6.5" tall, **$48**
Bottom Left: Beaded Melon #711 tulip vase, 7.25" tall, **$45**; **Bottom Center:** Beaded Melon #711 vase, 5.25" tall, **$45**; **Bottom Right:** Beaded Melon #711 pitcher, 6" tall, **$58**

Backwards C atomizers, Special Order for DeVilbiss, 1948
Left: #S750-36, Rose Overlay, **$75**; **Right:** #S750-37, Blue Overlay, **$75**

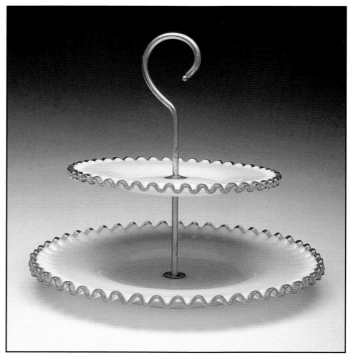

Ivy Overlay, 1949 to 1952
Left: Beaded Melon #711 tulip vase, 9.5" tall, **$65**; **Right:** #186 tulip vase, Charleton decoration, 9.25" tall, **$98**

#7294 2 tier tray, 8.5" wide plate and 12.5" wide plate, Emerald Crest, metal center handle, 1949 to 1955, **$85**

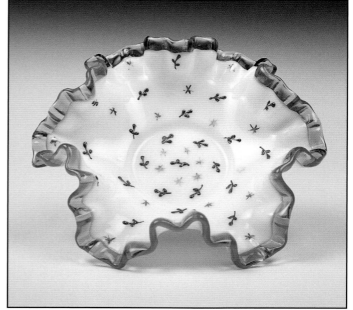

Emerald Crest, 1949 to 1955
Top Left: #7269EC cruet, 5.5" tall, **$125**; **Top Right:** #36 fan vase, 4.5" tall, **$24**
Bottom Left: #401 flower pot, 4.5" tall, **$58**; **Bottom Right:** #680 open sugar, 3.25" tall, **$24**

#203 bowl, 7" wide, Emerald Crest, Charleton decoration, 1949, **$48**

1950 TO 1959
MILK GLASS AND MORE

An important era in Fenton's history took place in 1950 with the introduction of Milk Glass Hobnail. This glass contributed to a large portion of Fenton's sales during this time period. Colored Hobnail continued in popularity and a square version was added but it didn't meet with much success. A new crest line called Snowcrest was introduced with the edge being milk glass and applied to Amber, Blue, Emerald Green, and Ruby Overlay.

On July 1, 1952, Fenton changed from a three digit number to a four digit number. For instance, previously the #389 marked the entire Hobnail line and every item had the same number. Now, the new code separated out all of the pieces. In the new system, the first two numbers signified a two digit design or pattern. The next two numbers marked the item and the last two digits were the color code. Let's take the #3830TO code. The 38 is for Hobnail, the 30 is for the 10" basket and TO indicates it was made in Topaz Opalescent. In the beginning the last two digits were always letters but now they could be a combination of a letter and a number.

The closure of Paden City Glass caused Fenton to obtain another new customer. Rubel & Company of New York had previously done business with Paden and now turned to Fenton to make glass for them. A special room that had previously been built as additional storage space, now would be put to use. This agreement would continue for several years until the situation was no longer profitable for either.

Fenton reached a milestone in 1955 by celebrating their 50th anniversary. Several new colors were added to the line: Cased Lilac, Rose Pastel, and Turquoise. More and more items were added to the Milk Glass Hobnail collection. Different colors of crests were also increased. The Cactus pattern in Milk Glass and Topaz was introduced in 1959.

An astonishing amount of $2.25 million in sales was achieved in 1957. Sales would continue strong the next year and surpassed that amount by almost half a million. A new warehouse was built in 1958 that held a special conveyor referred to as a flow rack. Glass was stacked behind the conveyor so a clerk could easily grab a piece and place it in a box that moved down the system. This was a great time saver.

Aerial photo of Fenton factory; original photo taken by S. Durward Hoag in May 1951, 1955 catalog
Reprinted with permission from Fenton Art Glass Company

Hobnail, Square, Blue Opalescent, 1950 to 1955
Left: #3919BO plate, 7" wide, salad, **$68;**
Center: #3808BO cup - 4" wide and saucer-7" wide, **$125**;
Right: #3910BO plate, 11" wide, dinner, **$12**0

Ruby Snowcrest, 1950 to 1954
Top Left: #3159RS vase, 9.25" tall, **$85**
Bottom Left: #3150RS vase, 9.75" tall, **$125**;
Bottom Center: #3156RS vase, 6.5" tall, **$80**;
Bottom Right: vase #3151RS, 11"tall, **$145**

Amber Snowcrest, 1951 to 1952
Left: #170 hurricane electric lamp, 11" tall, Special Order for Light House Lamp and Shade Company, **$125**; **Center:** #1923 hat vase, 4.5" tall, **$45**; **Right:** #170 hurricane lamp, 11" tall, **$95**

Emerald Snowcrest, 1950 to 1954
Left: #3159GS vase, 9.5"tall, **$75**;
Right: #3151GS vase, 11" tall, **$125**

Blue Snowcrest, 1950 to 1951
Top Left: #1925 vase, 6.75" tall, **$95**; **Top Right:** #194 vase, 9.25" tall, **$145**
Center: #1925 vase, 4.75" tall, **$65**
Bottom Left: #3151 vase, 10.75" tall, **$225**; **Bottom Center:** #3154 vase, 4" tall, **$65**; **Bottom Right:** #3153 lamp, 9.25" tall, **$125**

Milk Glass
Top Left: Hobnail #3971MI miniature cornucopia candleholder, 3.5" tall, 1950 to 1956, **$20**; **Top Center:** Hobnail #3945MI tumbler, 2.5" tall, 1952 to 1967, **$10**; **Top Right:** Hobnail #3847MI punch cup, 2.5" tall, 1950 to 1965, **$18**
Bottom Left: Hobnail #3869MI cruet, 5" tall, 1950 to 1969, **$18**; **Bottom Center:** Hobnail #3889MI mustard, 3" tall, 1950 to 1968, **$35**; Daisy and Button #1994MI bootie, 2.25" tall, 1973, **$12**; **Bottom Right:** Hobnail #3825MI sherbet, 4.25" tall, 1954 to 1967, **$16**

Hobnail Milk Glass
Top Left: #3967MI water pitcher, 7.5" tall, 1953 to 1968, **$125**; **Top Center:** #3755MI swung vase, 12.5" tall, 1971 to 1987, **$45**; **Top Right:** #3887MI footed covered comport, 8.5" tall, 1953 to 1968, **$38**
Bottom Left: #3634MI oval basket, 6.5" long, 1963 to 1968, **$38**; **Bottom Center:** #3809MI condiment set: (#3806MI shakers, 3.25" tall, #3869MI cruet, 4.75" tall, #3889MI mustard, 3" tall, #3900MI creamer, 2" tall, #3900MI sugar, 2" tall, on a #3879MI tray, 7.75" wide), 1950 to 1973, **$98**;
Bottom Right: #3637MI basket, 9" tall, 1963 to 1977, **$65**

Hobnail, Cranberry Opalescent
Top Left: #3869CR cruet, 4.75" tall, 1950 to 1964, **$85**; **Top Right:** 3964CR pitcher, 4.5" tall, 1941 to 1955, **$65**
Bottom Left: #3837CR basket, 7" tall, 1940 to 1969, **$98**;
Bottom Center: #3870CR candleholder, 3.25" tall, handled, 1953 to 1969, **$55**; #3806CR shaker, 3.25" tall, 1954 to 1968, **$45**; **Bottom Right:** #3854CR vase, 4.5" tall, 1940 to 1969, **$85**

Hobnail, covered candy jar #3980, 6.5" tall, 4.5" wide, Milk Glass, 1951 to 1969, **$16**

Rib Optic, Cranberry Opalescent, 1952 to 1955
Top Left: #1604CR sugar, 3.25" tall, New World line, **$75**; **Top Center:** #1604CR creamer, 4.25" tall, New World line, **$95**; **Top Right:** #3248CR cone vase, 4.75" tall, **$98**
Bottom Left: #88 barber bottle, 7.5" tall, Made for LG Wright, **$175**; **Bottom Center:** #1605CR salt 5.25" tall, pepper 4.25"tall, New World line, **$100 pair**; **Bottom Center:** #1622CR ivy ball on Milk Glass base, 4.5" tall, **$125**; #1647CR wine tumbler, 3.75" tall, New World line, **$100**; **Bottom Right:** #1669CR cruet, 7.5" tall, New World line, **$200**; #1667CR wine bottle, 13.5" tall, New World line, **$175**

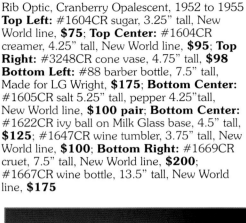

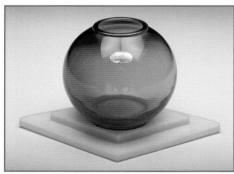

#705 ivy ball on base, 4.5" tall, Cranberry on Milk Glass, 1952 to 1953, **$95**

Ivy ball #1021, 8.75" tall, 4.5" wide, Ruby Overlay top, Milk Glass base, 1953 to 1966, **$49**

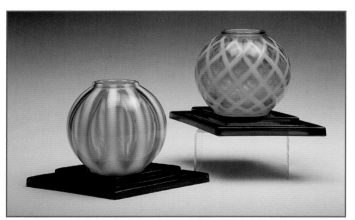

Ivy balls on trays,
Left: Rib Optic #1622GO 4.75" tall, Green Opalescent, 1953, **$125**; **Right:** Diamond Optic #1722LO 4.75" tall, Lime Opalescent, 1952 to 1954, **$150**

Rib Optic, Lime Green Opalescent, New World line, 1953 to 1954
Top Left: #1647LO wine tumbler, 4" tall, **$125**; **Top Right:** #1619LO plate, 9.25" wide, **$125**
Bottom Left: #1605LO salt 5.25" tall and pepper 4.25" tall, **$145** pair; **Bottom Center:** #1604LO sugar, 3.25" tall, **$90**; #1604LO creamer, 4.25" tall, **$110**; **Bottom Right:** #1669LO cruet (missing stopper), 6.25" tall, **$275**. Note: price includes having a stopper.

Coin Dot, Lime Green Opalescent, 1952 to 1954
Left to Right: #1456LO vase, 6" tall, **$115**; #1454LO vase, 4.5" tall, **$50**; #1457LO vase, 7" tall, **$100**; #1459LO vase, **$125**
Reprinted with permission from the Schiffer Publishing, Ltd.

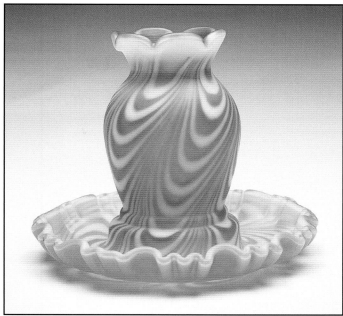

Swirled Feather one piece fairy light #2092RA, tall, Cranberry Opalescent Satin, 1953 to 1955, **$450**

Black Rose, 1953 to 1955
Left: #7350BR vase, 5" tall, **$85**; **Center:** #5155BR hand vase, 10.5" tall, **$350**; **Right:** #7398BR hurricane lamp, 8" tall, **$300**

Hen collection, 1953 to 1954
Top Left: #5188 hen egg server, 12" long, Milk Glass with Emerald Green head, **$500**; **Top Right:** #5188 hen egg server, 12" long, Milk Glass with Amethyst head, **$500**
Bottom Left: #5189 hen egg server, 12" long, Amethyst with Milk Glass head, **$550**; **Bottom Center:** #5185 chick, 5.5" long, Emerald Green top with Milk Glass base, **$95**; **Bottom Right:** #5185 chick, 5.5" long, Amethyst top with Milk Glass base, **$95**

Hens on nest, #5183
Left: Amethyst with Milk Glass head, 6.25" tall, 6.5" wide, 9" long, **$125**; **Right:** Milk Glass, 6.25" tall, 6.5" wide, 9" long, **$45**

Swirled Feather, Green
Opalescent Satin, 1952
Left: One piece fairy light #2092,
$395; **Right:** Covered candy
box #2083, **$200**

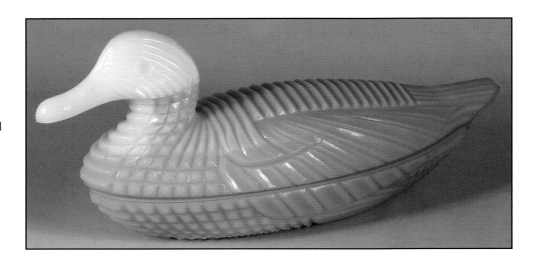

Atterbury Duck #70-2, Milk
Glass head, Jade (Kitchen
Green) body, covered animal
dish, Made for LG Wright,
1950s, **$150**

Fish Vases #5156, two tone,
1953 to 1954, **$250 each**
Left: Milk Glass with
Amethyst accents;
Right: Amethyst with Milk
Glass accents

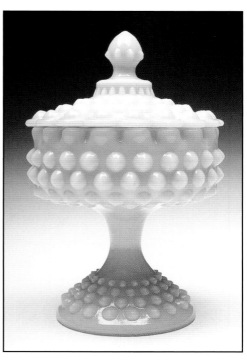

Hobnail #3986 boxtle: cologne and powder combination, 7.1" tall, 1953 to 1954
Left: French Opalescent, **$225**; **Right:** Blue Opalescent, **$350**

Hobnail #3887RP footed covered comport, 8.5" tall, Rose Pastel, 1954 to 1957, **$85**

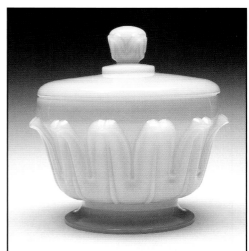

Opaque Pastels, 1950s
Left: Hobnail #3924GP bowl, 10" wide, Green Pastel, 1954 to 1955, **$38**; **Center:** Hobnail #3974TU candleholder, 3" tall, Turquoise, 1955, **$35**; **Right:** #5116RP leaf plate, 8.5" wide, Rose Pastel, 1954 to 1955, **$45**

Lambs Tongue #4381BP covered candy, Blue Pastel, 1954 to 1955, **$95**

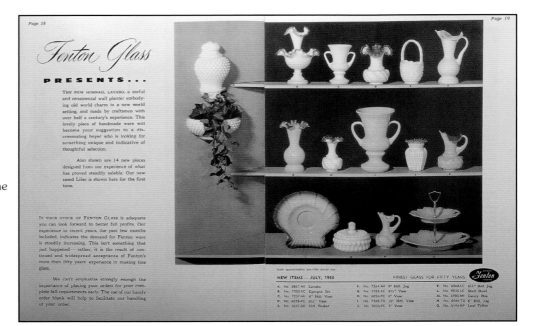

New items for July 1955, from the 1955 catalog
Reprinted with permission from the Fenton Art Glass Company

Cased Lilac, 1955 to 1956
Left: #7255LC vase, 8.75" tall, **$75**;
Center: #9020LC shell bowl, 10.25" wide, **$85**; **Right:** #7264LC pitcher, 9" tall, **$95**

Teardrop, Turquoise, 1955 to 1956
Left: #6909TU condiment set, **$125**; **Right:** #6985TU flat covered candy, **$58**
Reprinted with permission from the Schiffer Publishing Ltd.

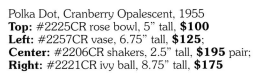

Polka Dot, Cranberry Opalescent, 1955
Top: #2225CR rose bowl, 5" tall, **$100**
Left: #2257CR vase, 6.75" tall, **$125**;
Center: #2206CR shakers, 2.5" tall, **$195** pair;
Right: #2221CR ivy ball, 8.75" tall, **$175**

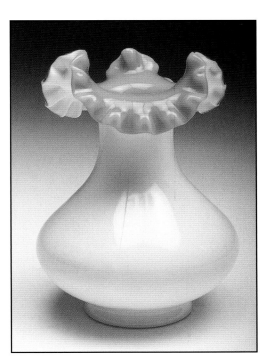

#7252GD vase, 7.5" tall,
Goldenrod, 1956, **$65**

Goldenrod, 1956
Left: #7258GD vase, 8"tall, **$50**;
Right: Beaded Melon #711, basket, 10" tall, **$135**
Note: This color was very hard to maintain with
color varying from a light yellow to a dark yellow.

Beaded Melon #711 rose bowl, 5" tall,
Goldenrod, 1956, **$40**

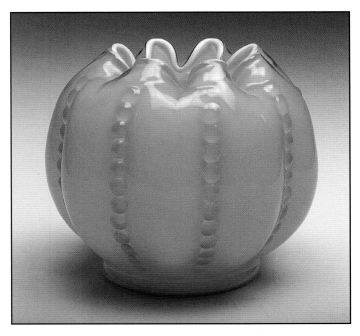

#7330ST, Silver Turquoise square footed bowl, 8.25" tall, 1956 to 1959, **$98**

Silver Turquoise, 1956 to 1959
Left: #7202ST epergne, 10.5" tall, **$100**;
Center: #7225ST bonbon, 6" wide, **$18**;
Right: #7237ST basket, 7.5" tall, **$85**

Silver Crest, late 1950s
Left: #7342SC tumbler, 6" tall, **$68**; **Center:** #7467SC pitcher, 9" tall, **$275**; **Right:** #7342SC tumbler, 6" tall, laying down to show foot, **$6**8

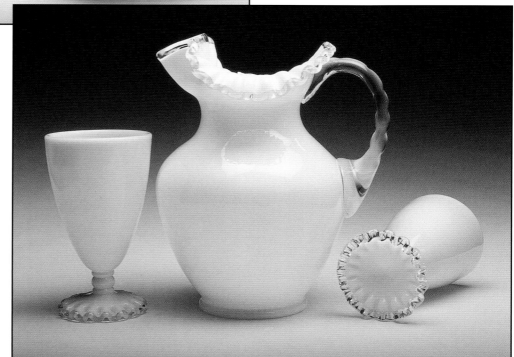

Daisy and Fern, Cranberry Opalescent, Made for LG Wright, 1950s
Top Left: #98-6 rose bowl, 4" tall, **$60**; **Top Right:** #96-2 sugar shaker, 4.5" tall, **$95**
Bottom Left: #96A-2 syrup, 6.75" tall, **$295**; **Center:** finger bowl, 4.75" wide, **$95**; **Right:** #94-2 cruet, 7" tall, **$225**

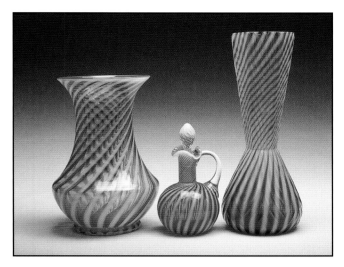

Spiral Optic, Cranberry Opalescent
Left: #183 vase, 9.25" tall, 1939, **$195**; **Center:** #95-4 cruet, 6.5" tall, Made for LG Wright, 1950s, **$175**;
Right: #3261CR vase, 11.75" tall, 1956 to 1959, **$195**

Jamestown Blue, 1958 to 1959
Top Left: Pillar vase #9055JB, Overlay, 4.75" tall, **$49**;
Top Center: Polka Dot, Rose bowl #2424JT, 3.25" tall, **$48**
Bottom Left: Cream pitcher #2461JT, Overlay, 4.25" tall, **$40**;
Center: Vase #7456JB, Overlay, 6" tall, **$49**;
Right: Polka Dot, Pinch vase #2452JT, 8" tall, **$75**

Polka Dot #2450JT vase, 6" tall, Jamestown Blue, 1958 to 1959, **$48**

Hobnail, Green Opalescent, 1959 to 1961
Left: #3887 footed covered comport, 8.5" tall, **$110**;
Center: #3762 pitcher, 5.75" tall, **$65**;
Right: #3731 footed bowl, 7" tall, 10" wide, **$100**

Emerald Green, Condiment sets, set on black metal stand
with maple ball feet and top of handle, Special order for
Rubel & Co., 1950s
Left: jam and jelly jars, 3.75" tall, **$125 set**; **Right:** oil
bottles, 6.75" tall, **$125 set**

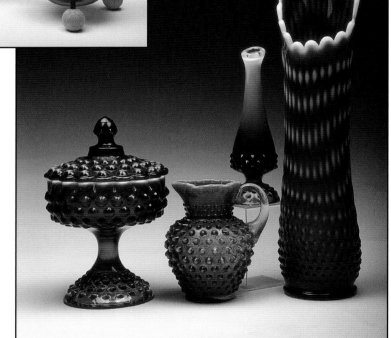

Hobnail, Plum Opalescent, 1959 to 1962
Left: Covered candy #3887PO, 8.5" tall, **$145**; **Top
Center:** Bud vase #3756PO, 7.5" tall, **$48**; **Bottom
Center:** Syrup pitcher #3762PO, 5.5" tall, **$75**; **Right:**
Swung vase #3759PO, 16.5" tall, **$195**

Cactus, Topaz Opalescent, 1959 to
1961
Left to Right: #3454TO vase, 5"
tall, **$48**; #3456TO flared vase, 7"
tall, **$85**; #3459TO fan vase, 6" tall,
$175; #3457TO vase, 7" tall, **$85**;
#3455TO flared vase, 5" tall, **$60**
*Reprinted with permission from the
Schiffer Publishing, Ltd.*

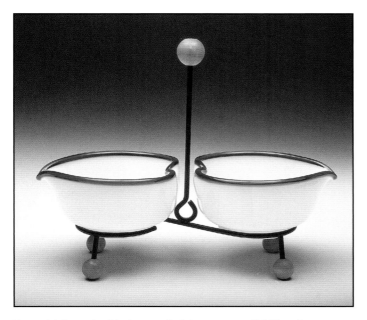

Emerald Crest double heart salad dressing set, 5.25" wide, set in black metal tray with maple handle and feet, Special Order for Rubel, 1950s, **$85**

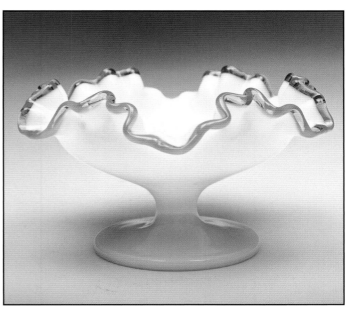

Emerald Crest, Comport #7329, 7.75" wide, low footed, 1954 to 1956, **$24**

Milk Glass, 1950s
Top Left: #9199MI turtle ring tree, 4" tall, **$20**;
Top Right: #9299MI owl ring tree, 4.5" tall, **$20**;
Bottom Left: #9080MI honey box, 4.5" wide, **$38**;
Bottom Right: #5180MI, owl decision maker, 4.5" tall, **$49**

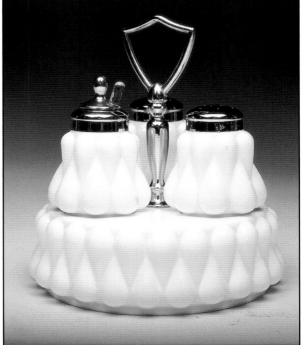

Teardrop, Condiment set #6909MI, Milk Glass, 1955 to 1962, **$75**
Shakers- 2.75" tall, 2.5" wide; Mustard- 3.5" tall, 2.5" wide; Crystal spoon- 3.25" long; Tray- 7" tall, 5.5" wide.

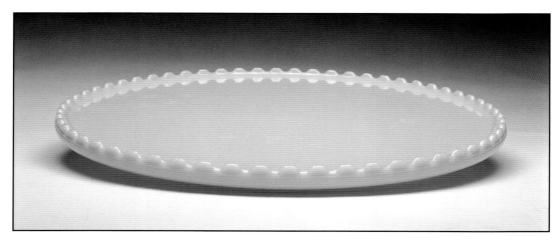

Dentist tray, Ivory, industrial use, 14" wide, 1950s, **$45**

American Beauty, Student lamp, 18.5" tall, 11.5" wide, Wild Rose Overlay, made for LG Wright, brass base, 1950s, **$250**

1960 TO 1969
A NEW AGE OF COLOR

In 1960 more improvements took place and continued over the next several years. In the middle 1960s, Fenton started issuing their catalogs in full color and, as a result, greatly improved their sales.

In order to further expand on their sales, Fenton entered into an arrangement with wholesalers and catalog companies to sell glass that wasn't part of their regular line. Fenton's name wasn't associated with any of this glass so as not to interfere with sales of their regular retailers. The name of Olde Virginia Glass was established in 1960. This line continued until the end of the 1970s, when catalog sales were no longer profitable.

The monumental hiring of Charlie Goe as Fenton's chemist in 1960 would have a huge influence in future sales at Fenton. One of his first important colors was the development of Vasa Murrhina. In 1961, Fenton decided to name a pattern in honor of Jacqueline Kennedy, wife of President John F. Kennedy. The Jacqueline pattern resembled overlapping petals.

In 1963, the Fenton Gift Shop was reorganized to be a separate company, operating completely independent of the Fenton Art Glass Company. The gift shop is the largest account of the company. Dave Fetty came to work at Fenton in 1965 after being employed at Blenko for a number of years.

1966 brought more changes to Fenton. The Verlys moulds, owned by Holophane of Newark, Ohio, were purchased that year. Additional moulds previously owned by US Glass were also bought by Fenton. Some of these included the Rose pattern and Alley cat. Previously, Fenton had only made lamp parts for other companies. Now lamps began to be made as part of their own line. Howard Seufer came to work in the position of Methods Engineer and in later years was Quality Control Manager. Bob Hill, formerly from Wheaton Glass, was hired by Fenton. Also about this time the company offices were moved and hot metal was expanded.

As with any company, sometimes things happen and there is no explanation. While sales were good in 1966, suddenly there was a big drop in 1967 and this continued through 1968. Things turned around in 1969 and suddenly sales were back on track. There had been a decrease in Milk Glass sales but now it was back to selling well.

Tony Rosena, a designer, came to work for Fenton in 1967 from Jeannette Glass. The first piece he designed for Fenton was the #3986MI Milk Glass Hobnail covered urn. Today this urn is very hard to find. Tony was also instrumental in the hiring of Louise Piper. She had started her decorating career at Jeannette Glass and was now working for Jeannette Shade and Novelty Company. Tony had known Louise while they were both employed at Jeannette Glass. When he heard that Fenton was looking to re-establish a decorating department, Tony instantly thought of Louise and contacted her about coming to work at Fenton. Louise's first hand-painted decoration was Violets in the Snow and it debuted in July 1968. Tony also developed the Valencia line based on a Czechoslovakian Moser piece that Frank had purchased at an antique shop. Valencia made its appearance in 1969.

A happiness bird made from a former Paden City mould appeared in the Fenton catalog in 1969. That same year, K-Mart signed an agreement with Fenton to sell the Olde Virginia line in their stores. Rose Presznick approached Fenton about remaking some carnival glass for her to sell at her museum. She was a long time collector of carnival glass and wrote several books on the subject. Fenton agreed and carnival glass was reborn in 1968. At first there were numerous complaints from collectors about this new glass on the market. Fenton soon decided to mark this new carnival with the Fenton name inside an oval to distinguish it from the old pieces. This satisfied the collectors and no more complaints occurred. The new Fenton mark became so popular that Fenton decided to start marking all of their glass beginning with the next decade.

Charlie Goe's fascination with the old glass formulas continued. For a number of years he had devoted time to trying to revive the Burmese formula. Finally in October 1969, Charlie excitedly went and found Bill Fenton. He was convinced that he had finally gotten the formula right. Charlie and Bill waited as the Burmese came out of the lehr. Charlie had done it. The Burmese was gorgeous. Unfortunately, later that day Charlie died of a heart attack. As sad as the occasion was, it brought joy to everyone that Charlie had at least seen his beautiful glass.

Apple Blossom, 1960 to 1961
Left: #7377AB ashtray, 6.5"
wide, **$48**; **Right:** #7224
bowl, 10.25" wide, **$125**
Front: #7271AB
candleholders, 3" tall, **$98** pair

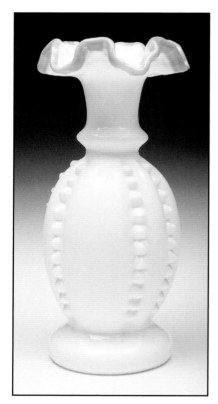

Apple Blossom, 1960
to 1961
Left: Basket
#7336AB, 8.25"
wide, **$145**; **Center:**
Vase #7354AB, 4"
tall, double crimp,
$45; **Right:** Heart
nappy #7333AB,
6.76" wide, **$75**

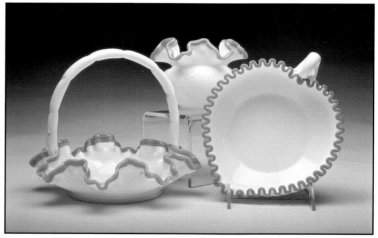

Apple Blossom Beaded vase,
8.75" tall, 1960 to 1961, **$195**

Jacqueline
Top: #9156WR vase, 5.75" tall,
Wild Rose, 1961 to 1962, **$75**;
Top Center: #9166 pitcher,
Powder Blue, 6" tall, 1961
to 1962, **$100**; **Top Right:**
#9156CL vase, 5.75" tall, Coral,
1961 to 1962, **$70**
Bottom Left: #9166BV pitcher,
6" tall, Powder Blue Overlay,
1961 to 1962, **$110**; #9152PN
tulip vase, 7.5" tall, Pink Opaline,
1960, **$85**; **Bottom Center:**
#9100HA creamer, 3.25" tall,
Honey Amber, 1961 to 1962,
$28; #9152YN tulip vase, 7.5"
tall, Yellow Opaline, 1960 to 1961,
$75; **Bottom Right:** #9166AG
pitcher, 6" tall, Apple Green, 1961
to 1962, **$100**

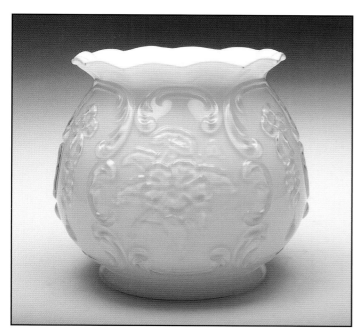

Wild Rose and Bow Knot vase #2855, 4.75" tall, Honey Amber Overlay, 1961 to 1968, **$38**

Bubble Optic, Overlays, 1961
Left: Pinch vase #1358AG, 8.75" tall, Apple Green, **$65**;
Right: Vase #1359WR, Wild Rose, 11" tall, **$125**

Bubble Optic, Overlays, 1960s
Left: Vase #1356OB, 7.5" tall, Opaque Blue, 1962, **$95**;
Center: Pinch vase #1358BV, Powder Blue Satin, 8.75" tall, 1961, **$85**;
Right: Vase #1350CL, 5" tall, Coral, 1961, **$89**

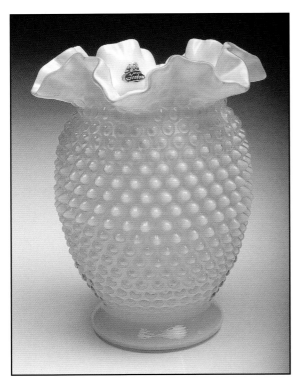

Hobnail #3858 vase, 8" tall, Powder Blue Overlay, 1961 to 1962, **$48**

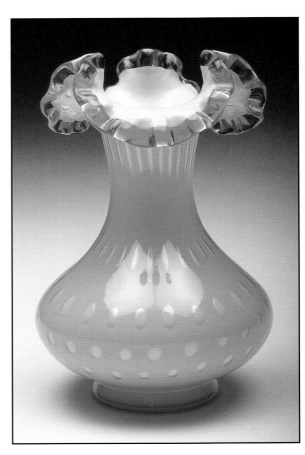

Bubble Optic #1356AG vase, 7.75" tall, Apple Green Overlay, 1961, **$6**8

Bubble Optic #1358BV pinch vase, 8,75" tall, Powder Blue, 1961, **$95**

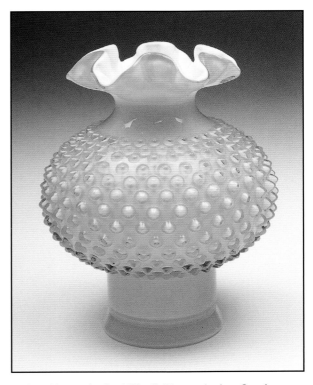

Hobnail lamp shade, 10" tall, Honey Amber Overlay, not cut, left as a vase, 1961 to 1963, **$75**

Wheat #5858 vase, 7.5" tall
Top Left: Apple Green Overlay, 1961, **$60**;
Top Right: Coral Overlay, 1961, **$85**
Bottom Left: Wild Rose, 1961 to 1962,
$65; **Bottom Center:** Honey Amber
Overlay, 1961 to 1963, **$48**; **Bottom
Right:** Opaque Blue, 1962, **$60**

Lady selector in the
factory
*Archival photo
reprinted with
permission from the
Fenton Art Glass
Company*

#1680 candy box, 7.25" tall, Opaque
Blue, 1962, **$100**

Colonial Blue, 1962 to 1968
Top: Pineapple #9045CB goblet, 6" tall,
$18
Left: Thumbprint #4442CB, tumbler,
5.5" tall, **$12**; **Center:** Hobnail
#3804CB, three piece fairy light, 8.5" tall,
$48; **Right:** Diamond Optic #1790CB,
courting lamp, 10.5" tall, **$60**

Colonial Blue, 1962 to 1979
Top Left: Daisy and Button #1994CB bootie, **$14**; **Top Right:** Roses #9271CB ashtray, 7" wide, **$24**
Bottom Left: Hobnail #3756CB bud vase, 9.5" tall, **$12**; **Bottom Center:** Hobnail #3995CB cat slipper, **$12**; **Bottom Right:** #3667CB bell, 5.5" tall, **$14**; Hobnail, #3608CB Fairy light, **$24**

Hobnail #3867WR, lavabo set, 13"tall, Wild Rose Overlay, on original store display stand, 1962, **$395**

Wildrose Overlay Satin, Made for LG Wright, 1962
Left: Maize #40-2 bowl, 5" tall, **$145**; **Right:** #1-1D barber bottle, 7.5" tall, hand painted, **$175**

Hobnail Milk Glass
Top Left: #3606MI creamer, 4" tall, 1961 to 1966, **$12**; **Top Center:** #3762MI syrup pitcher, 5.5" tall, 1958 to 1966, **$28**; **Top Right:** #3837MI basket, 8" tall, 1950 to 1966, **$35**
Bottom Left: #3606MI covered sugar, 5.25" tall, 1961 to 1966, **$14**;
Bottom Center: #3674MI candlestick, 6" tall, 1961 to 1966, **$28**; #3733MI heart relish, 6.5" wide, 1958 to 1989, **$35**;
Bottom Right: #3752MI vase, 10.75" tall, 1958 to 1989, **$45**

Hobnail bowls and candleholders, 1967 catalog
Reprinted with permission from the Fenton Art Glass Company

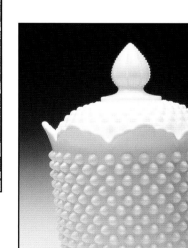

Tony Rosena, a designer formally from Jeannette Glass, came to work at Fenton in 1967. He was instrumental in bringing Louise Piper to Fenton.

Hobnail #3680MI cookie jar, 10.5" tall, Milk Glass, 1962 to 1969, no logo, **$85**

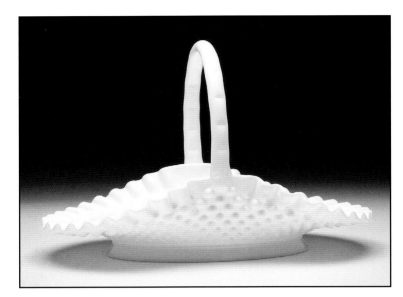

Hobnail #3839MI oval basket, 12" long,
Milk Glass, 1962 to 1969, no logo, **$58**

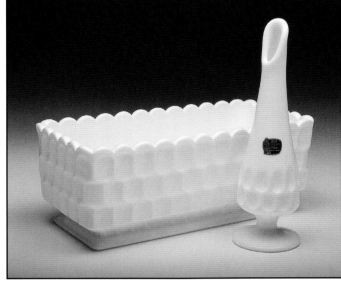

Olde Virginia Glass line, Thumbprint, Milk Glass, 1962 to 1969
Left: #4490MI planter, 10" long, **$18**;
Right: #4456MI bud vase, 8.25" tall, **$9**

Thumbprint, Milk Glass, Olde Virginia Glass line, 1960 to 1969
Left: Covered comport #4484, footed, **$48**;
Right: Hurricane lamp #4498, **$60**

Blue Crest, 1963
Left: #7329BC low compote, 4" tall, **$38**;
Right: #7429BC tall compote, 6.25" tall, **$60**

Flame Crest, 1963
Left: #7429FC compote, 6.25" tall, **$75**;
Right: #7329FC compote, 4" tall, **$40**
Reprinted with permission from the Schiffer Publishing, Ltd.

Colonial Green, 1963 to 1976
Top: Roses #9284CG covered candy, 8.5" tall, **$18**; **Top Center:** Roses #9256CG bud vase, 12" tall, **$8**; **Top Right:** Santa #5106CG fairy light, 5.5" tall, **$24**
Center Left: Hobnail #3995CG cat slipper, 6" long, **$10**; **Center Right:** Daisy and Button #1990CG boot, 4.5" tall, **$9**
Bottom Left: Hobnail #3872CG candle bowl, 6.5" wide, **$9**; **Bottom Right:** Thumbprint #4426CG bowl, 8" wide, **$12**

Thumbprint Decorative pieces, 1967 catalog
Reprinted with permission from the Fenton Art Glass Company

Thumbprint, covered candy jar #4486, 5" tall, 6.5" long, 4.75" wide, footed, Colonial Amber, 1962 to 1974, **$10**

Colonial Amber, 1964 to 1980
Back Left: Swirl #9176 ashtray, 9" wide, **$8**; **Top Right:** Roses #9223CA compote, 6.25" tall, **$10**;
Bottom Left: Hobnail #3756CA bud vase, 9" tall, 1967 to 1980, **$6**; Swan #5127, 3.75" tall, **$8**; **Bottom Center:** Roses #9251CA fan vase, 4.5" tall, **$10**; Valencia #8356CA vase, 12.5" tall, 1969 to 1975, **$8**; **Bottom Right:** Roses #9256CA bud vase, 10.75" tall, **$9**

Vasa Murrhina, Aventurine Green,
1964 to 1967
Left: #6457GB vase, 7" tall, **$48**;
Right: #6435GB basket, 7" tall, **$65**

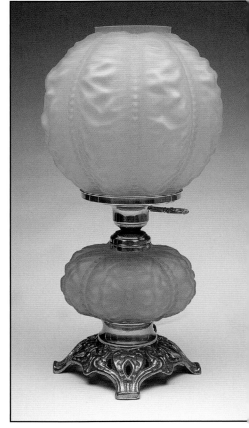

Beaded Curtain lamp, 27" tall, Amber
Overlay, Made for L.G. Wright, 1965, **$295**

Vasa Murrhina
Left: #6437GB, basket, 11.5" tall, Aventurine Green with
Blue, 1964 to 1968, **$95**; **Center:** #6459RG vase, 14.75"
tall, Rose with Aventurine Green, 1964 to 1968, **$125**;
Right: #6465AO, pitcher, 10.25" tall, Autumn Orange, 1965
to 1967, **$85**
Front Left: mushroom, 2.5" tall, Autumn Orange, 1984, **$70**;
Front Right: #5012GB, elephant, 2" tall, Aventurine Green,
1984, **$85**

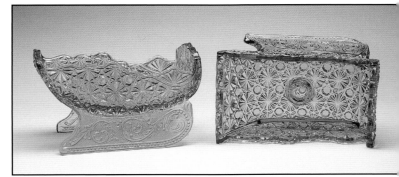

Daisy and Button #22-55 sleigh
candleholder, 8" long, 1965, Made
for LG Wright, Amber, **$125** pair

Embossed Roses #74 electric lamp, 18" tall, Ruby Satin, 1960s, Made for L.G. Wright, **$295**

Steps of making glass, 1967 catalog
Reprinted with permission from the Fenton Art Glass Company

Plated Amberina, Diamond Optic, Satin finish, 1962
Left: Courting Lamp #1790, **$225**;
Right: Vase #1751, 7" tall, **$85**

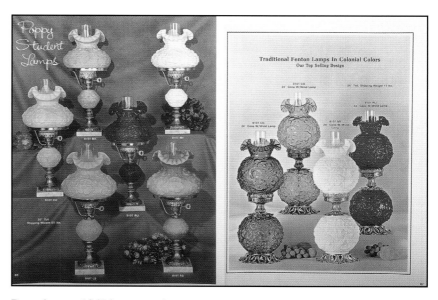

Roses lamps, 1967 lamp supplement
Reprinted with permission from the Fenton Art Glass Company

Made for LG Wright Glass Company, 1960s
Left: Three piece fairy light #57-20, Peach Blow, 5.5"tall, 6.75" wide, **$185; Right:** Oval cruet #1-2D, 7" tall, Blue Overlay Satin, **$85**

Made for LG Wright Glass Company, Hand painted Overlays, 1960s
Left: Barber bottle #1-17D, Amethyst, 7.5" tall, **$85; Center:** Cruet #1-7D, Vine, Amber, 7" tall, **$50; Top Right:** Rose bowl 1-6D, Dark Blue, 3.5" tall, **$45; Bottom Right:** Barber bottle #1-17D, Dark Blue, 8.5" tall, has chrome plated drip top, **$98**

Pitchers, Custard, Hand painted, Made for LG Wright Glass Company, 1960s
Left: Creamer #73-5, 5.25" tall, Gold Floral, **$35; Right:** Water #73-3, 9.25" tall, Wood Rose, **$135**

Made for LG Wright, Water goblets
Left: Flower Band #6345, 6.5" tall, Colonial Blue, 1962 to 1964, **$20**;
Center: Priscilla #55-62, 6.25" tall, Ruby, 1963 to 1966, **$28**;
Wildflower #67-5, 6" tall, Green, 1960s, **$15;**
Right: Acorn #77-17, 6" tall, Amber, **$10**

Made for Red Cliff, Water goblets, 1960s to 1970s
Left: Knobby Bull's Eye, 6.75" tall, Crystal, **$12**;
Right: Sydenham, 6.5" tall, Colonial Blue, **$20**

Lamp grouping, Cranberry Opalescent, Made for LG Wright, 1960s
Left: Coin Dot, Charleton decoration, 12" tall, **$250**;
Center: Daisy Optic, 16.5" tall, **$450**;
Right: Opal Dot, 16" tall, **$275**

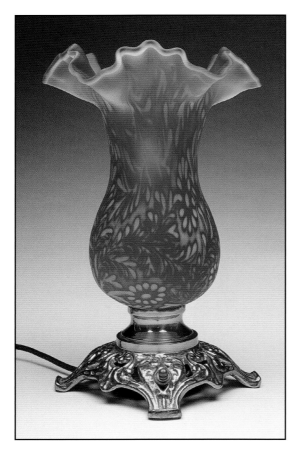

Daisy and Fern, #725 hurricane lamp, 10.75" tall, Cranberry Opalescent Satin, Made for L.G. Wright, 1960s, **$295**

Daisy and Fern, Topaz Opalescent, Made for LG Wright, 1960s
Left: #725 hurricane lamp, 10.75" tall, **$295**;
Right: #100-1 pitcher, 9.25" tall, **$295**

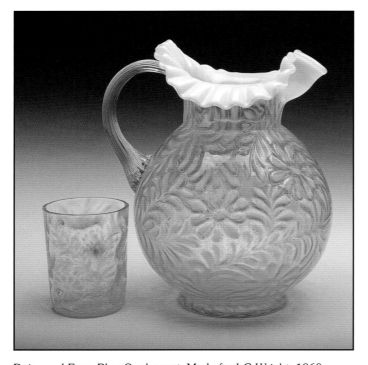

Daisy and Fern, Blue Opalescent, Made for LG Wright, 1960s
Left: #97-2 tumbler, 3.75" tall, **$28**;
Right: #84-2 pitcher, 9.5" tall, **$195**

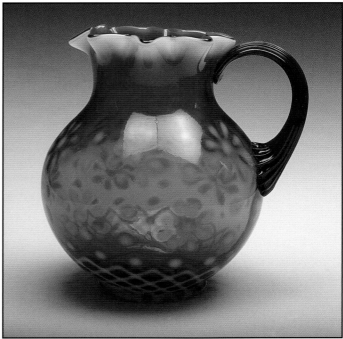

Christmas Snowflake Optic, #85-12, pitcher, 6.5" tall, Cobalt Opalescent, Made for LG Wright, 1960s, **$125**

Thumbprint, Cranberry, Special Order for LG Wright, 1967
Left: #86-1 apothecary jar, 7.75" tall, **$225**; **Center:** #89-1 barber bottle, 7.5" tall, **$125**; **Right:** #87-1 apothecary jar, 10" tall, **$350**

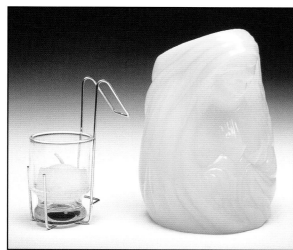

Frank and Bill discussing an order in 1967
Archival photo reprinted with permission from the Fenton Art Glass Company

Madonna #5107JO prayer light, 6.25" tall, Jonquil Yellow, 1968, **$95**

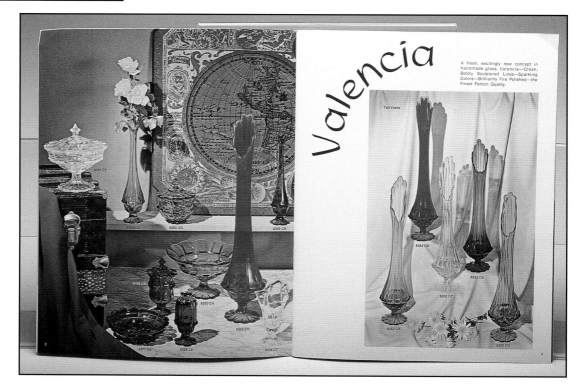

Valencia vases, 1969 catalog
Reprinted with permission from the Fenton Art Glass Company

Louise Piper was hired in 1968 and restarted Fenton's decorating department. One of her first decorations was Violets in the Snow. One of her first decorations for Burmese after it was recreated in 1970 was the Rose and Tree Scene. She retired from Fenton in 1989 at the age of 81.

Mermaid vases, 1968 to 1969, **Value Not Established on either one**
Left: Jonquil Yellow; **Right:** Colonial Blue

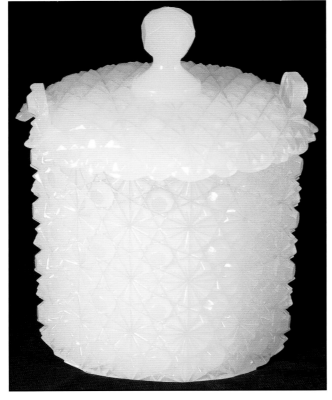

Daisy and Button, covered candy #1890JO, Jonquil Yellow, 1968, **$85**

Floral Bouquet #9430 vase, 5" tall, 5.5" wide, Teal Green, Olde Virginia Glass line, 1960s and 1970s, OVG mark, **$20**

Detail of OVG logo

Gold Crest, Bowl #7429 with metal cherub base, 6.5" tall, 7.75" wide, made for decorator shop, 1963 to 1965, **$35**

Lamps, Roses, Overlay, 1967
Left: Buffet #9205, Colonial Green, 18" tall, **$98**;
Right: Gone with the Wind #9207, Colonial Blue, 23.5" tall, **$198**

Valencia #8398 cigarette box, 1969 to 1972
Left: Colonial Green, **$15**; **Right:** Colonial Blue, **$24**

Violets in Snow
Top: #7252DV vase, 7" tall, 1968 to 1970, **$45**
Left: Wavecrest, #6080DV candy, 4.5" tall, 1968 to 1970, **$100**;
Center: #7484DV candy box, 4.5" tall, 1979 to 1980, **$50**;
Right: #9504DV basket weave candle light, 8.5" tall, 1982 to 1983, **$150**

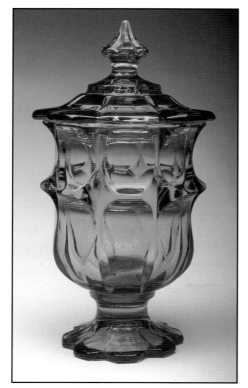

Valencia, Cigarette jar #8398CA, 7.5" tall, 3.5" wide, Colonial Amber, footed, 1969 to 1972, **$12**

Violets in the Snow, 1969 catalog
Reprinted with permission from the Fenton Art Glass Company

Violets in Snow, decoration developed by Louise Piper, 1968 to 1980s
Top: Fairy light #7300DV, 4.35" tall, **$49**
Bottom Left: Bud vase #9056DV, 8.5" tall, **$28**; Vase #7254DV, 3.75" tall, 1975 to 1984, **$28**; **Bottom Center:** Candlestick #7474DV, 5.5" tall, 1968 to 1971, **$25**; **Bottom Right:** Comport #7429DV, 6" tall, 8" wide, 1968 to 1983, **$40**

Silver Crest Petticoat Glass, 1969 catalog
Reprinted with permission from the Fenton Art Glass Company

Black Crest, late 1960s
Back Left: #7210BC plate, 10.25" wide, **$95**;
Back Right: #7217BC plate, 8.25" wide, **$60**
Front Left: #7336BC basket, 6.5" tall, **$100**;
Front Right: #37237BC basket, 7.5" tall, **$195**

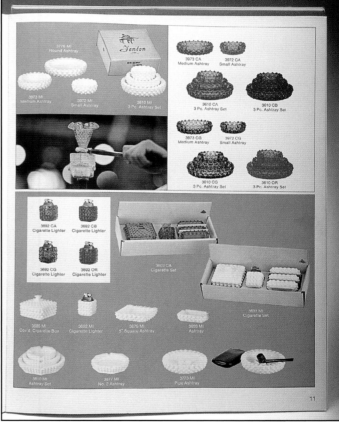

Hobnail smoking items, 1967 catalog
Reprinted with permission from the Fenton Art Glass Company

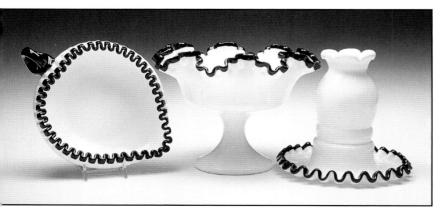

Black Crest, late 1960s
Left: #7333BC heart relish, 6.5" wide, **$125**;
Center: #7429BC compote #7429BC, 6"tall, **$85**;
Right: 37392BC fairy light, 6" tall, **$150**

Orange, 1969 to 1970s
Top Left: Hobnail #3608OR 2 piece fairy light, 4.75" tall, 1969 to 1978, **$18**; **Top Right:** Daisy and Button boot #1990OR, 4.5" tall, 1971 to 1973, **$10**
Bottom Left: Hobnail #3756OR bud vase, 11" tall, 1969 to 1978, **$8**; **Bottom Center:** Hobnail #3995OR cat slipper, 6" long, 1969 to 1978, **$12**; Thumbprint #4453OR swung vase, 8" tall, 1969 to 1973, **$12**; **Bottom Right:** Hobnail #3854OR rose bowl, 4.5" tall, 1969 to 1977, **$12**

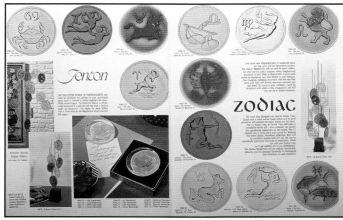

Zodiac paperweights, 1969 catalog supplement
Reprinted with permission from the Fenton Art Glass Company

Vessel of Gems vase #8253, 6.75" tall, 6.75" wide, former Verlys mould
Left: Orange, 1968, **$38**; **Right:** Milk Glass, 1969, **$24**

Zodiac Medallions, 1969 to 1970, designed by Tony Rosena, **$18 each**

Vessel of Gems vase #8253, 6.75" tall, 6.75" wide, Crystal with white stain, former Verlys mould, 1968, **$39**

Wild Strawberry #9088TS candy box, 9" tall, Brown Stain, 1969, **$45**

1970 TO 1979
THE REVIVAL

Burmese entered the Fenton catalog in 1970 with six pieces and was very successful with customers asking for more. More plain pieces were offered with the addition of a Maple Leaf design.

Collector plates were very popular on the market at this time and Fenton was determined to capture some of these sales. The Craftsman and Christmas in America series came out in 1970. The following year, the Mothers Day plates were issued. All of these plates sold extremely well for Fenton.

Tom Fenton joined the company full time in 1972 and became the plant manager. Also that same year George came aboard full time and was doing research for the company. Mike became the new purchasing agent in 1973. Frances Burton was hired as a decorator in 1973 and was trained by Louise Piper. Don and his brother Randy, sons of Bill Fenton, joined the company in 1975. They both were involved with the sales department.

Sudodh Gupta, a native of India, was hired to be Fenton's new chemist in 1971. Wayne King was hired to be his assistant. He was able to remake the Chocolate glass and this became part of the Bicentennial line in 1976. Other colors of Independence Blue, Patriot Red and Valley Forge White became part of Fenton's patriotic line to honor our American Bicentennial. The other colors of Custard, Lime Sherbet, Rosalene, Rose Satin, and Lilac Satin also entered the Fenton line.

The gift shop underwent a huge remodel in 1971. The parking lot was also increased to accommodate more customers coming to the factory.

In 1974 Robert Barber was hired to develop a special line. The Robert Barber Collection came out in 1975. Sales were good and another offering was made. These items didn't sell well and were returned. As a result the whole line was discontinued. For another year, Barber continued working at Fenton before being let go and then finding employment at Pilgrim Glass.

To address the needs of collectors interested in Fenton, Otis and Ferril Rice formed the first Fenton group in 1976. They called their group, Fenton Art Glass Collectors of America.

Bill Fenton's daughter, Christine joined the company in 1975 as part of customer service. She helped make the switch to an 800 number. Today she is responsible for the gift shop personnel and data processing. Frank's dream of establishing a Fenton museum came to be in 1977. It was set up on the second floor of the factory. Frank's wife, Elizabeth, fell ill in 1978 and he stepped down as president so he could spend more time with her. Bill assumed the presidency that year and continued in that position until 1986.

The new color for 1977 was Crystal Velvet. This color was crystal with a special matte sheen. Blue Opalescent Hobnail was reintroduced in 1978. The new color of Rosalene was introduced in 1978 along with continued good sales of Burmese. Decorators Kim Plauche (now Kim Barley) and Robin Spindler were hired in 1979. Milk Glass sales were starting to decrease while the new transparent colors were taking off.

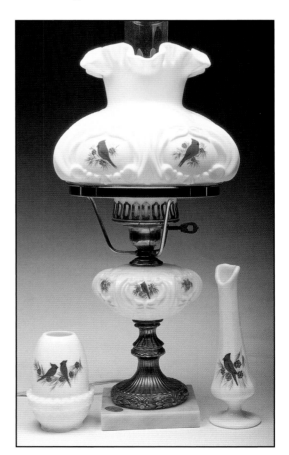

Cardinal in Winter, 1979 to 1980
Left: Fairy light #7300CW, 4.5" tall, **$35**;
Center: Student Lamp #9308CW, 19.5" tall, **$125**;
Right: Bud vase #9056CW, 7.5" tall, **$22**

Blue Marble, 1970 to 1973
Top: Daisy and Button #1990MB boot, 4.5" tall, **$15**
Bottom Left: Roses #9256MB bud vase, 12" tall, **$14**;
Bottom Right: Hobnail #3872MB candle bowl, 6.5" wide, **$18**

Purple Carnival, 1970s
Left: Paneled Daisy #9185CN covered candy, 8.5" tall, **$45**;
Center: Hobnail #3949CN tumbler, 4.25" tall, **$20**;
Right: Hobnail #3360CN pitcher, 10.75" tall, **$125**

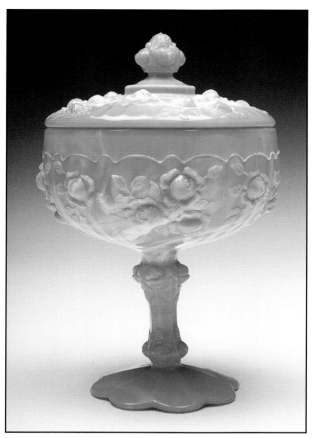

Roses #9284MB candy box, 9.5" tall, Blue Marble, 1970 to 1973, **$40**

#Y9180CN Chessie box, 8" tall, Amethyst Carnival, Special Order for Chesapeake and Ohio Railroad, 1970, **$175**

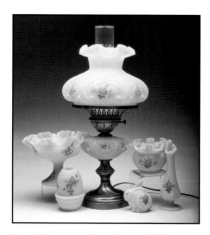

Blue Roses on Blue Satin, 1978 to 1982
Left Top: Comport #7429BL, 5.75" tall, 7.75" wide, **$20**; **Bottom Left:** Fairy light #7300BL, 4.5" tall, **$35** **Center:** Student lamp #9309BL, 18" tall, **$125**; **Top Right:** Vase #7254BL, 3.5" tall, **$22**; **Bottom Right:** Bunny #5162BL, 3.5" tall, 3" long, **$30**; **Far Right:** Bud vase #9056BL, 7.5" tall, **$18**

Waterlily covered candy jar #8480BA, 7.5" tall, 6" wide, footed, Blue Satin, 1971 to 1980, **$24**

Blue Satin, 1971 to 1979
Left: Poppy #9138BA basket, 10" tall, **$54**; **Center:** #2454BA vase, 6.25" tall, **$28**; **Right:** Waterlily #8434BA basket, 8" tall, **$30**

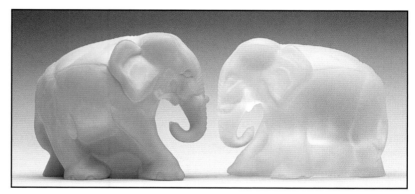

5123 work elephant, 3" tall, 1972
Left: Blue Satin, **$250**; **Right:** Crystal Satin, **$150**

Hobnail, Milk Glass decorated
Top Left: Blue Bells #3608BB fairy light, 4.5" tall, 1971 to 1973, **$48**;
Top Center: Blue Bells #3795BB toothpick, 3" tall, 1972, **$25**;
Top Right: Holly #3608DH fairy light, 4.5" tall, 1971 to 1976, **$45**;
Roses #3633RW nut dish, 7" wide, 1974 to 1976, **$29**;
Center Left: Holly #3667DH bell 5.5" tall, 1971 to 1976, **$35**;
Bottom Left: Holly #3700DH covered shoe, 6" long, signed Louise Piper, 1971 to 1976, **$85**; Blue Bells #3950RW bud vase, 10" tall, 1974 to 1976, **$35** ;
Bottom Center: Roses #3837RW basket, 7" tall, 1974 to 1976, **$65**;
Holly #3674DH candlestick, 6" tall, 1971 to 1972, **$28**;
Bottom Right: Roses, #3950BB bud vase, 9.5" tall, **$35**

Hobnail covered candy #3886, Milk Glass, 6.5" tall, 6.5" wide, footed, **$45 each**
Top: Holly DH, 1974 to 1975
Bottom Left: Blue Bells BB, 1971 to 1972;
Right: Pink Roses RW, 1974 to 1975

Burmese, 1970s
Top Left: Maple Leaf #7468BD cruet, 1972, **$145**; **Top Center:** Scenic #7437DB basket, 7.5" tall, 1974, **$125**; **Top Right:** Pink Butterflies #7424 rose bowl, 4" tall, 1977, Special Order for Frederick and Nelson, 1977, **$150**
Bottom Left: Roses #7255RB tulip vase, 10" tall, 1977, **$125**; Roses #7461RB creamer, 4.25" tall, 1971, **$50**; **Bottom Center:** Maple Leaf #7392BD one piece fairy light, 5.75" tall, 1970 to 1971, **$225**; Ribbed #9055BR vase, 4.75" tall, 1971, **$95**; **Bottom Right:** Hobnail #3752BR vase, 10.5" tall, 1971, **$225**

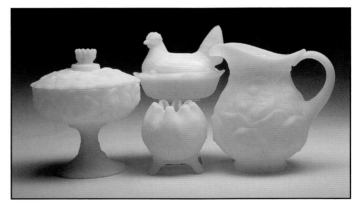

Jacqueline, Burmese, Experimental, 1970,
Value Not Established
Left: Pitcher #9166BR, 48 ounce; **Right:** Creamer #9100BR

Custard Satin, 1972 to 1979
Top Center: #5186CU hen on nest, 4" tall, **$28**
Bottom Left: Waterlily #8480CU covered candy, 7.5" tall, **$35**; **Center:** Grape #8457CU footed rose bowl, 4.25" tall, **$18**; **Right:** Waterlily #8464CU water pitcher, 7.5" tall, **$35**

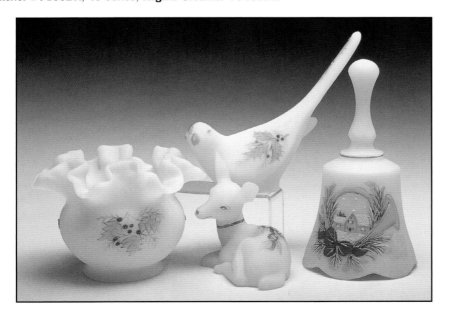

Custard
Top Center: Holly #5197CH happiness bird, 6" long, 1972 to 1979, **$38**
Bottom Left: Holly #7254CH vase, 3.75" tall, 1972 to 1979, **$20**; **Center:** #5160 fawn, 3.75" tall, Custard with pine cones, 1970s, **$45**; **Right:** Joy to the World #7669VZ bell, 6.5" tall, Custard, musical, 1987, **$45**

Mother's Day plate, 1972
catalog supplement
*Reprinted with permission
from the Fenton Art Glass
Company*

Mothers Day Plates, Milk Glass Satin, 7.5" wide, **$10 each**
Top: Madonna and Child with Pomegranate #9377WS, 1977, 7th in the series;
Center: The Holy Night #9376WS, 1976, 6th in series;
Right: Madonna of the Rose Hedge #9379WS, 1979, 9th in series, Madonna of the Rose Hedge

Hobnail, Ruby
Left: #3716RU bonbon,
7.75" wide, shallow, 1972
to 1973, **$18**; **Center:**
#3843RU wine goblet, 4.5"
tall, 1977 to 1979, **$20**;
Right: #3924RU bowl, 9"
wide, 1981 to 1986, **$38**

Holly on Ruby, 1972 to 1982
Left: Medallion #8288RH covered candy,
8.5" tall, **$68**; **Right:** #7237RH basket,
7" tall, **$48**
*Reprinted with permission from the
Schiffer Publishing, Ltd.*

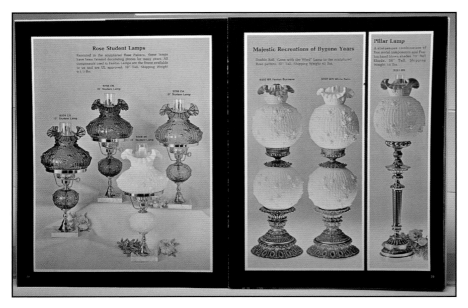

Rose student lamps, 1973 catalog
Reprinted with permission from the Fenton Art Glass Company

White Daisies, 1973 catalog
Reprinted with permission from the Fenton Art Glass Company

Thumbprint #4469WD ashtray, 7.5" wide, White Daisies, 1973, **$24**

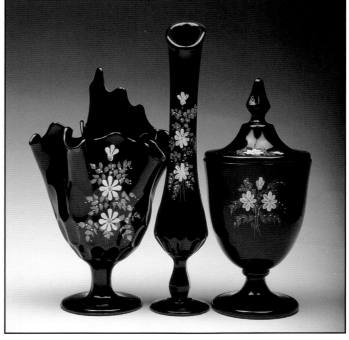

White Daisies on Black, 1973
Left: Thumbprint vase #4454WD, 9.75" tall, **$34**;
Center: Thumbprint bud vase #4453WD, 12" tall, **$20**;
Right: Candy jar #7380WD, 9.5" tall, **$38**

Lime Sherbet Satin, 1973 to 1979
Top Center: Butterfly #8230LS, bonbon, 9" long handle to
handle, **$15**
Bottom Left: Persian Medallion #8408LS fairy light, 6.5" tall,
$48; Hobnail #3608LS fairy light, 4.75" tall, **$28**;
Right: Poppy #9138LS basket, 9.5" tall, **$45**

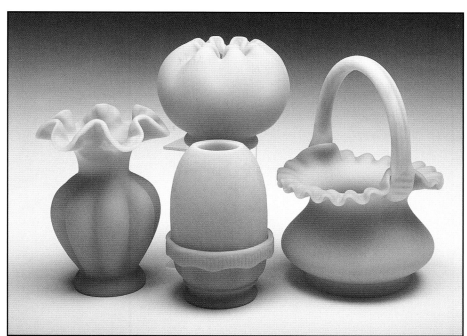

Rose Satin, 1974 to 1977
Top Center: #7424RS rose bowl, 3.5"
tall, **$24**
Left: Melon #7451RS vase, 5.5" tall, **$38**;
Center: #7492RS fairy light, 5" tall, **$40**;
Right: #7437RS basket, 7.5" tall, **$58**

Chou Ting #8407 fairy light,
5.85" tall, White Satin, 1975, **$35**

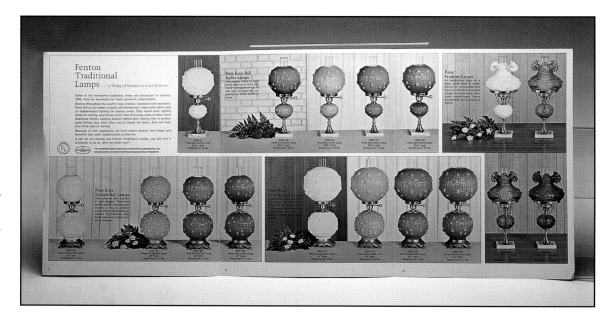

Rose student lamps,
1975 catalog
*Reprinted with
permission from the
Fenton Art Glass
Company*

Black, 1970s
Left: Empress vase #8252BK,
7.75" tall, **$85**; **Right:** Mandarin
vase #8251BK, 9.5" tall, **$95**

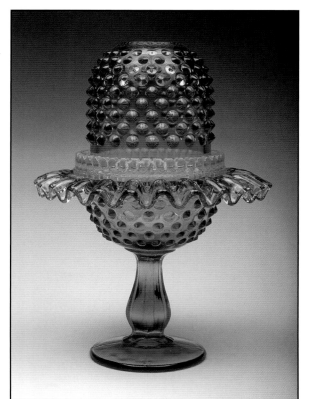

Black, 1970s
Left: Thumbprint, handkerchief
vase #4454BK, 7.75" tall, 1969 to
1974, **$20**; **Right:** Waterlily, basket
#8434BK, 7" tall, 7" wide, 1974 to
1979, **$35**

Hobnail, Fairy Light #3804CG, 8.75"
tall, 6.25" wide, Colonial Green, three
piece, footed, clear insert, 1975 to
1977, **$35**

Robert Barber was hired in 1974 to develop a special line. His designs included Hanging Hearts, Pulled Feather and Cascade. The line didn't sell well and Barber was let go in 1976. He went on to work at Pilgrim Glass.

Robert Barber, 1975 to 1976, Samples,
Value Not Established
Left: Barber bottle #8960CI, Custard Iridized;
Right: Tankard, Custard

Robert Barber, 1975 to 1976, Samples,
Value Not Established
Left: Vase, Custard Iridized;
Right: Pitcher, Custard

Rope hangers for Fenton planters, 1975 catalog
Reprinted with permission from the Fenton Art Glass Company

Robert Barber vases, 1975
Left: Hanging Heart #0003BH, 8" tall, Bittersweet, limited to 750, **$300;**
Center: Cascade #5006CV, 7.75" tall, Blue, **$375;**
Right: Summer Tapestry #0005ST, 10.25" tall, Custard Iridized, **$295**

Robert Barber vases, Turquoise, 1975
Left: Hanging Heart #0008TH, 9.75" tall, limited to 600, **$275;**
Center: Hanging Heart #0002TH, 11" tall, limited to 600, **$300;**
Right: Pulled Feather #0004BF, 8.25" tall, limited to 1000, **$300**

Cascade vase, 8" tall, Cobalt and White satin, Robert Barber
collection, 1975, **$395**

Robert Barber vases, 1975
Left: Labyrinth #0010, 10" tall,
Cobalt and White satin, Limited
edition of 700, **$275**;
Center: Feather #001, 12.25" tall,
Hyacinth, Limited edition of 450,
$495; **Right:** Hanging Heart #002,
10.75" tall, Turquoise satin, **$295**

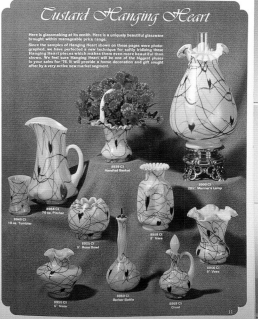

Custard Hanging Heart,
1976 catalog supplement
*Reprinted with permission
from the Fenton Art Glass
Company*

Hanging Hearts, 1976
Left: #8937TH basket, 7.25" tall,
Turquoise Blue, **$98**, **Right:** #8939CI
basket, 10.5" tall, Custard, **$145**

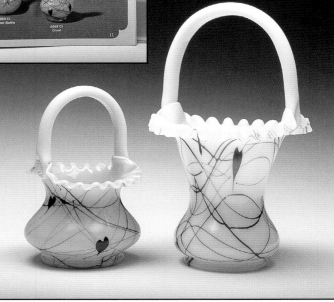

Bicentennial collection, 1976
catalog supplement
*Reprinted with permission from
the Fenton Art Glass Company*

Chocolate Glass, Bicentennial, 1975 to 1976
Left: Lafayette and Washington plate #9410CK, 8" wide, **$28**;
Center: Patriot planter #8499CK, 4" tall, 4.25" wide, **$30**;
Right: Eagle plate #9418CK, 8" wide, **$24**

Bicentennial, 1976
Left: Patriot's #8467PR bell, 6.5" tall, Patriot Red, **$35**; **Center:**
Jefferson #8476IB compote, 10.25" tall, Independence Blue
Carnival, **$175**; **Top Right:** #8446PR Stein, 6.75" tall, Patriot
Red, **$48**; **Bottom Right:** Eagle #9418PR paperweight, 3.75"
tall, Patriot Red, **$30**

Chocolate Glass, Bicentennial, 1975 to 1976
Left: Bell #8467CK, 6.5" tall, **$24**; Eagle
paperweight #8470CK, 3.75" tall, 4" wide, **$28**;
Center: Stein #8446CK, 6.75" tall, **$35**; **Right:**
Patriot planter #8499CK, 4" tall, 4.25" wide, **$30**

Amethyst Carnival, former Verlys shapes, 1970s
Top Left: Atlantis vase #5150CN, 6.5" tall, 1971 to 1972, **$85**;
Top Right: Love Bird vase #8258CN, 4.5" tall, 1974, **$50**
Bottom Left: Mums planter bowl #8226CN, 4.25" tall, 7.25"
wide, 1970 to 1973, **$60**; **Bottom Right:** Mermaid #8254CN
vase, 6.5" tall, 1970 to 1972, **$98**

Left: #5174GN, rabbit, 6" tall, Springtime Green
Carnival, 1977, **$75**; **Right:** #5178CN, owl, 7" tall,
Amethyst Carnival, 1971, **$95**

Rosalene, 1977
Top Left: Ogee #9394RE covered candy box, 7" tall,
$125; **Top Center:** Heart #8406RE fairy light, 7.25"
tall, **$58**; **Top Right:** Flowered #8422RE comport,
7" tall, **$45**
Bottom Left: Chessie #9480RE candy box, 8"
tall, **$250**; Happiness bird #5197RE, 6" long, **$30**;
Bottom Center: Chou Ting #8407RE ceremonial
light, 5.75" tall, **$60**; **Bottom Right:** Waterlily
#8480RE candy box, 7.5" tall, **$95**; Swan #5127RE,
3.75" tall, **$24**

Butterflies on Milk Glass, 1977 to 1978
Back: #7300BY, fairy light, 4.5" tall, **$45**; **Left:**
Medallion #8267BY, bell, 6.5" tall, **$28**; **Center:**
#7254BY, vase, 4" tall, **$25**; **Right:** Medallion #8288BY,
candy dish, 8.5" tall, **$48**

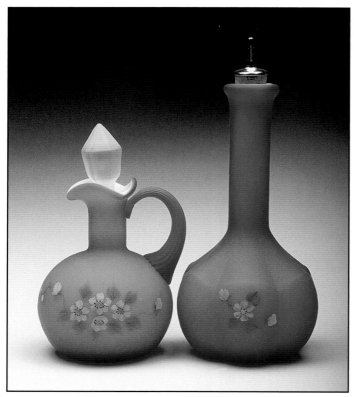

Mermaid vase #8254RE, Rosalene, **Value Not Established**

Dark Blue Overlay, hand painted, Made for L G Wright, 1977
Left: #1-2D cruet, 6.5" tall, **$75**;
Right: #1-1D barber bottle, 7.5" tall, **$135**

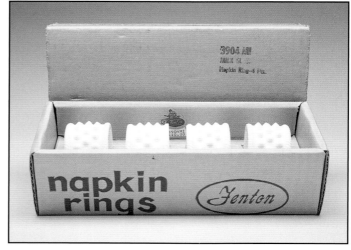

Hobnail #3904MI napkin rings, Milk Glass, 2" wide, shown in original box, 1976 to 1978, **$98**

Rosalene, 1977, **Value Not Established**
Left: Knobby Bull's Eye, covered candy #9385RE; **Right:** Coin Dot vase #1456RE

Daisies on Cameo, 1978 to 1982
Left: Bud vase #9056CD, 11" tall, **$18**; Temple jar #7488CD,
6" tall, **$35**; **Top:** Comport #7429CD, 6" tall, 7.5" wide, **$20**;
Center: Vase #7254CD, 3.75" tall, **$16**; Tulip vase #7255CD,
11" tall, **$45**; **Top Right:** Vase #7252CD, 7" tall, **$35**; **Bottom
Right:** Covered powder #7484CD, 5" tall, 4.5" wide, **$26**;
Basketweave vase #9356CD, 11" tall, **$20**

Daisies on Cameo, 1978 to 1982
Left: Fairy light #9304CD, Basketweave, 4.5" tall, **$45**;
Center: Fairy light #7300CD, 4.5" tall, **$35**;
Right: Candlestick, Basketweave, 4.25" tall, **$25**

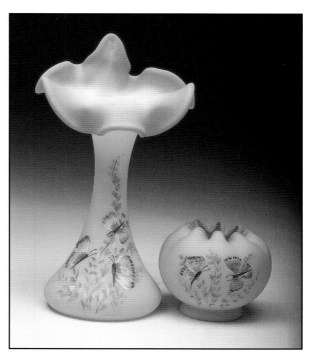

Pink Butterflies, Burmese, special order for Frederick
and Nelson department store in Seattle, Washington,
Designed by Louise Piper, 1977
Left: Tulip vase #7255, 10" tall, **$195**;
Right: Rose bowl #7424, 4" tall, **$98**

Lavender Satin, 1977 to 1978
Top: #5163LN bird, 3" tall, **$38**
Bottom Left: Water Lily #8456LN bud vase,
11" tall, **$28**; **Bottom Center:** #5108LN owl
fairy light, 4" tall, **$38**; **Bottom Right:** Baroque
#9388LN candy dish, 6.5" tall, **$48**

Silver Crest #7436 baskets, 6.5" tall
Top: Yellow Roses, Special Order for Sears, 1977, **$45**
Bottom Left: purple flowers, 1977, **$40**;
Bottom Right: Violets in Snow, 1970s, **$48**

Daisies on Cameo, 1978 to 1982
Top: #5197CD, Happiness bird, 5.5" tall, **$35**
Left: #9356CD, bud vase, 11" tall, **$24**;
Center: #5166CD, frog, 2.25" tall, **$30**;
Right: #7254CD, vase, 4"tall, **$18**

#5163 bird, 3" tall, 1978 to 1984
Top Left: Rosalene, **$45**; Lime Sherbet, **$35**; **Top Center:** Amethyst Carnival, **$28**; **Top Right:** Daisies on Cameo, **$32**
Center Left: Blue Satin, **$35**; Violets in the Snow, **$40**; **Center:** Lavender Satin, **$48**; **Center Right:** Pink Blossoms on Custard, **$32**
Bottom Left: Roses on Custard, **$32**; Blue Roses on Blue Satin, **$42**; **Bottom Center:** Crystal Velvet, **$25**; Chocolate Roses on Cameo, **$35**; **Bottom Right:** Daisies on Custard, **$30**

Decorator hand painting the #5163 bird
Archival photo reprinted with permission from the Fenton Art Glass Company

Christmas Morn, 1978 Christmas supplement
Left: #7300CV fairy light, 4.75" tall, **$60**;
Right: #7466CV, bell, 6" tall, **$38**

Subodh Gupta, a native of India, was hired in 1971 to be Fenton's glass technologist. One of his first colors to be recreated was Chocolate.

Cactus, #3407AO water set, Aqua Opalescent, 1979, **$450** seven piece set
Left: pitcher, 48 ounce;
Right: water goblet, 10 ounce

Spiral Optic Cameo Opalescent, 1978 to 1980
Top Left: #3157CO vase, 6.5" tall, **$30**;
Top Right: #7300CO fairy light two piece, 4.65" tall, **$40**
Bottom Left: #3137CO basket, 7.5" tall, **$50**; **Bottom Center:** #9499CO logo, 5"long, **$40**; **Bottom Right:** #3180CO candy box, 6.5" tall, **$85**

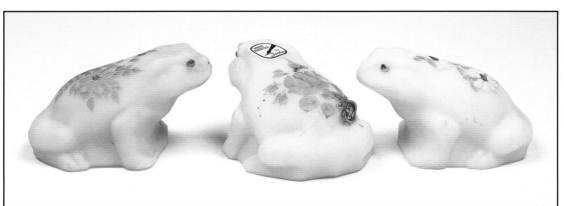

#5166 frog, 2.25" tall, 1979 to 1980, **$35** each
Left: Daisies on Cameo;
Center: Blue Roses on Blue Satin; **Right:** Daisies on Custard

Chocolate Roses, 1979 to 1982
Top: Wavecrest #6056DR, vase, 5.75" tall, **$25**
Left: #9056DR bud vase, 7.75" tall, **$18**;
Center: #5163DR bird, 3" tall, **$38**; **Right:**
#7252DR vase, 7.5" tall, **$35**

#5165 sitting cat, original offering, 1979
Top Row: Chocolate Roses on Cameo Satin,
$45; Violets in the Snow, **$48**
Center Row: Custard, **$20**; Crystal Velvet, **$25**;
Blue Satin, **$35**; Lime Sherbet Satin, **$30**
Bottom Row: Daisies on Cameo Satin, **$38**;
Blue Roses on Blue Satin, **$40**; Pink Blossoms on
Custard, **$38**; Daisies on Custard, **$38**; Roses on
Custard, **$35**

Violets in the Snow
Left: Silver Crest #7474DV candlestick,
5.75" tall, 1968 to 1971, **$35**; **Center:**
#8494DV square planter, 4" tall, 1978 to
1979, **$45**; **Right:** #9056DV bud vase,
8" tall, 1976 to 1983, **$24**

Roses on Custard Satin, 1979 to 1981
Top Left: Covered powder #7484RC, 5" tall, 4.5" wide, **$24**
Bottom Left: Bud vase #9056RC, 8" tall, **$15**; Fairy light #7300RC, 4.25" tall, **$35**; **Center:** Hammered Colonial Lamp #7204RC, 16" tall, **$98**; **Top Right:** Vase #7451RC, 5.25" tall, **$16**; **Bottom Right:** Picture frame #7596RC, 4.5" tall, **$12**

Pink Blossom on Custard Satin, 1978 to 1981
Top Left: Bud vase, scalloped foot, 8" tall, **$22**; Footed nut dish #7229PY, 4" tall, **$18**; **Bottom Left:** Bud vase #9056PY, 7.5" tall, **$20**; Fairy light #7300PY, 4.5" tall, **$35**; **Center:** Picture frame #7596PY, 4.5" tall, **$12**; Student lamp #9308PY, 19.5" tall, **$125**; **Top Right:** Vase #7252PY, 7" tall, tri corner, **$35**; **Bottom Right:** Vase #7554PY, 4" tall, **$20**; Rose bowl #7254PY, 3.5" tall, **$15**

Log Cabin on Custard Satin, 1977 to 1979
Left: Vase #7252LC, 7" tall, **$45**; **Center:** Fairy light #7300LC, 4.5" tall, **$58**; Student lamp 37412LC, 21" tall, **$225**; **Right:** Temple jar #7488LC, 6" tall, **$60**

Chocolate Roses on Cameo Satin, 1979 to 1982
Top Left: Comport #7429DR, 6" tall, 7.5" wide, **$20**; **Top Right:** Bud vase #9056DR, 7.5" tall, **$18**; Basketweave bud vase #9356DR, 11" tall, **$20**
Bottom Left: Fairy light #7300DR, 4.5" tall, **$38**; Egg #5140DR, 3.35" tall, **$20**; Frog #5166DR, 2" tall, 3.75" long, **$25**; Hammered Colonial Lamp #7215DR, 22" tall, **$125**; **Right:** Temple jar #7488DR, 6" tall, **$45**; Wavecrest vase #6056DR, 5.5" tall, **$25**

Daisies on Custard Satin, 1979 to 1980
Left: Vase #7252DC, 7" tall, **$38**;
Top Left: Fairy light #7300DC, 4.5" tall, **$32**; **Top Center**: Donkey #5125DC, 4.75" tall, 4.5" long, **$35**; **Bottom Center**: Bud vase #9056DC, 8.25" tall, **$20**; Footed nut dish #7229DC, 3.75" tall, **$18**; **Bottom Right:** Medallion candy box #8288DC, 8.25" tall, **$45**

Bunny #5162, 3" tall, 1970s
Top Left: Violet in Snow DV, 1978 to 1980, **$35**; **Top Center:** Orange Rose on Cameo, **$30**; Roses on Custard satin RC, 1978 to 1980, **$30; Top Right:** Yellow Roses on Milk Glass YR, 1969 to 1970, **$35**
Bottom Left: Amethyst Carnival CN, 1978, **$30**; **Bottom Center:** Chocolate Roses on Cameo DR, 1979 to 1980, **$32**; **Bottom Right:** Blue Satin BA, 1978 to 1980, **$28**

Roses on Ruby, Fairy light #1700RD, 4.5" tall, 3.25" wide, Top: Ruby with white roses, Bottom: Crystal, 2 piece, 1978 to 1991, **$38**

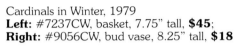

Cardinals in Winter, 1979
Left: #7237CW, basket, 7.75" tall, **$45**;
Right: #9056CW, bud vase, 8.25" tall, **$18**

Spiral Optic, Blue Opalescent, 1979
Left: #3137BO basket, 8" tall, **$48**;
Right: #3164BO pitcher, 8"tall, **$65**

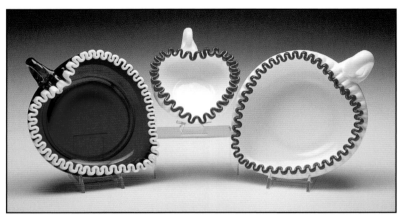

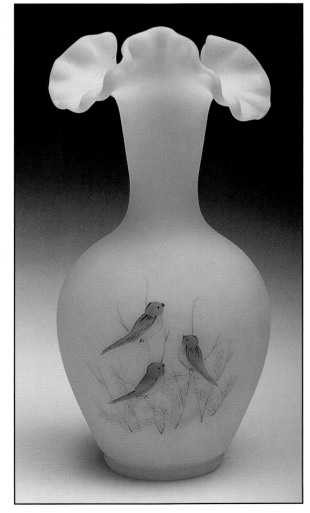

Heart relishes Valentines
offering, 1979
Left: Ruby Snowcrest #7333,
6.5" wide, **$65**; **Center:**
Ruby Crest, $ 4.25" wide,
$45; **Right:** Ruby Crest
#7333, 6.25" wide, **$55**

Blue birds on Custard Satin,
Fairy light #7300BC, 4.5" tall,
3.25" wide, two piece, 1977
to 1979, **$40**

Blue Birds #7257BC vase,
9.75" tall, Custard, 1979, **$75**

#5108 owl fairy light, 3.75" tall
Top: Crystal Velvet, 1979 to 1989, **$35**
Bottom Left: Blue Satin, 1975 to 1979, **$40**;
Bottom Right: Lime Sherbet Satin, 1979, **$38**
Note: metal insert fits in bottom to hold candle

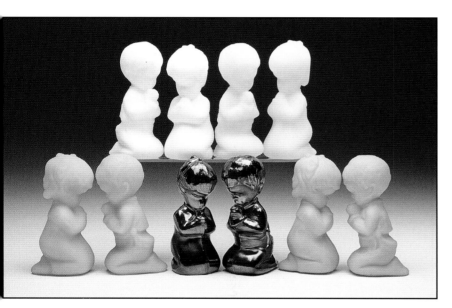

#5100 praying kids, old style, 3.75" tall
Top Left: White Satin, 1978 to 1981, **$28** pair;
Top Right: Custard Satin, 1978 to 1981, **$30** pair
Bottom Left: Lime Sherbet Satin, 1978 to 1980, **$30** pair;
Bottom Center: Plum Carnival, 1978, **$50** pair;
Bottom Right: Blue Satin, 1978 to 1982, **$35**

Praying Kids, 1984 catalog supplement
Reprinted with permission from the Fenton Art Glass Company

1980 TO 1989
MOVING FORWARD AND LOOKING BACK

1980 was another milestone for Fenton. They celebrated their 75th anniversary of being in business. A special offering of Velva Rose was planned with all the pieces being marked with the 75th anniversary. The decision was made to change the logo to designate the 1980s decade. An 8 was placed under the word Fenton inside the oval. Bill Fenton's youngest daughter, Shelley, joined the sales department in 1982. Three years later, she became the assistant sales manager. Later, Shelley became involved with the layout and design of catalogs, a job she still does today.

Burmese continued to be strong for Fenton and a new collection, called Dogwood, was added in 1981. The years of 1980 and 1981 both set new sales records. But as good as those years were, sales dramatically dropped in 1982 and continued to slump through 1985. Fenton worked hard to be more diversified and established their Back to Basics program. Sales finally turned around in 1986.

Lots of changes were in store for Fenton in the early 1980s. Gary Levi, owner of the Levay Company worked with Fenton to establish a limited edition offering in 1980. The Katja and American Legacy lines were started in 1982. Sales failed to materialize and the lines were dropped in 1983.

Nancy Fenton came to work at Fenton in 1982 in the sales department and was also a merchandising coordinator. Today she is Director of Design. A new line to celebrate the different types of glass was called the Connoisseur collection and came out in the June 1983 supplement. Avon approached Fenton in 1984 about making a vase for them to sell in their Gallery brochure. It was to be based on a Stevens and Williams cameo vase. While the Fenton version was only hand-painted, from a distance the vase does look like it could be cameo. A series of Glass Pets was offered in 1985 and would be the start of many different animals sold in years to come. Another anniversary was celebrated in 1985 to mark their 80th birthday in business. At this time the cobalt crest pattern called Blue Ridge was reintroduced.

Looking to capture sales from the home party lines of Avon, Princess House, and Tiara, Fenton launched their own called Gracious touch in 1986. The line failed to meet expectations and was discontinued in 1990.

George Fenton became the company president in 1986 when his uncle Bill retired. Another new avenue of sales was tried in 1987 with a home shopping network called QVC. Bill became a regular host on the show in 1988. Items were first offered from their regular catalog but it was soon realized that it was important to offer special issue items to be successful. Shelley worked to develop new products for QVC. Sales to JC Penny also produced another avenue of special sales for Fenton. Doris Lechler, Dorothy Taylor, and Mary Walrath all had Fenton make special order items for them. Long time designer and decorator Louise Piper retired in 1989. Bob Hill was made supervisor of the mould shop that same year.

Vase, 9" tall, Azure Blue Satin, Special Order for Avon Gallery Originals, 1984, **$95**

Pekin Blue, 1980
Left: #7588PK temple jar, 10" tall,
$48; **Center:** Empress #8252PK
vase, 7.75" tall, **$48**; **Right:** Mandarin
#8251PK vase 9.5" tall, **$60**

Jade, 1980
Left: #7588JA temple jar, 10" tall, **$48**;
Center: #5168JA owl, 3" tall, **$28**;
Right: #7488JA temple jar, 6" tall, **$30**

Antique Stains
Left: Currier and Ives #8409AW, fairy
light vase, 6.25" tall, Antique White,
1980, **$12**; **Center:** Nativity #9401TB
fairy light, 4.5" tall, Antique Blue stain,
1981, **$38**; **Right:** Currier and Ives
#8409TN, fairy light vase, 6.25" tall
Antique Brown stain, 1980, **$18**

Red Slag, Special Order for Levay, 1980
Top: #5170 butterfly, **$85**
Left: #5177 alley cat, **$600;**
Center: #5151 bear, **$110**;
Right: #9188 grape tobacco jar, 1980, **$350**

Purple Slag, Special Order for Levay, 1980
Top Center: Strawberry #8295 toothpick, 3" tall, **$30**
Left: Heart and Vine #8237 bowl, 7.25" wide, **$45**; **Right:** Cherry interior/Orange Tree exterior #9136 basket, 9.5" tall, **$100**

Special Order for Nouveau Art Glass Company, Rueven Collection, 1980s
Top: #5152 whale, 5" long, Crystal Velvet, **$65**
Top Left: #5160 fawn, Crystal, 3.5" tall, **$65**; **Top Center:** #5152 whale, 5" long, Black over Crystal, **$48**; #5162 bunny, 3.25" tall, Crystal, **$68; Top Right:** #5163 bird, 2.75" tall, Crystal, **$6**8
Bottom Left: #5161 swan, 4" tall, Crystal, **$58**; #5160 fawn, tall, Black over Crystal, **$48**; **Bottom Center:** # 5158 elephant, 3.6" tall, Crystal Velvet, **$68**; #5169 duckling, 3.5" tall, Crystal Velvet, **$65**; **Bottom Right:** #5165 sitting cat, 3.75" tall, Crystal Velvet, **$95**

Velva Rose, 1980 to 1982
Back: Dolphin #7580VR covered candy, 8.5" tall, **$50**
Bottom Left: Paneled #9432VR basket, 10.5" tall, **$65**; **Center:** Beaded Daisy #8250VR miniature bowl, 4" wide, **$24**; **Right:** Paneled #9488VR covered candy, 10.5" tall, **$45**

Blue Dogwood on Cameo Satin, 1980 to 1982
Top Left: #5165BD cat, 3.5" tall, **$48**; **Top Right:** #5163BD bird, 3.5" tall, **$38**
Bottom Left: #7252BD vase, 7.25" tall, **$30**; **Bottom Center:** #5162BD bunny, 3.25" tall, **$38**; #5169BD duckling, 3.5" tall, **$38**; **Bottom Right:** #9334BD basket, 7.5" tall, **$35**

Blue Roses on Blue Satin, 1981 to 1982
Top Center: #9574BL basket weave chamber stick, 4.5" tall, **$38** Left; #7288BL ginger jar, 7.5" tall, **$95**; **Center:** #7594BL picture frame, 3.25" tall, **$18**; #5140BL, egg, 3.5" tall, **$20**; **Right:** #7311BL hurricane lamp, 10.75" tall, **$75**

Jade, 1980
Top Left: Praying Girl #5100JA, 3.75" tall, **$24**;
Top Right: Praying Boy #5100JA, 3.75" tall, **$24**
Bottom Left: Owl #5168JA, 3" tall, **$29**;
Center: Bird #5163JA, 2.75" tall, **$35**; **Right:**
Sitting Cat #5165JA, 3.5" tall, **$35**

Jade, 1980
Left: Empress vase #8252JA,
7.75" tall, **$48**;
Right: Mandarin vase
#8251JA, 9.5" tall, **$60**

Christmas fairy lights #7300, 4.75" tall,
Custard Satin, **$58 each**
Left to Right: Christmas Morn
#7300CV, 1978; Nature's Christmas
#7300NC, 1979; Going Home, 1980;
All is Calm #7300AC, 1981; Country
Christmas #7300OC, 1982

Nativity with Antique Stains, 1981 to 1983
Top Left: Ornament #9413TB, 4" wide,
Antique Blue, **$18**; **Bottom Left:** Fairy
light #9401FL, 4.5" tall, Florentine Brown,
$40; **Center:** Plate #9412FL, 8" wide,
embossed on back: Matthew 2:11, Florentine
Brown, **$40**; **Top Right:** Ornament
#9413FL, 4" wide, Florentine Brown, **$18**;
Bottom Right: Fairy light #9401, 4.5" tall,
Florentine Brown, **$45**

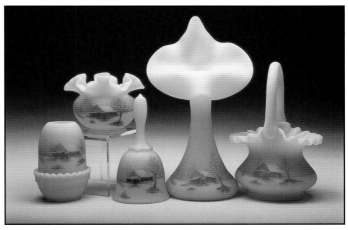

Wildflower on Cameo, 1983
Top: Temple jar #7488FD, 6" tall, **$45**
Bottom Left: Comport #7431FD, 6" tall, 7.25" wide, **$22**;
Center: Vase #7241FD, 3.5" tall, blue flower, **$22**;
Right: Vase #7530FD, 6" tall, **$30**
Note: This pattern was introduced with brown flowers but after 6 months was changed to be a blue flower

Sunset on Cameo, 1981 to 1982
Top Left: Vase #7241SS, 3.5" tall, **$35**
Bottom Left: Fairy light #7300SS, 4.5" tall, **$58**;
Center: Bell #7564SS, 6" tall, **$32**; Tulip vase #7255SS, 11" tall, **$75**;
Right: Basket #7437SS, 8" tall, **$95**

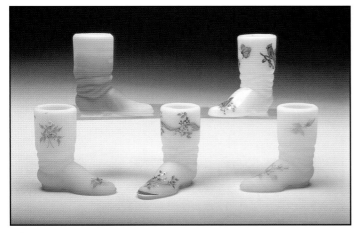

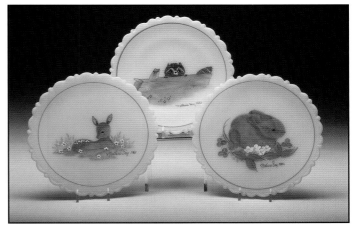

Miniature Boots, #9590, 2.75" tall, 1980s to 1990s
Top Left: Burmese Satin BR, 1982, **$24**; **Bottom Left:** Pink Blossoms on Custard satin PY, 1981, **$22**; **Center:** Ivory Satin #C95902I hand painted flowers and ribbons, Made for QVC, 1994, **$24**; **Top Right**: Blue Birds and Butterflies on Custard Satin, **$26**; **Bottom Right**: Blue Roses on Custard satin BQ, 1981, **$24**

Mother's Day and Wildlife Plates, 8" wide, Custard Satin, **$28 each**
Top: Where's Mom #7418RQ, Raccoon looking over log, 1983
Bottom Left: Gentle Fawn #7418FN, 1981;
Bottom Right: Nature's Awakening #7418NA, Brown bunny, 1982

Footed Comport #7431 grouping, 5.75" tall, 7.25" wide
Top: Blue Garland on Custard satin BA, 1982, **$24**; **Left:** Pink Roses on Blue Satin, 1985, **$28**; **Right:** Yellow Roses on Custard Satin, **$26**

Blue Roses on Custard, 1981
Left: #9536BQ basket, 5" tall, **$28**;
Center: #9592BQ toothpick, 2.5" tall, **$24**;
Right: #7554BQ vase, 4.5" tall, **$25**

Pink Blossom on Custard, 1981
Left: #7488PY temple jar, 6.5" tall, **$48**;
Center: Medallion #8267PY bell, 6.75" tall, **$28**;
Right: Medallion #8288PY candy jar, 8" tall, **$48**

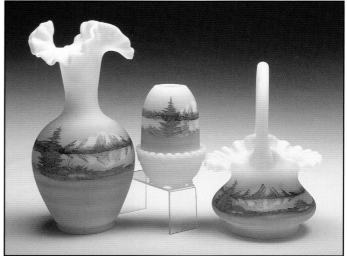

Mountain Reflections, 1981
Left: #7257MV vase, 10" tall, **$100**;
Center: #7300MV fairy light, 4.75" tall, **$65**;
Right: #7437MV basket, 8" tall, **$95**

Down by the Station, 1983
Left: Fairy light #7300TT, 4.5" tall, **$60**;
Center: Plate #7418TT, 8" wide, **$35**;
Right: Temple jar #7488TT, 5.75" tall, **$48**

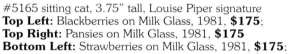

#5165 sitting cat, 3.75" tall, Louise Piper signature
Top Left: Blackberries on Milk Glass, 1981, **$175**;
Top Right: Pansies on Milk Glass, 1981, **$175**
Bottom Left: Strawberries on Milk Glass, 1981, **$175**;
Bottom Center: Maple Leaves on Black, 1985, **$195**;
Bottom Right: Holly and Berries on Opal Satin, 1989, **$165**

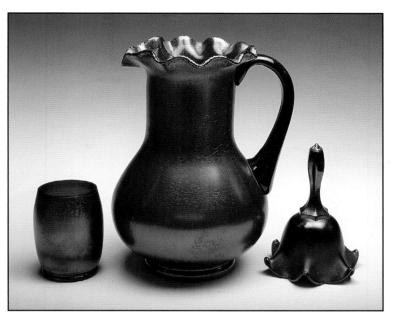

Purple Stretch, Special Order for Levay, 1981
Left: #7509VY tumbler, 4" tall, **$35**;
Center: #7509VY pitcher, 10" tall, **$295**;
Right: #7563VY bell, 6" tall, **$48**

Peach Opalescent Carnival, Special Order for MTL (Michael Taylor Limited), 1981
Left: Beaded Daisy plate, 5.5" wide, **$35**;
Center: Beaded Daisy #8250PI, miniature rose bowl, 3" tall, **$35**;
Right: Atlantis vase #5150PI, 6.5" tall, **$80**

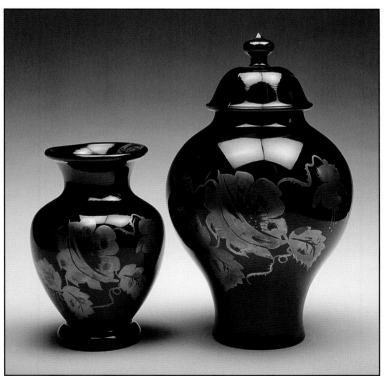

Silver Poppies, Black, Fenton's regular catalog and also sold at J.C. Penney 1981 to 1982
Left: #7550PE vase, 6.5" tall, **$24**;
Right: #7588PE temple Jar, 9.75" tall, **$65**

Sophisticated Lady, Black, 1982
Left: #7561SX vase, 10.5" tall, **$195**;
Center: #7655SX vase, 8" tall, **$250**;
Right: #7651SX vase, 10.25" tall, **$195**

Black, 1980s
Top: Kitten #5119BK, 2.25" tall, 4" long, 1989, **$32**
Left: Sitting cat #5165BK, 3.75" tall, 3" wide, 1995, **$28**;
Center: Duckling #5169BK, 3.25" tall, 2.5" wide, **$25**;
Right: Owl Decision Maker #5180BK, 4" tall, 3" wide,
1969 to 1972, **$30**

Sculptured Ice Optic
Left: ball vase, 9" tall,
Glacial Blue, **$40**; **Right:**
#8551CY vase, 10.25"tall,
Crystal, 1982, **$25**

Iris Collection on Bone
White, 1982
Top: #7521IN bowl, 4.5"
tall, **$38**;
Bottom Left: #7539IN
basket, 8" tall, **$60**;
Bottom Center: #7550IN
vase, 6.5" tall, **$38**;
#7564IN bell, 6" tall, **$24**;
Bottom Right: #7559IN
vase, 7.5" tall, **$38**

Cactus, Red Sunset Carnival, Special Order for Levay, 1982
Top: #3441RN tulip vase, 7.25" tall, **$85**
Bottom Left: #3434RN basket, 10" tall, **$125**; **Bottom Center:** #3427RN rose bowl, 4" tall, **$78**; #3463RN cruet, 6.25" tall, **$125**; **Bottom Right:** #3407RN pitcher, 10" tall, **$200**

Candleglow, 1983 to 1984
Top Left: Hobnail #3853YL vase, 3.25" tall, sample, **$30**
Top Right: #G1603YL creamer, 4.5" tall, American Legacy, **$25**
Left: #G1645YL goblet, 6.25" tall, American Legacy, **$24**; #G1644YL wine, 5" tall, American Legacy, **$20**;
Center: #G1603YL sugar, 4" tall, American Legacy, **$25**;
Right: G1659YL vase, 7" tall, American Legacy, **$35**

Spiral Optic vase #3161OH, 11.25" tall, Heritage Green Overlay, 1983, **$60**

Overlays, 1983 to 1985
Top Left: #2034OH basket, 8" tall, Heritage Green Overlay, **$48**; **Top Right:** #1866OF pitcher, 5.5" tall, Federal Blue Overlay, **$30**
Bottom Left: Dogwood #9650OD, vase, 11" tall, Dusty Rose Overlay, **$125**; **Bottom Center:** Dogwood #9658OP vase, 7.5" tall, Periwinkle Blue Overlay, **$75**; **Bottom Right:** #3161OY vase, 11" tall, Yellow Overlay, **$85**

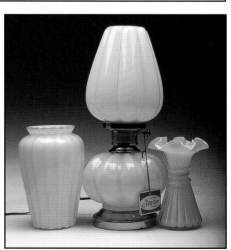

Candleglow Yellow Overlay, 1983 to 1985
Left: Vase #1650OY, 8.5" tall, **$49**;
Center: Student Lamp #2001OY, 10.75" tall, **$115**; **Right:** Wheat vase #5858OY, 7.25" tall, **$48**

Dianthus on Custard, 1983 to 1984,
Left: #5160DN fawn, 3.75" tall, **$45**; **Center:** #7488DN temple jar, 6.5" tall, **$65**; **Right:** #5151DN sitting bear, 4" tall, **$60**

Cobalt, sand carved, 1983 to 1984
Back: Thumbprint #4469LK ash tray, 6.5" wide, love birds, **$45**
Front Left: #7488KY temple jar, 5.75" tall, butterfly on branch, **$60**; **Right:** #7561ZX vase, 10.75" tall, floral, **$95**

Vasa Murrhina, Cranberry Iridized, Connoisseur collection, 1983
Left: #6462IM cruet, 7.25" tall, **$135**;
Right: #6432IM basket, 8.5" tall, **$100**

Vase, 10.5" tall, Cobalt Overlay, hand painted scenic, Louise Piper signature, 1983, **$450**

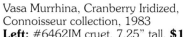

Katja, Flame, 1983 to 1984
Left: #K7765KO vase, 6.5" tall, **$45**; **Center:** #K7755KO vase, 5.5" tall, **$35**;
Right: #K7744KO, vase, 8.75" tall, **$45**

Katja, 1983 to 1984
Left: #K7765KN vase, 6.5" tall, Hickory, **$40**; **Center:** #K7751KO vase, 3.5" tall,
Flame, **$35**; **Right:** #K7766KE vase, 7.75" tall, Aquamarine, **$50**

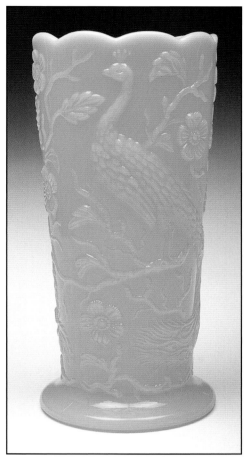

Peacock #8257PK, 8" tall,
Pekin Blue, 1980, **$48**

#3193PV top hat vase, 6.25" tall, 8.5" wide,
Plated Amberina, Connoisseur Collection,
Limited edition of 1500, satin finish, 1984, **$125**

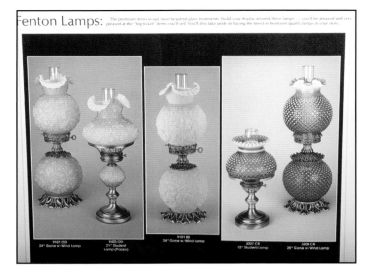

Fenton lamps, Poppy and Hobnail, 1984 catalog supplement
Reprinted with permission from the Fenton Art Glass Company

Petite Fleur, 1984
Left: Melon #7549PF bowl, 8.25" wide, **$20**; **Right:** Wheat #5838PF basket, 8" tall, **$35**

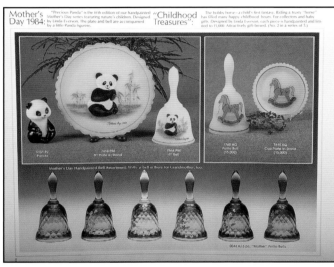

Mother's Day 1984 and Childhood Treasures, 1984 catalog supplement
Reprinted with permission from the Fenton Art Glass Company

Childhood Treasures, Custard Satin, 1980s
Left to Right: Teddy Bear cup plate #7615TE, 3.5" wide, 1983, **$16**; Teddy Bear bell #1760TE, 4.25" tall, 1983, **$20**; Frisky Puppy cup plate 7615PN, 3.5" wide, 1987, **$16**; Frisky Puppy bell #1760PN, 4.25" tall, 1987, **$20**; Clown plate #7615CL, 3.5" wide, 1985, **$16**; Clown bell #1760CL, 1985, 4.25" tall, **$20**; Playful Kitten cup plate #7615KD, 3.5" wide, 1986, **$16**; Playful Kitten bell #1760KD, 4.25" tall, 1986, **$20**

Artist Series, Custard Satin, 1980s
Left to Right: Hummingbird cup plate #7615HW, 3.5" wide, 4th in series, 1986, **$16**; Hummingbird bell #1760HW, 4.25" tall, 4th in series, 1986, **$20**; House hunting cup plate #7615AC, 3.5" wide, 7th in series, 1989, **$16**; House Hunting bell #1760AC, 4.25" tall, 7th in series, 1989, **$20**; Flying Geese cup plate 7615FG, 3.5" wide, 3rd in series, 1985, **$16**; Flying Geese bell #1760FG, 4.25" tall, 3rd in series, 1985, **$20**; Serenity cup plate #7615AT, 3.5" wide, 6th in series, 1988, **$16**; Serenity bell #1760AT, 4.25" tall, 1988, **$20**

Hobnail, Aqua Opalescent Carnival, Special Order for Levay, 1982
Left: #3645IO bell, 5.5" tall, **$25**; **Right:** #3869IO cruet, 5" tall, **$48**

Stiegel Green Overlay, Special Order for JC
Penney, 1984
Left: #1866, pitcher, 5.5" tall, **$40**; **Right:**
Coin Spot #2034, basket, 8" tall, **$65**

Hobnail, Plum Opalescent, Special Order
for Levay, 1984
Back Left: #3804PO footed fairy light, 8.5" tall, **$195**;
Back Right: #3656PO vase, 5.5" tall, **$75**
Front Left: #3926PO bonbon, **$28**;
Front Center: #3667PO bell, 6" tall, **$45**;
Front Right: #3733PO heart relish, 8.5" long, **$145**
*Reprinted with permission from the Schiffer
Publishing Ltd.*

#5158 elephant, 3.6" tall
Top Left: Berries and
Blossoms, 1984 to 1986,
$35; **Top Right:** Crystal
Velvet, 1984 to 1988, **$28**
Bottom Left: Roses on
Custard, 1981 to 1984,
$35; **Bottom Center:**
Cobalt Carnival, 1984,
$40; **Bottom Right:**
Frosted Asters, 1984 to
1986, **$75**

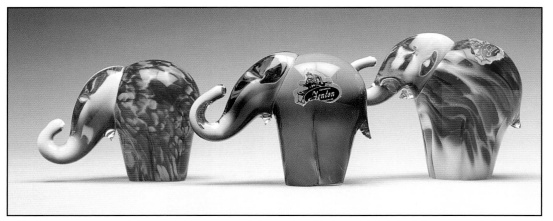

#5012 free hand elephant, 3.35" long,
Left: Autumn Orange Vasa Murrhina, 1984, **$95**;
Center: Federal Blue, 1980, **$115**; **Right:** Rose Mist Vasa Murrhina, 1984, **$145**

#5011 bird, 2" tall, Vasa Murrhina, Aventurine Green with Blue, 1984, **$85**

Love Bouquet, Special order for Mary Walrath, Burmese, 1982 to 1986
Top Left: #7558WQ vase, 6" tall, **$60**;
Top Right: #9230WQ basket, 4.75" tall, **$75**
Bottom Left: #9558WQ rose bowl, 3" wide, **$38**; #9591WQ slipper, 5" long, **$35**; **Bottom Center:** #7255WQ tulip vase, 10.5" tall, **$125**;
Bottom Right: #7662WQ bell, 4.5" tall, **$38**; #9590WQ boot, 2.75" tall, **$30**

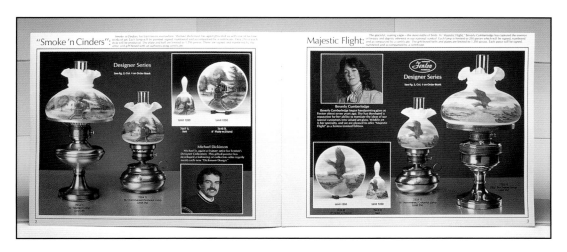

Smoke'n Cinders and Majestic Flight, designer series, 1984 catalog supplement
Reprinted with permission from the Fenton Art Glass Company

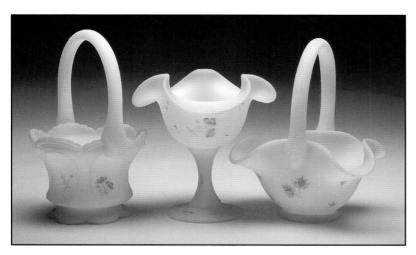

Opal Satin with Periwinkle blush, 1985 to 1986
Left: Meadow Blooms #9639JU basket, 8" tall, **$30**;
Center: Meadow Blooms #1628JU compote, 6" tall, **$18**;
Right: Autumn Leaves #7635LB basket, 8" tall, **$35**

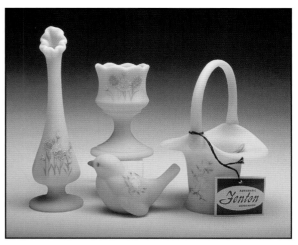

Blue Satin hand painted
Top Center; #7275FA votive candleholder, 4.25" tall,
Frosted Asters, 1983 to 1985, **$15**
Left: #9056F bud vase A, 8.25"tall, Frosted Asters,
1983 to 1985, **$18**; **Center:** #5163JS bird, 3" tall,
Pink Roses on Blue Satin, 1985, **$45**; **Right:** #9035JS
basket, 7.5" tall, Pink Roses on Blue Satin, 1985, **$45**

#5119 kitten, old style, 4" long
Top Left: Natural, 1985 to 1988, **$85**;
Top Right: Berries and Blossoms, 1985 to 1987, **$65**
Bottom Left: Sunset Peach, 1985 to 1987, **$65**;
Bottom Center: Frosted Asters, 1985, **$85**;
Bottom Right: Pink Blossoms on Custard, 1985 to 1987, **$6**8

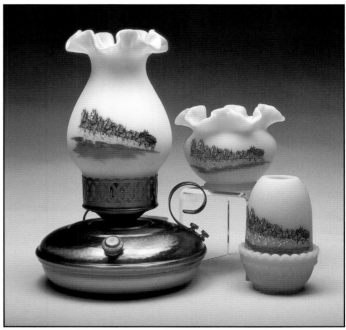

Budweiser, Cameo Satin, 1983
Left: Lamp #7311XA, 10.5" tall, **$295**;
Center: Vase #7254XA, 3.5" tall, **$60**;
Right: Fairy light #7300XA, 4.75" tall, **$145**

#9480 Chessie box, 8" tall, Iridized Crystal, 1985
Left: plain, **$145**; **Right:** hand painted, **$225**

Sitting bear #5151, 3.5" tall
Top Left: True Blue, 1985 to 1986, **$75**;
Top Right: Crystal with Cobalt center, Special Order for Puget Sound Fenton Finders, 1980s, **$50**
Bottom Left: Natural Brown, 1985 to 1987, **$75**;
Bottom Center: Red Slag, 1984, **$110**;
Bottom Right: Schwarz, 1991, **$65**

#5111NK clown, 4.75" tall, Cobalt Carnival, 1985, **$65**

#5232CY Nipper dog, 3" tall, Crystal, Special Order for GE Electronics, mid 1980s, **$60**

Christmas Fantasy Series, fairy lights #7300, 4.75" tall. Limited edition of 7500, **$58 each**
Left to Right: Heart's Desire WP, Custard Satin, 1985; Sharing, Opal Satin, 1987; Anticipation AI, Custard Satin, 1983; Expectation GE, Opal Satin, 1984

Fenton Classic, Christmas Fantasy, 1985 catalog supplement
Reprinted with permission from the Fenton Art Glass Company

Diamond Lace #4809GK epergne, 10" tall, Green Opalescent with Cobalt crest, 1985, **$350**

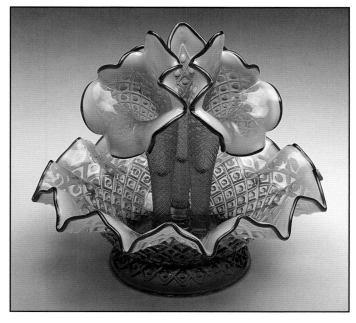

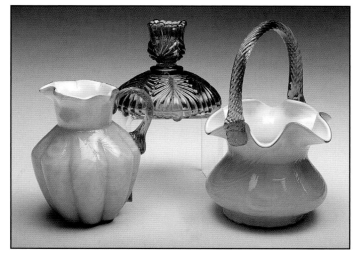

Top Center: Beauty #9674HG candleholder, 4" tall, Heritage Green, 1982 to 1983, **$15**
Bottom Left: #1866OF pitcher, 5.25" tall, Federal Blue Overlay, 1983 to 1985, **$28**; **Right:** #2034OF basket, 8" tall, Federal Blue Overlay, 1983 to 1985, **$45**

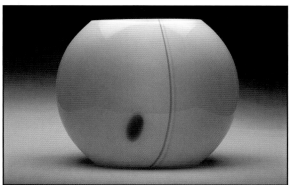

Masterworks vase #8801NV, 9.5" tall, designed by Delmer Stowasser, 1985, **$98**

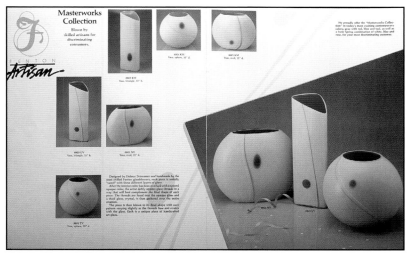

Masterworks, 1985 catalog
Reprinted with permission from the Fenton Art Glass Company

Overlays, 1984 to 1987
Top Left: #3501OF apple, 3.25" tall, Federal Blue Overlay, 1984, **$70**;
Top Right: #1924 hat vase, 3" tall, Dusty Rose Overlay, Special Order for Collectors Showcase, 1986, **$45**
Bottom Left: #5019OD, apple, 4" tall, Dusty Rose Overlay, 1984, **$60**; #1924 hat vase, 3" tall, Teal Overlay, **$40**;
Bottom Right: #1924 hat vase, 3" tall, Periwinkle Overlay, Special order for Collectors Showcase, 1985 to 1987, **$40**

Heart candy #9519, 6" long, 5.5" wide
Left: Provincial Blue OO, 1987, **$14**; **Right:** Rosalene RE Satin, 1989, **$20**

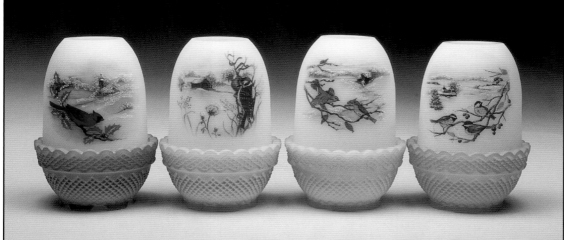

Birds in Winter, fairy lights #7300, 4.75" tall, Opal Satin, limited edition of 4500, **$68 each**
Left to Right: Cardinal in Churchyard BC, 1987; Downy Woodpecker BL, 1989; Blue Bird in Snowfall NB, 1990; Chickadee Ballet BD, 1988

Decorated Custard satin
Left: Deer Scene fairy light #7300PG, 4.5" tall, 1989, **$65**; **Center:** Vase #7252, 7" tall, Amish horse and carriage, **$68**; **Right:** Mug #7540, Blue flowers, 3.25" tall, **$20**

Fairy lights, Crystal Velvet, 1983 to 1984
Left: Inverted Strawberry, #9407VE, 5" tall, 3.5" wide, two piece, **$26**; **Right:** Madonna, #5107VE, 6" tall, 4.5" wide, one piece with original metal and glass insert inside, **$30**

Bells, Crystal Velvet, 1981 to 1983
Left: Faberge, #8466VE, 6.75" tall, **$14**;
Center: Craftsman, #9660VE, 7" tall, **$24**;
Right: Inverted Strawberry, #9407VE, 6.25" tall, **$19**

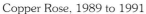

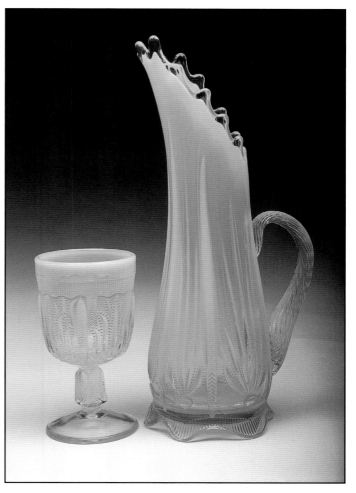

Cactus, Topaz Opalescent, Water Set #3407TO, Collector's Extravaganza, 1988
Left: Goblet, 6" tall, 10 ounce, **$35**;
Right: Pitcher, 13.5" tall, 48 ounce, **$225**

Copper Rose, 1989 to 1991
Top Left: Wave Crest, #6080KP candy box, 4.5" tall, 6" wide, **$68**; **Bottom Left:** Comport #6322KP, 5.5" tall, **$24**; Ram's Head candlestick #9372KP, 4.5" tall, **$22**; **Center:** Vase #8817KP, 8" tall, **$85**; **Top Right:** Rose bowl, 3" tall, **$24**; **Bottom Right:** Heart candy box #4106KP, 5" wide, **$35**

Kissing Kids #5101, 4.5" tall
Top Left: Crystal Velvet, 1981, **$45 pair**;
Top Right: Candleglow Yellow YL, 1983 to 1984, **$75 pair**
Bottom Left: Heritage Green HG, 1983 to 1984, **$48 pair**;
Bottom Center: Opal Satin, hand painted, late 1980s, not in
regular line, **$85 pair**;
Bottom Right: Amethyst Carnival, 1978, **$60 pair**

Crystal Velvet
Top Center: #5214VE Scottie, 2.75" tall, 1986 to 1987, **$75**
Bottom Left: Water Lily #8480VF covered candy, 7.5" tall, 1977
to 1979, **$35**;
Bottom Center: #5134VF snail, 3" tall, 1985 to 1987, **$25**;
Right: Mandarin #8251VF vase, 9.5" tall, 1977 to 1979, **$75**

42 pc bell assortment, 1986-87 catalog
Reprinted with permission from the Fenton Art Glass Company

Silhouettes, 1986-87 catalog
Reprinted with permission from the Fenton Art Glass Company

Natural Series, Opal Satin, 1985 to 1988
Top Left: #5165NG gray cat, 3.75" tall, **$85**;
Top Right: #5163NY yellow bird, 2.75" tall, **$65**
Bottom Left: #5163NO orange bird, **$55**;
Bottom Right: #5119NX kitten with gray paws, **$85**

Natural Animals, 1986-87 catalog
Reprinted with permission from the Fenton Art Glass Company

Natural Series, #5214 scottie, 2.75" tall, Opal Satin, 1986 to 1987
Left: Gray, **$45**; **Right:** Plain, **$45**

Sand Carved
Top Center: Mother and Child #7661MD vase, 8.5" tall, Rose Velvet, 1984, **$75**
Left: Danielle #8812JY vase, Teal Overlay, 10.5" tall, limited to 1000, Connoisseur Collection, 1986, **$125**; **Center:** #7542FJ Rose Quartz vase, 5" tall, Connoisseur Collection 1983, **$60**;
Right: Gabrielle #8802LY vase, 12.5" tall, Cobalt Overlay, Connoisseur Collection, limited to 800, 1985, **$150**

Natural Series, #5159SP brown spaniel,
3" wide, Opal Satin, 1985 to 1987, **$60**

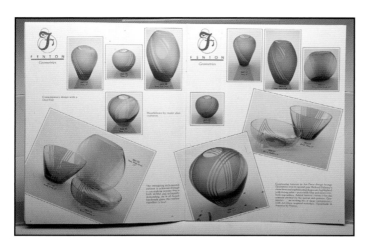

Geometrics, 1986-87 catalog
Reprinted with permission from the Fenton Art Glass Company

Geometrics vase #8806EP, Periwinkle, 7" tall, designed by Richard Delaney, 1986 to 1987, **$60**

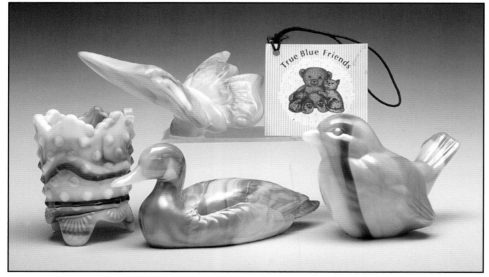

Blue Slag
Top: #5170OZ butterfly, 3.5" long, Cobalt slag, 1980s, **$50**
Left: Almost Heaven #3795, Hobnail toothpick, 2.75" tall, 1989, **$24**; True Blue #5147IK mallard, 5" long, 1986, **$85**; True Blue #5163IK bird, 2.75" tall, 1986, **$95**

Crystal
Left: Fine Cut and Block #9159CY swung vase, 12" tall, 1986, **$18**;
Center: Fine Cut and Block #9180CY candy dish, 8.25" tall, 1980, **$25**;
Right: Hobnail #3986CY covered urn, 11.25" tall, 1968, **$85**

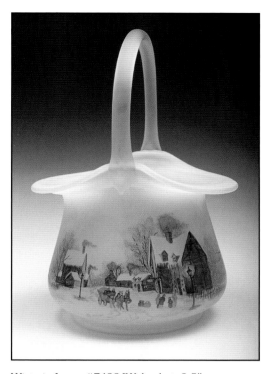

Wisteria Lane #7439JW, basket, 9.5"
tall, limited to 5000, 1986, **$145**

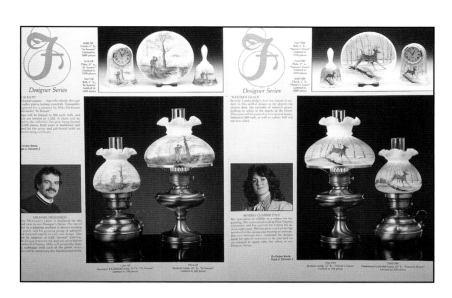

In Season and Nature's Grace,
Designer series, 1985 catalog
supplement
*Reprinted with permission from
the Fenton Art Glass Company*

Wisteria Lane vase #7661JW, 8.5" tall,
designed by Michael Dickinson, limited to
5000, 1986, **$125**

Wildrose #77-41 goblet, 6.25" tall,
Special Order for Madonna Inn, 1986 to
1987
Top Left: Topaz, **$18**;
Top Right: Candleglow Yellow, **$15**
Bottom Left: Lilac, **$15**;
Bottom Center: pink, **$15**;
Bottom Right: Apple Green, **$15**

#5225 puppy, old style, 4" long
Top Left: Crystal, 1987 to 1988, **$40**;
Top Right: Victorian Roses, Opal Satin, 1987 to 1988, **$35**
Bottom Left: Natural, 1987 to 1988, **$65**; **Bottom Center:** Pastel Violets on Custard, 1987, **$35**;
Bottom Right: Natural, 1988, **$65**

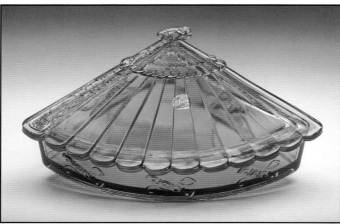

Fan box #765, Covered candy, 2.25" tall, 9.5" wide, Dusty Rose, Special order for Tiara, 1988 to 1990, **$35**

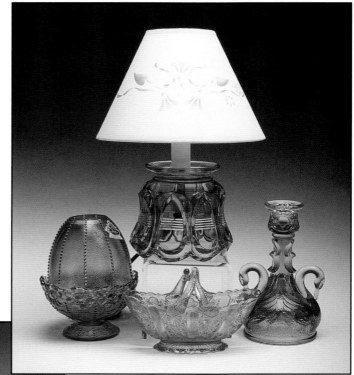

Dusty Rose, 1980s
Top Center: Barred Oval #8303DK lamp, 10.5" tall, 1987, **$38**
Bottom Left: Daisy #8405DK fairy light, 6" tall, 1984, **$35**; **Center:** Daisy and Button #1939DK, oval basket, 6"long, 1987, **$20**; **Right:** Swan #5172DK, candleholder, 6.25" tall, 1987, **$20**

Wheat #5858 vases, 7.5" tall
Top Left: Federal Blue, 1983, **$60**; **Top Right:** Opaline, Petite Fleur, 1984, **$48**
Bottom Left: Marigold Carnival, flared top, 8.5" tall, 1981, **$85**; **Bottom Center:** Country Cranberry, 8.5" tall, unfinished top, 1982 to 1987, **$98**;
Bottom Right: Dusty Rose Overlay, 1987 to 1988, **$60**

Burmese
Top Left: Wild Rose and Bow
Knot #2854BE tulip vase, 8.25"
tall, Special Order for Levay,
1979, **$98**; **Top Center:** Butterfly
and Flowering Branch #7634EB
basket, 8.5" tall, 1985, **$125**; **Top
Right:** Peacock #8257BR vase,
7.8" tall, 1986 to 1987, **$98**
Bottom Left: Shell #8808SB
vase, 8" tall, limited to 950, 1985,
$175; Paneled Daisy #8294BR
toothpick, 3.5" tall, 1986 to 1987,
$24; **Bottom Center:** Dogwood
#7501PD three piece fairy light,
6.75" tall, 1981 to 1982, **$135**;
Roses fawn #5160RB, 3.5" long,
1986, **$48**; **Bottom Right:**
Wavecrest #6059RB vase, 8.5" tall,
limited to 112, Special order for
Lois Radcliff, 1985, **$135**

French Opalescent, 1987 to 1988
Left: Provincial Bouquet #3196FS
vase, 13" tall, **$85**;
Right: Victorian Roses #3195VJ
vase, 7" tall, **$60**

Sapphire Blue, Made for Gracious Touch,
1987 to 1990
Top Center: #5163BX bird, tall, **$40**
Bottom Left: Hobnail #3674BX
candleholder, 5.75" tall, **$24**;
Center: #9799BX logo, 5" long, **$35**;
Right: Hobnail #3664BX pitcher, 10"
tall, **$125**

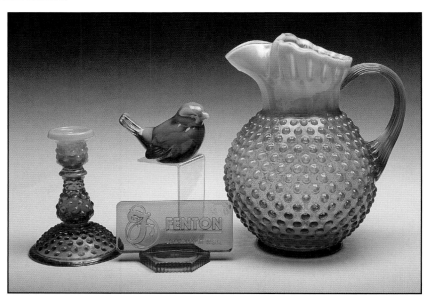

Blue Royale, 1988 to 1991
Left: #3201KK lamp, 14.25" tall, **$100**;
Center: #1432KK pitcher, 6.5" tall, **$45**;
Right: #1516KN vase, 8.5" tall, **$38**

Reflections, Peaches 'N Cream,
1986-87 catalog
*Reprinted with permission from
the Fenton Art Glass Company*

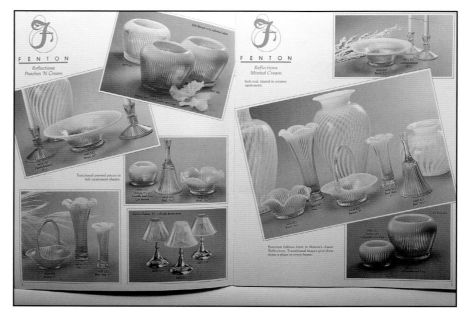

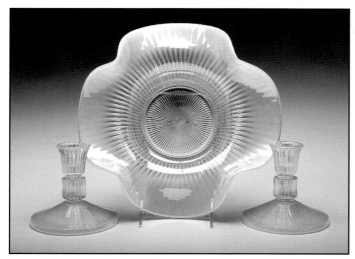

Sheffield, Peaches and Cream, 1987 to 1988
Back: #6625UO bowl, 11.25" wide, **$38**
Front: # 6672UO candlesticks, 4.5" tall, **$35 pair**

Hobnail, Pink Opalescent, 1988, **$350** for 15 piece set (punch bowl, base and 12 cups)
Punch bowl, 7.75" tall, 14" wide; base, 3.5" tall, 8.75" wide; total height 10.75"; Cup, 2.25" tall

Heart relishes, Made for Gracious Touch, 1988
Left: #Q7333MR Milk Glass with Dusty Rose
crest, 6.5" wide, **$28**; **Right:** #Q7333DM
Dusty Rose with Milk Glass crest, 6.5" wide, **$32**

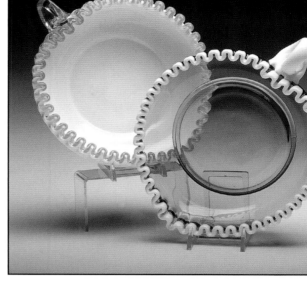

Hobnail #3733 heart relish, 6.5" wide, Dusty
Rose crest and Cobalt handle, 1988, **$85**

Top: Holly Berry #5106HL Santa fairy light, 5.75" tall, Opal
Satin, 1988, **$40**
Bottom Left: Winter #8637XT, basket, 7.5" tall, Opal Satin,
1985, **$28**; **Bottom Center:** Winter #7475XT, candlestick,
6" tall, 1985, **$20**; Holly Berry #5115HL bird, 2.85" tall, Opal
Satin, 1988, **$32**; **Bottom Right:** Holly Berry #9238HL,
paneled basket, 7" tall, 1988, **$30**

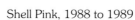

Shell Pink, 1988 to 1989
Top Center: Peacock and Dahlia plate, 6.5" wide, **$28**
Left: Wild Rose and Bowknot #Q2802PE lamp, 18.5" tall,
Made for Gracious Touch, 1988, **$135**; **Bottom Center:**
Daisy and Button #1995PE cat slipper, 6" long, **$20**; **Right:**
Rose Corsage #8376MP hurricane lamp, 11" tall, **$38**

Flute and Dot #9050 vase, 5.5" tall
Top Left: Candleglow Yellow Overlay, 1983 to 1984, **$35**; **Top Center:** Periwinkle Blue Overlay, 1985, **$48**; Federal Blue Overlay, 1983, **$30**; **Top Right:** Blue Splatter, experimental color, 1988, **$60**
Bottom Left: Blue Royale, 1988, **$38**; Blue Burmese, 1984, **$58**; **Bottom Center:** Colonial Amber, 1987 to 1988, **$25**; **Bottom Right:** Teal Royale, 1988, **$35**; Dusty Rose Overlay, 1983 to 1984, **$48**

Two Ring vases, 6" tall
Top Left: Curtain #2057OO Provincial Blue Opalescent, 1987 to 1988, **$35**; **Top Center:** Curtain #2057JF French Opalescent, Country Garden, 1987 to 1988, **$30**; **Top Right:** Coin Dot #1466BO, Blue Opalescent, 1960 to 1961, **$48**
Bottom Left: Coin Dot #1466CR, Cranberry Opalescent, 1956 to 1966, **$60**; **Bottom Center:** Rib Optic #1549AO, Autumn Gold Opalescent, 1993 to 1994, **$38**; #7456 Jamestown Overlay, 1957 to 1959, **$50**; **Bottom Right:** Dot Optic #1354CR, Cranberry Opalescent, 1990 to 1993, **$45**

#5148 mouse, 2.85" tall
Top Left: Natural Brown, 1985 to 1988, **$60**; **Top Center:** Opal Satin, hand painted, 1990, **$48**; **Top Right:** Happy Santa, 1990, **$48**
Bottom Left: Morning Glories on Sea Mist Green, 1997, **$30**; **Bottom Center:** Blue Burmese, 2000, **$45**; True Blue, 1985 to 1986, **$55**; **Bottom Right:** Red Slag, 1984, **$85**

Rosalene, 1980s
Left: Basket Weave #8354RE vase, 8.25" tall, Connoisseur Collection, limited to 2500, 1989, **$85**; #9667 bell, 7" tall, Fenton Gift Shop, 1989, **$32**; **Center:** #7605RE epergne, 13" tall, Connoisseur Collection, limited to 2000, 1989, **$450; Right:** Diamond #7060RE pitcher, 7" tall, Connoisseur Collection, limited to 2500, 1989, **$75**

Teal Royale
Top Center: #5228 bridesmaid, 6.5" tall, Made for Gracious Touch, 1989, **$60**
Left: Flute and Dot #9050OC vase, 5.25" tall, 1987 to 1988, **$18**; **Center:** Spanish Lace #Q3570TX candleholder, 4" tall, snow crest, Made for Gracious Touch, 1989, **$22**; **Right:** Roses #9237OC basket, 8" tall, 1987 to 1988, **$40**

Jacqueline
Top Left: #C9452AB vase, 4.5" tall, Cobalt Overlay, Made for QVC, 2001, **$45**; **Top Center:** #9452MG vase, 4.5" tall, Mulberry, 1989, **$48**; **Top Right:** #9166XC pitcher, 5.5" tall, Persian Blue, 1989, **$75**
Bottom Left: #9166RU pitcher, 6.25" tall, Ruby, 1982, **$100**;
Bottom Center: #9442 bowl, 8.75" wide, Fuchsia Opalescent, 1994, **$85**; **Bottom Right:** #C9165CZ vase, 5.5" tall, Cranberry with Milk Glass crest, Frank Fenton signature, Made for QVC, 1998, **$98**
Front Left: #6569EZ vase, 2.75" tall, Jade Iridized, **$28**; **Front Right:** #6569TZ vase, 2.75" tall, Twilight Blue Iridized, 1992 to 1993, **$28**

Samples from Fenton Gift Shop, late 1980s
Left: Pulled Feather with Hanging Hearts vase, 5.25", Favrene, **$295**; **Center:** Pulled Feather vase, 4.5" tall, Favrene, **$225**; **Right:** Hanging Heart egg, 4.75" tall Cobalt, **$195**

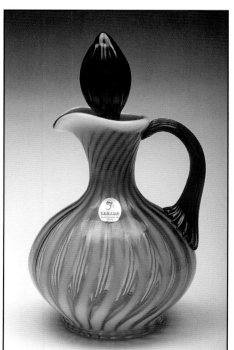

Spiral Optic #Q0207 cruet, 7" tall, Royal Blue Opalescent, Made for Gracious Touch, 1989, **$65**

1990 TO 1999
DAWN OF A NEW AGE

1990 marked another anniversary for Fenton. For their 85th anniversary an offering of Burmese in a variety of decorations was in their June supplement. Also this year, their logo was altered again to reflect the new decade. A 9 replaced the 8 under the Fenton word inside the oval.

Bob Hill's wife, Pat, was hired to work in the selecting and packing departments before going full time as a Selector in 1992. More changes were also implemented on how Fenton marketed their glass. In the spring supplement of 1992, a special Valentine offering debuted with the Heart Optic collection. The Family Signature series was started in 1993 with an emphasis placed on a certain type of glass that would be signed by a designated family member. The Showcase dealer program was launched in 1994 with 235 dealers, allowing those shops with high sales to offer an item exclusively made for them. Today this total is over 1,000 shops. To honor the people in the Gulf war in 1991, a Proud to be American series was offered with a portion of the proceeds going to the USO.

Stacy Williams was hired in 1993 as a decorator. Lynn Fenton Erb was the first fourth generation family member to became part of the family business. She joined Fenton, as part of the sales and marketing department, in 1994. To promote their own new products, family, designers and workers, Fenton decided to issue their own publication. This quarterly magazine was titled, *Glass Messenger* and made its debut in 1996. Lynn was actively involved in the planning of this new magazine. That same year, Louise Piper passed away.

Jon Saffell, a former designer at Fostoria Glass joined Fenton in 1994 and immediately set about making several sculptured animals along with holiday related items.

Major improvements were made at Fenton with the closure of the old disposal site and the development of the new basement storage in 1997.

Scott Fenton, son of Tom Fenton, was the second fourth generation family member to join the family business. He went full time in 1997 and went right to work in sales and marketing. Scott can actively be seen at the many retail gift shows across the country every year.

A new mould was made in 1998 based especially on an occupation of a family member. Mike Fenton's daughter, Natalie was a professional ballerina and Jon Saffel sculpted a likeness of her to become the first ballerina figurine for Fenton. Special orders were also done for both the Cracker Barrel restaurant chain and Martha Stewart catalogs.

The longtime L.G. Wright Glass Company closed and a monumental auction was held in May 1999 to liquidate all their remaining glass and moulds. Fenton purchased a great number of their moulds; many of which are now starting to be used. That same year, Dave Fetty officially retired but he can still be seen at Fenton consulting on many of their projects.

Black Rose, 1990s
Back Left: Hobnail #3837RZ basket, 7.5" tall, Frank Fenton signature, Made for QVC, 1992, **$75**; **Back Center:** #7202 epergne, 10" tall, Special Order for Zeta Todd, 1990, **$225**; **Back Right:** #0329A Beaded Melon tulip vase, 10" tall, Fenton Gift Shop, 1993, **$95**; **Front Left:** #7436 basket, 6.5" tall, Special Order for Zeta Todd, 1990, **$100**; **Front Right:** C7575U1 ewer, 6.25" tall hand painted, Bill Fenton signature, Made for QVC, 1991, **$60**

#5241 lion, 2.8" tall, 1990
Top: Black, **$35**; **Center:** Red Carnival, **$40**; **Right:** Blue Royale, **$30**

Burmese, 1990s
Top Left: Raspberry 7731QH basket, 8" tall, Made for 85th anniversary, 1990, **$78**; **Top Right:** Roses # 7790RB vase, 6.4" tall, **$60**
Bottom Left: Roses #7791RB vase, 6.5" tall, Made for 85th anniversary, 1990, **$50**; **Bottom Center:** Apple paperweight, 3.75" tall, Special order for Lois Ratcliff, 1991, **$85**; **Center:** Tree Scene #7732QD basket, 6.5" tall, Made for 85th anniversary, 1990, **$78**; **Center:** Petite Floral #7202QJ epergne, 9.5" tall, Made for 85th anniversary, 1990, **$145**; #7732 basket, 6.5" tall, Fenton Gift Shop, 1990, **$115**; **Bottom Right:** Petite Floral #7701QJ cruet, 7" tall, Made for 85th anniversary, 1990, **$110**

Crackle, Iridized, 1992
Left: Pinch vase #7647P8, Pink, 8.25" tall, **$49**;
Top Center: Vase #7645P8, Pink, 5.5" tall, **$35**;
Bottom Center: Vase #7645L4, Sea Mist, 4" tall, **$25**;
Right: Pitcher #7483L4, Sea Mist, 11" tall, **$95**

#5163 bird, 4" long
Top Left: Gilded Star flowers, Pearlized Milk Glass, 1993, **$35**; **Top Right:** Meadow Blossoms, Opal Satin, 1991 to 1993, **$35**
Bottom Left: Sea Mist Green, 1996, **$28**;
Bottom Center: Twilight Blue, 1994, **$30**;
Bottom Right: Teal Carnival, 1989, **$35**

Daisy and Fern, Cranberry Opalescent
Left: Beaded Melon #1844CR tulip vase, 10" tall, 1991, **$95**; **Center:** #1852CR vase, 11.75" tall, 1991 to 1993, **$125**; **Right:** 1872CR ewer, 32 oz., 6.75" tall, 1982 to 1992, **$48**

Spiral Optic, Cranberry Opalescent
Left: #C3051CR epergne, 9.5" tall, 2 pieces, Made for QVC, 1991, **$195**; **Center:** #3161CR vase, 11.25" tall, 1990 to 1991, **$98**; **Right:** #3163CR ewer, 5.5" tall, 1990 to 1991, **$45**

Bubble Optic tulip vase, 8.5" tall, Blue with Green Vasa Murrhina crest, Sample, 1992, **$125**

Cat Capers, #5165 sitting cat, 1992
Top Left: Green Iridized, hand painted floral, **$30**; **Top Right:** Green Iridized, **$32**
Center Left: Pink Iridized, hand painted floral, **$30**; **Center Right:** Pink Iridized, **$32**
Bottom Left: Blue Iridized, hand painted floral, **$30**; **Bottom Right:** Blue Iridized, **$32**

Left: Basket #6572QX, 10"
tall, 7.25" wide, paneled, hand
decorated Roses, Rosalene, 1992,
QVC, **$75**; **Center:** Basket
#6572BK, 10.5" tall, 7" wide,
paneled, Black, 1994, **$45**; **Right:**
Tulip Vase #7255QX, 11.25" tall,
Hand decorated Roses, Rosalene,
1991, QVC, **$68**

Rosalene, 1990s
Top Left: Rose Buds #7000WA
perfume bottle, 6.25" tall, 1998, **$65**;
fish paperweight #5193RE, 4.5" tall,
limited to 2000, 1991, **$25**; **Top
Right:** Rose Buds Natalie #5270WA
ballerina, 6.5" tall, 1998, **$95**
Bottom Left: angel #5114, 6" tall,
Fenton Gift Shop, 1993, **$38**; Rose
Buds kissing girl #5101QX, 4.65"
tall, and kissing boy 4.65" tall, 1992,
Fenton Gift Shop, **$75 pair**; **Bottom
Center:** #5165 sitting cat, 3.85"
tall, Fenton Gift Shop, 1992, **$65**;
Twinning Floral #1684RP ginger jar,
7" tall, Connoisseur Collection, 1992,
$85; Rose Buds #7009WA powder
box, 4.75" wide, 1998, **$50**; **Bottom
Right:** Diamond Lattice #1710R5
perfume bottle, 5.5" tall, limited to
1250, 1993, **$75**

Gold Series made for Heisey Club of
America, Rosalene, limited edition of
450 sets, 1992
Top Left: tiger paperweight #103,
2.75" tall, 8" long, **$98**; **Top Right:**
sow #1, 3" tall, 4.5" long, **$80**
Center: cygnet #5, 2.1" tall, 2.5"
long, **$30**
Bottom Left: filly #1, 8.75" tall,
5" long, **$135**; **Bottom Center:**
Airedale #1, 6" tall, 5.25" long,
$100; **Bottom Right:** rabbit #1538,
2.6" tall, 3.6" long, **$75**

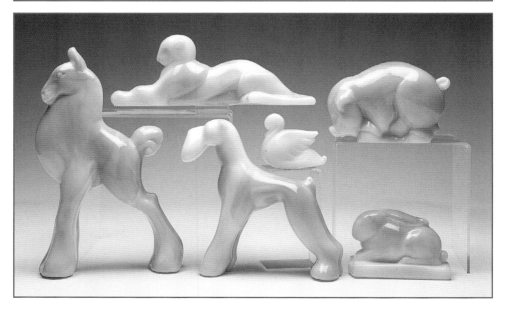

Gold Series made for Heisey Club of America, Rosalene, 1992
Top Left: hen #2, 4.25" tall, 3.5" long, **$70**; **Top Right:** duckling #22, 2.75" tall, 2.5" long, **$35**
Bottom Left: giraffe #2, 10.25" tall, 3" long, **$125**; **Bottom Center:** standing colt #1522, 5" tall, 2.75" long, **$48**; fish bookend #1554, 7" tall, 5" long, **$85**; **Bottom Right:** gazelle #104, 10.75" tall, 3.5" long, **$115**

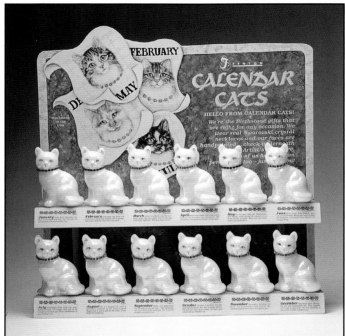

Calendar cats, #5165, Opal Iridized with rhinestone necklace, 1993 to 2001, **$20** each

#5125 donkey, 4.75" tall and #1524 cart, 5.5" long
Top: Rosalene, 1992, **$98 set**
Bottom: Champagne, 2000, **$65 set**

#5119 kitten, new style, 3.8" long
Top Left: Crystal, 1993 to 1995, **$20**;
Top Right: Baby Gift- boy, 1998 to 2000, **$28**
Bottom Left: Pink Iridized, 1993, **$24**; **Bottom Center:** Twilight Blue, Special Order for Singleton Bailey, 1994, **$45**; **Bottom Right:** Spruce Green, Made for QVC, 1998, **$40**

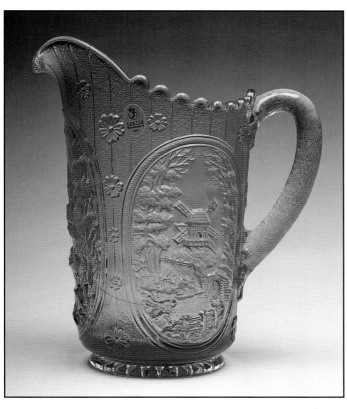

Wind Mill pitcher, 7" tall, Dusty Rose, Made for Tiara, 1993, **$30**

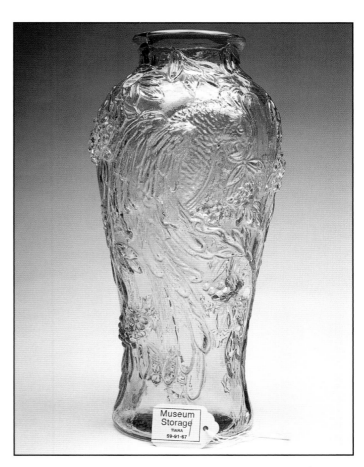

Paradise #926 vase, 10" tall, Dusty Rose, Hostess Gift at $250 level, Made for Tiara, 1991, **$48**

Victoria #849 vase, 16.5" tall, Platinum, Designer's Touch, Made for Tiara, 1991, **$60**

Primrose #424 vase, 17.5" tall, Periwinkle, Hostess Gift at $500 level, Made for Tiara, 1991, **$60**

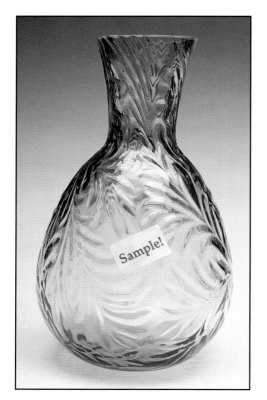

Fern Optic vase, 10" tall,
Premier Blue, Made for
Tiara, sample, 1991, **$75**

Made for QVC, 1993
Left: #C5178DN owl, 7" tall, Rose Pearl, **$85**;
Right: #C5174XV rabbit, 6" tall, Persian Pearl, **$85**

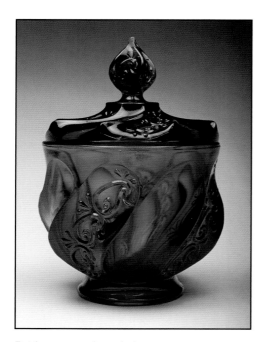

Paisley, covered candy jar
#6780TB, 7" tall, 4.75" wide,
Twilight Blue, 1992 to 1994, **$32**

Pansies on Cranberry, 1994 to 1997
Top Left: #3239CW basket, 6.5" tall, **$75**; **Top Right:** #1672CW ewer, 11" tall, **$175**
Bottom Left: #1559 CW vase, 9.75" tall, Bill Fenton signature, **$95**; #1700CW fairy
Light, 4.5" tall, two piece, **$75**; **Bottom Center:** #1685CW tulip vase, 8.5" tall, **$85**;
Bottom Right: #1557CW vase, 4.5" tall, **$48**; #1554CW vase, 9" tall, **$99**

Cranberry, Hand painted
Top Left: Open Heart Arches #CV0704Q basket, 8.5" tall, Bill and George Fenton signatures, Made for QVC, 1994, **$100**; **Top Right:** Empire #1211RW pitcher, 10" tall, Connoisseur Collection, limited to 950, 1992, **$99**
Bottom Left: Drapery #C91554Q vase, 8" tall, Made for QVC, 1994, **$85**; **Bottom Center:** #1796BY vase, 7.25" tall, Cherry Blossoms, Connoisseur collection, limited to 950, 1987, **$125**; #2085TM candy box, 4.5" tall, limited to 2500, 1990 to 1991, **$80**; **Bottom Right:** #1640C1 vase, 10.5" tall, Family Signature Series with George Fenton signature, sales limited to April 30, 1993, **$125**

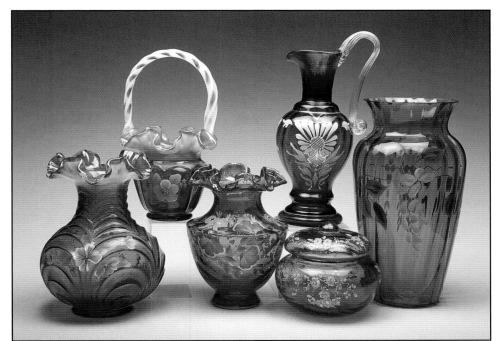

Fuchsia, 1994
Top Left: Spiral Optic #3077EH, basket, 11" tall, **$98**;
Top Right: Spiral Optic #1216, vase, 9.5" tall, George Fenton signature, **$98**,
Bottom Left: Drapery #2058EH, vase, 5.5" tall, **$38**; **Center:** Drapery #2001EH, lamp, 17" tall, **$275**; **Bottom Right:** Spiral Optic #1215EH, pitcher, 6.25" tall, **$75**

Special order for Pacific NW Fenton Association
Top **Left to Right:** #5165 sitting cat, 3.75" tall, Black, 1994, **$125**; #5225 puppy, 1995, 4" long, **$115**; #5151 bear, 3.5" tall, 1996, **$60**; #5148 mouse, 3" tall, 1997, **$48**
Bottom Left to Right: #5251 squirrel, 2.75" tall, 1998, **$45**; #5149 luv bug, 3" tall, 1999, **$45**; #5162 bunny, 2000, 3.25" tall, **$35**; #5169 duckling, 3.5" tall, 2001, **$55**

Puddle Parade, Duckling #5169, 3.5" tall, Pearlized Opal, 1994, **$45 each**
Top Left: Daffodil;
Bottom Left: Miss Daphne;
Bottom Center: Delbert; Ditsy;
Top Right: Dolly Sue;
Bottom Right: Dugan

#5141 Southern Belle, 8" tall
Left to Right: Rosalene, 1994, **$85**; Crystal Iridized, 1994, **$50**; Burmese hand painted, limited to 2000, 1997, **$75**; Persian Pearl, 1994, **$60**

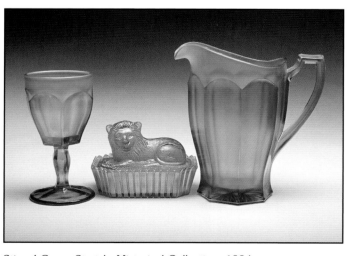

Stiegel Green Stretch, Historical Collection, 1994
Left: #5561SS goblet, 6.25" tall, **$18**; **Center:** #2799SS lion box, 5.25" long, **$45**; **Right:** #5562SS pitcher, 7.75" tall, **$75**

Southern Belles #5141, 7.75" tall, 5" wide, 4" long, Mary C. Walrath Collection, **$68 each**
Left to Right: Marianne #3, limited to 286 made Persian Blue Iridized, 1994; Anna #1, Light Gold Carnival, limited to 254 made, 1994; Carol #2, Petal Pink iridized, limited to 299 made, 1994

Cranberry with Mary Gregory style decoration, limited to 1500, Designed by Martha Reynolds, 1998
Left: Pitcher #3275DM, "Bird Watcher," 6.5" tall, **$85**;
Center: Basket #1533DI, "Breezy Day," 11.5" tall, **$98**;
Right: Perfume #2906RK, "The Swan," **$65**

Cranberry with Mary Gregory style decoration, Limited to 1500, Designed by Martha Reynolds, 1997
Left: Basket #1539DQ, "Swinging," 8" tall, **$85**;
Center: Fairy light #1505DW, "Meadow Flowers," 4.75" tall, **$75**;
Right: Guest set #1500DI, "Breezy Day," 7.5" tall, **$115**

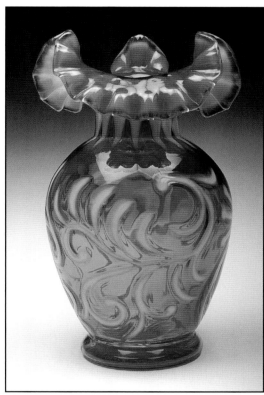

Buttons and Braids #3558CR vase, 8.5" tall, Cranberry Opalescent, George Fenton signature, Showcase Dealer exclusive, 1995, **$125**

#5220 pig, 2.5" tall
Top Left: Heav'n N Nature Sing, Opal satin, hand painted, 1985 to 1986, **$28**; **Top Right:** Pearly Sentiments, Opal Iridized, 1988, **$20**
Bottom Left: True Blue, 1985 to 1986, Iridized Blue Slag, 1985 to 1986, **$48**; **Bottom Center:** Sea Mist Green, 1997, **$18**; **Bottom Right:** Red Carnival, 1996, **$28**

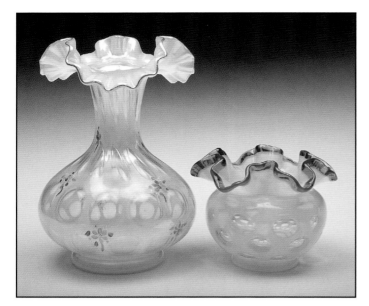

Coin Dot, Made for QVC, 1990s
Left: #C1478C2 vase, 8" tall, Stiegel Blue Opalescent, hand painted, iridized, 1991, **$48**; **Right:** #C1454DB rose bowl, 4"tall, Opaline with Cobalt crest, 1996, **$30**

Chessie Boxes, #9480, 8" tall
Top Left: Topaz, Special Order for McMillen & Husband, limited edition of 88, date **$145**; Top **Bottom:** Dusty Rose Carnival, 1997, **$95**
Bottom Left: Teal Carnival, 1988, **$115**; **Bottom Center:** Sea Mist Green, 1998, **$125**; **Bottom Right:** Red Carnival, 1991, **$95**

Mary Gregory on Cranberry, 1996
Left: #1532RK basket, 6.75" tall, "The Swan," limited to 2000, **$65**; **Right:** #1554RP vase, 9" tall, "Day Dreaming," limited to 1500, **$125**

Miniature flower pots, 2.25" tall, sampled for Martha Stewart, 1997
Top: Yellow Slag, **$10**; **Left:** Orange slag, **$12**; **Right:** Blue Slag, **$10**

Hand painted Cranberry, 1997 to 2002
Top Left: White Poppies #3076C6 basket, 8" tall, 2001, **$85**;
Top Right: #1432 pitcher, 7" tall, pink and white flowers with a ribbon, Fenton Gift Shop, **$60**
Bottom Left: Provincial Floral #3071RG vase, 8.75" tall, 2000, **$85**; **Bottom Center:** #C46114, creamer, 4.5" tall, white and yellow flowers, Made for QVC, 1997, **$45**; **Bottom Right:** #1642JM egg, 5" tall, bird on branch, limited to March 31 sales, Spring Supplement 1996, **$85**; **Bottom Right:** #1218 vase, 9.25" tall, feather shape with iris, Fenton Gift Shop, 2001, **$125**

Ann Stull is a longtime Fenton gift shop clerk. She is a huge help in assisting collectors find particular items when they need to make a phone order.

Heart Spot Optic
Top Left: #1214CR vase, 5.5", **$48**; **Top Center:** #2732CR basket, 7" tall, 1993, **$75**; **Top Right:** #2774CR, pitcher, 5.5" tall, 1995, **$60**
Bottom Left: #2755CR vase, 5.5", 1995, **$48**;
Bottom Center: #4965CR basket, 6.5" tall, 1997, **$75**; #6580CR perfume, 7" tall, 1992, **$95**; **Bottom Right:** #2903CR fairy light, 6.5" tall, 1996, **$135**

Historic collection, Rubina Verde, 1997
catalog June supplement
*Reprinted with permission from the
Fenton Art Glass Company*

Black Snowcrest, Fenton Gift Shop (these
are the plain versions of what was hand
painted for QVC), 1997
Left: #6587, basket, 6.5" tall, **$45**;
Center: #7686, basket, 10" tall, **$54**;
Right: #2454, vase, 6" tall, **$40**

Medallion Collection, on wooden base,
1997
Top Left: #5136X8 Elephant, 3.5" tall,
Cobalt, **$60**; **Top Right:** #5147X9
Mallard, 5" long, Green, **$60**
Bottom Left: #5226Y6 Fox, 4.25" tall,
Black, **$68**; **Bottom Center:** #5163Y4
Bird, 2.75" tall, Ruby, **$48**; **Bottom
Right:** #5258Y8 Owl, 6" tall, Black, **$98**

Romance, 1997
Top: #8267RW bell, 6.5" tall, **$20**
Bottom Left: #4639RW basket,
7.5" tall, **$25**;
Right: #9357RW vase, 3.5" tall, **$15**

Favrene
Top Center: Daisy #8807FR vase, 10.75" tall, brass
lid and handles, Connoisseur Collection, limited to
1350, 1997, **$295**; **Bottom Left:** Seasons #9259FY
vase, 8.5" tall, Connoisseur Collection, limited to
1350, 1998, **$275**; **Bottom Center:** Symphony
#7480FW covered box, 4.75" tall, Honor Collection,
limited to 1950, 2001, **$195**; Floral #9855EV
vase, 7.75" tall, Connoisseur Collection, limited to
1250, 1996, **$195**; **Bottom Right:** Pulled Feather
#9931KW vase, 8.5" tall, Connoisseur Collection,
limited to 1250, 2002, **$275**

#1645 September Morn, 7" tall, 1990s
Left to Right: Peachalene, gloss, Special
Order for Singleton Bailey, **$95**; Rosalene,
gloss, Special Order for Fenton Art Glass
Collectors of America, **$125**; Peachalene
satin, Special Order for Singleton Bailey, **$85**;
Celeste Blue Stretch in cupped bowl, Cobalt
5 legged base, Fenton general catalog, **$195**;
Celeste Blue satin, Fenton Gift Shop, **$60**;
Rosalene satin in Burmese Love Bouquet
bowl, Special Order for Mary Walrath, **$175**

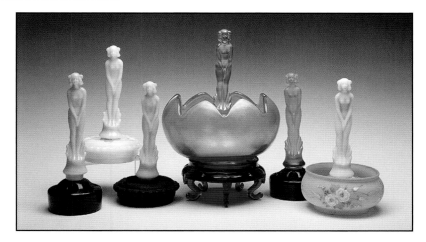

#2950 ginger jars, 8" tall, 1990s
Top Left: Diamond Optic, Burmese satin, 1998,
$250; **Top Center:** Coin Dot, Twilight Blue,
Made for QVC, 1993, **$195**; **Top Right:** Rib
Optic, Topaz Opalescent, 1999, **$175**
Bottom Left: Coin Dot, Cranberry Opalescent,
hand painted, Made for QVC, Bill Fenton
signature, 1992, **$250**; **Bottom Right:** Favrene,
sand carved butterfly, Special Order for Fenton
Art Glass Collectors of America, 1997, **$295**

Golfing scene, Sports Theme collection, 1998
Left: #1502JU lamp, 12.5" tall, **$150**;
Right: #8600JU clock, 6" tall, **$85**

Susan Bryan is a
featured Fenton gift
shop artist. She is found
frequently hand painting
items in the gift shop.

#5249 Santa holding a kitten, 8.5" tall
Left: Burmese, hand painted, 1998, **$100**; **Center:** Tyrolean, Opal
Satin, 2000, **$75**; **Right:** Olde World, Opal Satin, 1998, **$100**

#5299 Santa holding a list, 8" tall, Opal Satin,
Left: Northern Lights, 1998, **$85**; **Center:** Poinsettia Glow, 1996, **$85**;
Right: Olde World, 1997, **$75**

Bear set #5270AX, Plum Carnival, limited to 1250 numbered and
matched sets, 1998, **$150 set**
Top: reclining #5233, 3.75" long;
Bottom Left: day dreaming #5239, 4" long;
Bottom Right: sitting 5151, 3.5" tall

#5136 circus elephant, 3.75" tall
Top Left: French Opalescent, hand painted, 1997, **$30**; **Top Right:** Amber Carnival, 2000, **$24**
Bottom Left: Medallion, 1996, **$45**; **Bottom Center:** Plum Opalescent, 1998, **$48**; **Bottom Right:** Spruce Green Carnival, 1998, **$24**

#5177 alley cat, 10.75" tall
Top Left: Aquamarine, 2000, **$95**; **Top Right:** Country Peach Iridized, Special Order for Levay, 1983, **$115**
Bottom Left: Red Slag, Special Order for Levay, 1984, **$600**; **Bottom Center:** Purple Slag Satin, 1998, **$395**; **Bottom Right:** Azure Blue Satin, 1997, **$125**

Ballerina #5270 Natalie, 6.5" tall, 1998
Left: Rosalene, **$65**; **Right:** Champagne Satin, **$45**

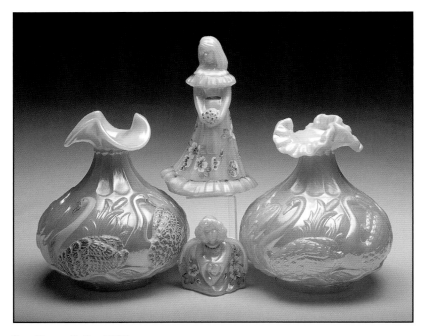

Sea Green Satin, 1998
Top Center: #C52285T bridesmaid, 7" tall, hand painted, Made for QVC, Shelley Fenton signature, **$85**
Bottom Left: #9458 swan vase, 8" tall, hand painted, **$98**; **Center:** #C55335T Guardian angel, 3.25" tall, hand painted, Made for QVC, **$30**;
Right: Swan #9458GE vase, 8" tall, **$75**

Folk Art Animals, 1998 catalog Spring supplement
Reprinted with permission from the Fenton Art Glass Company

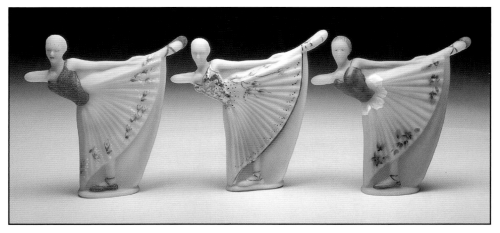

Ballerina #5270, "Natalie," 6.5" tall, Hand painted, 1998 to 1999
Left: Rosebuds on Burmese, Made for QVC, 1999, **$85**; **Center:** Rosebuds on Rosalene WA, 1998, **$85**; **Right:** Blue Burmese, limited to 700, 1999, **$95**
Note: The ballerina was named after Mike Fenton's daughter, Natalie, who was a ballerina. She modeled for Jon Saffell, while he sculpted the design for the mould.

#4683 bunny box, 7" long
Top: Opal Satin, 1996, **$45**
Center Left: Folk Art, limited to sales thru 3/31, 1996, **$65**; **Center Right:** Folk Art, Opal Satin, limited to sales thru 3/31, Spring Supplement 2001, **$60**
Front: Folk Art, Spring Supplement 1998, **$65**

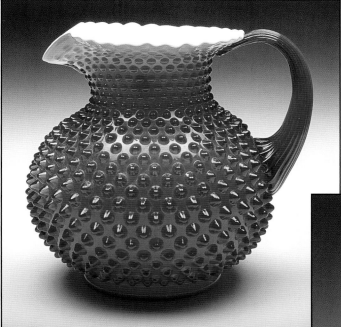

Hobnail #C3967AB
pitcher, 8" tall, Cobalt
Overlay, Made for QVC,
1998, **$85**

Mulberry, 1990s
Top: Evening Vine on Mulberry #5549EM vase, 8.75"
tall, limited edition 1750, decoration designed by Kim
Plauche, Connoisseur Collection, 2002, **$125**
Left: C1554H6 vase, 9" tall, George Fenton signature,
Made for QVC, 1997, **$98**; **Center:** Evening Blossom
#7603MD pomander jar, 5.5" tall, Limited edition 1250,
signatures of all the family members, Showcase dealer
exclusive, 1996, **$125**; **Right:** Mystical Bird #3090ZF
vase in brass stand, 14.5" tall, Limited edition 1250,
decoration designed by Martha Reynolds, Connoisseur
Collection, limited to 1250, 1999, **$295**

Tranquility, Aquamarine, Cobalt
& Morning Mist, 1999 catalog
Reprinted with permission from
the Fenton Art Glass Company

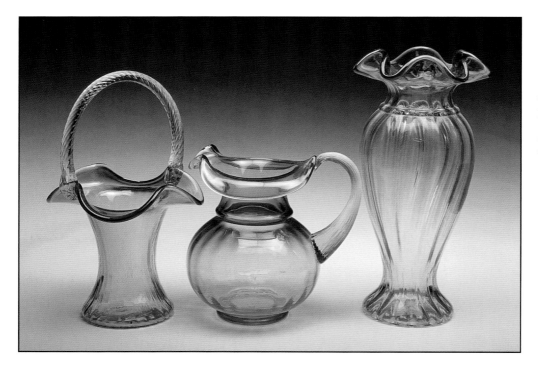

Tranquility, 1999
Left: #3230AL basket, 10" tall,
$75; **Center:** #3280AL pitcher,
6.5" tall, **$48**; **Right:** #3240AL
vase, 10.75" tall, **$65**

Butterfly #C6840KI covered candy
box, 2" tall, 6.6" wide, Cobalt
Carnival, Made for QVC- New
Century collection, 1999, **$50**

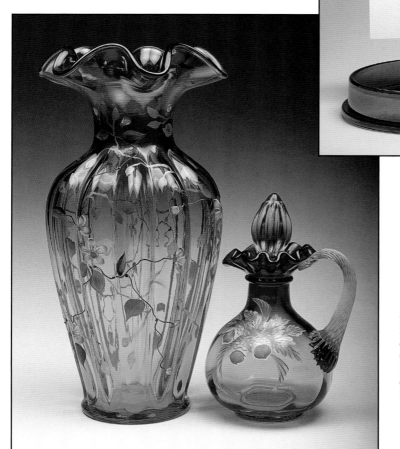

Gold Amberina, 1990s
Left: #3161JQ vase, 11" tall, decoration
designed by Martha Reynolds, Connoisseur
Collection, Limited edition of 750, 1994,
$175; **Right:** #3075AV cruet, 6.75" tall,
decoration designed by Robin Spindler,
Limited edition of 2500, 1999, **$150**

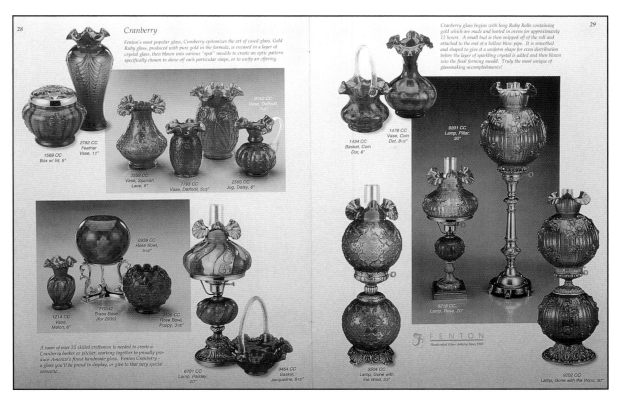

Cranberry glass, 1999 catalog
Reprinted with permission from the Fenton Art Glass Company

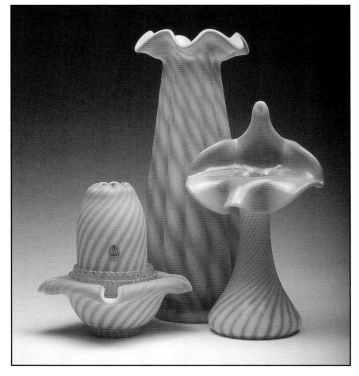

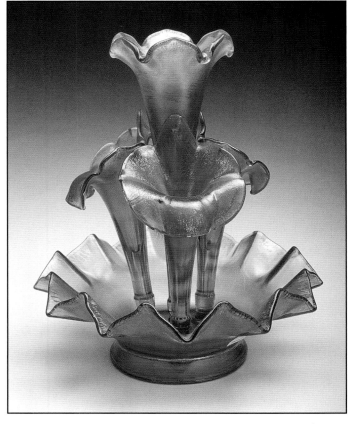

Spiral Optic, Rosalene, 1990s
Left: #CV256R7, three piece fairy light, 7" tall, Made for QVC, 1999, **$125**; **Center:** #C1220RS, vase, 14" tall, Made for QVC, 1993, **$135**; **Right:** #7255, tulip vase, 10.75" tall, Fenton Gift Shop (painted for QVC), 1999, **$95**

#7601XK epergne, 13.5" tall, 4 horn, Violet Stretch, 1999, **$295**

Happy Cat #5277, 6.25" tall, Special Order for Fenton Art Glass Collectors of America
Top Left: Sea Green Iridized, 1998, **$75**;
Top Right: Opal satin with butterfly, 2000, **$95**
Bottom Left: Ruby Crackle, 1999, **$115**;
Bottom Center: Topaz Satin, 1997, **$95**;
Bottom Right: Blue Burmese, 1995, **$95**

Figures on bust off bases (also referred to as on font)
Top Left: #5100RT praying boys (old style), 6.15" tall, Country Peach, 1983 to 1984, **$85**; **Top Center:** #5365TO miniature cat, 5" tall, Topaz, 1999, **$60** **Top Right:** #5243HZ curious cat, 6.5" tall, Pink Pearl, 1993, **$50**
Bottom Left to Right: #5165RU sitting cat, Ruby, 6.25" tall, 1990 to 1991, **$95**; #5165 sitting cat, hand painted, 6.25" tall, **$195**; #5293 lop ear bunny, 6.5" tall, 2003, **$75**; kitten, 5.75" tall, Favrene, 1999, **$125**; #5291 scaredy cat, 7.5" tall, 2002, Black, **$60**

#5225 puppy, 3" tall
Top: new style, French Opalescent Satin, 1999, **$24**
Center Left: new style, Topaz Opalescent, Special Order for Rossos, 1999, **$25**; **Center Right:** new style, Spruce Green Carnival, 2000, **$35**
Bottom Left: new style, Black over Opal Satin, 1999, **$45**;
Bottom Center: old style, Cobalt Carnival, 1987, **$35**;
Bottom Right: new style, Willow Green Satin, 2000, **$38**

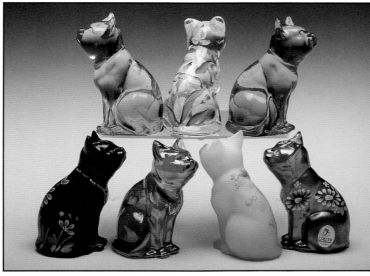

Curious Cat, #5243, 3.25" tall
Top Left: Salem Blue, 1990 to 1991, **$30**; **Top Center:** Begonias on French Opalescent, 2000, **$35**; **Top Right:** Lilac, 1990 to 1991, **$30**
Bottom Left: Black with flowers, 1990, **$35**; **Bottom Center:** Vining Hearts, 1993 to 1994, **$30**; Water Colors, 1990, **$35**;
Bottom Right: Spruce Green Carnival, hand painted, 1999, **$35**

Jon Saffel, Product Designer and Sculptor. Jon previously spent twenty-nine years at Fostoria in their design department. In 1994 he was hired by Fenton to design new products. He loved the designing of sculptured products. Jon has thrived at Fenton and has attracted new collectors to his type of work. He retired from Fenton in 2004 but has continued to do some work for them.

Angels, 5.8" tall
Left: Twinning Berries #5143JX boy, 1998 to 1999, **$38**;
Center: Northern Lights #5144VL girl, 2000, **$45**;
Right: Christmas #5144BM girl, 1997, **$48**

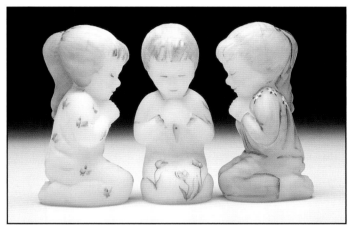

#5272 praying boy and girl, new style, 3.75", hand painted Opal Satin, designed by Jon Saffell, 1999
Left: girl, **$38**; **Center:** boy, **$38**; **Right:** girl, **$38**

Nativity family, 1st edition, designed by Jon Saffell
Top: angel from #5050NA Angel & Animals (angel, donkey and camel), 6.8" tall, 1999, **$145 three piece set**
Bottom Left: shepherd boy from #5055NS shepherd set (shepherd boy, shepherd and lamb) 4.25" tall, 2000, **$135 three piece set**; shepherd from #5055NS, 6.75" tall, 2000; **Bottom Center:** holy family, #5280NF, Mary, 4.8" tall, Joseph, 6.15" tall, baby Jesus, 1.6" tall, 1997, **$125 three piece set**; **Bottom Right:** wise men #5298WM, Balthazar, 6.25" tall, Melchcor, 5.1" tall, Gaspar, 6.75" tall, **$155 three piece set**
Front Left: donkey from #5050NA set, 3.35" tall, 1999;
Front Center: lamb from #5055NS shepherd set, 2.6" tall, 2000; **Front Right:** camel from #5050NA set, 3.5" tall, 2000

#5233 reclining bear, 3.75" long
Top Left: Misty Blue Satin, 1998, **$35**;
Top Right: Dusty Rose, 1993 to 1994, **$28**
Bottom Left: Blossoms on Plum Carnival, 1998, **$45**;
Bottom Center: Precious Panda, 1988, **$60**; **Bottom Right:** Santa, 1990, **$60**

Lamp, Reverse painted #5486, 19.5" tall,
11" wide, Dragonflies in Garden, Fall Lamp
Special, 1994, **$275**

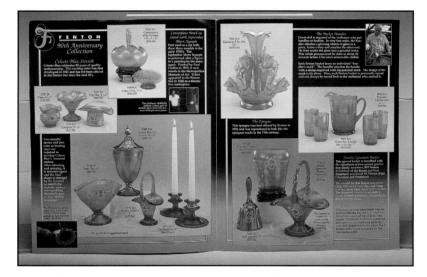

Celeste Blue Stretch, 90th anniversary collection, 1995 catalog supplement
Reprinted with permission from the Fenton Art Glass Company

Poppy Show vases, Iridized,
Made for Singleton Bailey,
1990s
Left: Cranberry Opalescent,
12" tall, single crimp, 1999,
$250; **Right:** Cobalt, Tulip
vase, 13.25" tall, 1995, **$195**

#7601KA epergne, 13.5" tall,
4 horn, Celeste Blue Stretch,
90th Anniversary collection,
1995, **$325**

#5109 Polar bears, 4.25" long
Top Left: Woodland Frost, French Opalescent Iridized, 2000 to 2001, **$28**; **Top Right:** Golden Pine Cones, Ivory Satin, 1995, **$35**
Bottom Left: Vermont Sky, Emerald Green, 2001, **$30**; **Bottom Center:** Snowflake Frosty Friends, Opal Satin, 2001, **$30**; **Bottom Right:** Golden Flax, Cobalt, 1995, **$30**

Christmas at Home, fairy lights #7300, 4.75" tall, Opal Satin, limited edition of 3500, **$65 each**
Left to Right: Christmas Eve HJ, 1991; Sleigh Ride HD, 1990; Family Tradition HQ, 1992; Family Holiday HT, 1993

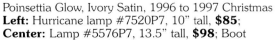

Poinsettia Glow, Ivory Satin, 1996 to 1997 Christmas
Left: Hurricane lamp #7520P7, 10" tall, **$85**;
Center: Lamp #5576P7, 13.5" tall, **$98**; Boot #9590P7, 2.5" tall, **$28**;
Right: Basket #2975P7, 8.25" tall, **$45**

Golden Pinecones, Ivory Satin, 1994 to 1995 Christmas
Left: Bell #7768VC, 6.25" tall, **$30**;
Center: Covered candy #7380VC, 9.25" tall, **$45**; **Top Right:** Fairy light #7300VC, 4.5" tall, **$45**; **Bottom Right:** Polar Bear #5109VC, 3" tall, **$40**

Unicorns #5253, 5" tall
Left: Red Carnival #5253RN, 1993, **$38**;
Center: Burmese #C5253RB, Made for
QVC, 1998, **$48**;
Right: Twilight Blue #5253TB, 1993, **$32**

Miniature Rabbit #5275, 2.5" tall, **$14**
Top Left: Aquamarine AA, 1998 to 1999;
Top Right: Champagne PY, 1997 to 1999
Bottom Left: Plum Carnival PX, 1998; **Bottom
Center:** Violet OE, 2000 to 2002; **Bottom Right:**
Willow Green GR, 2000 to 2001

Bunny #5162, 3" tall, 1980s
Top Left: French Opalescent hand painted,
$34; **Top Center:** Meadow Beauty,
#5162PD, French Opalescent Orange
Flower, 1997, **$34**; **Top Right:** Primrose
#5162DS, hand painted Pearlized Opal,
1994, **$30**
Bottom Left: Salem Blue SR, 1990 to
1991, **$26**; **Bottom Center:** Pearlized Opal
flowers on lattice #5162CD, Easter 1993,
$30; **Bottom Right:** Sapphire Blue BX,
Gracious Touch, 1987, **$24**

Top: Bunny tray #4670, 6" long,
Easter 1991
Left: Shell Pink PE, **$28**; **Right:**
Iridized Jade Opaline EZ, **$24**
Bottom: Miniature bunny #5209,
1.5" tall
Left: Sea Mist Green LE, 1996,
$12; **Center:** Sea Mist Slag 2A,
1994, **$16**; **Right:** Ocean Blue OB,
1993, **$12**

Hobnail Spiral Optic, Tulip vase #CV273CR, 8.5" tall, Cranberry Opalescent, Made for QVC, 1999, **$98** for vase only
Note: This is a Progressive set to show the various steps on how the vase is made, **$600 for set**

Bell Grouping
Top Left: #6662, Church on hills, Custard Satin, 6" tall, Princess House Collector's Edition, 1980, **$28**;
Top Right: #1773, Homestead, Opal Satin, 6" tall, Bob Evans Rio Grande, Ohio, 1994, **$28**
Bottom Left: #7463, Gibson girl decal, Sea Mist Green, 6.5" tall, Coca Cola, 1996, **$24**; **Bottom Center:** Mt. Rushmore, Opal Satin, 6" tall, **$35**;
Bottom Right: Magical Meadow #7463YE, Favrene Cobalt, 6.5" tall, sand carved horses, limited edition of 1500, 2002, **$50**

Christmas Star Series, Christmas fairy lights #7300. 4.75" tall, **$68 each**
Left to Right: Silent Night VS, Cobalt Satin, limited to 1500, 1994; Our Home is Blessed VT, Green Satin, limited to 1500, 1995; Star of Wonder #7300SN, Amber Satin, limited to 1750, 1996; The Way Home RX, Red Satin, limited to 1750, 1997

Birth of a Savior Series, Fairy lights #7300, 4.75" tall, limited to 2500, **$65 each**
Left to Right: The Arrival XS, Green Satin, 1998; The Announcement KP, Cobalt Satin, 1999; The Journey, Green Satin, 2000; The Celebration, Cobalt Satin, 2001

ANOTHER CENTURY BEGINS

The year of 2000 saw Fenton again making a change to their logo to reflect the new decade. A zero now replaced the 9 under the Fenton name. A special surprise birthday party was held on December 1, 2000, to honor Frank, marking 85 great years. As the family was looking forward to their 100th anniversary in 2005, they decided to launch a Centennial Collection. Starting in 2000 and leading up to 2005, each year two of the family members would pick out their favorite type of glass to have made and then signed by them. The second generation of Bill and Frank Fenton led off in 2000. Bill selected a Burmese vase and Frank, a Willow Green epergne. In 2001, Lynn and Scott Fenton, the fourth generation family members each had a piece done. Lynn selected a Nouveau perfume and Scott, a blown vase with a peacock design. For the last three years, all the members are of the third generation. In 2002, Shelley selected a hand painted Coral vase and Christine chose a Favrene Grape and Cable tobacco jar. Randy chose a Black Rain Tree vase and in memorial to his brother, Don, a Favrene vase was made for the 2003 offering. Mike selected a Rosalene lamp and Tom, a free hand elephant for the 2004 offering. George and Nancy's selection completed the Centennial Collection in 2005. George had a Mosaic vase done while Nancy selected a decorated Favrene vase set off in a brass holder.

Reaching out to people on the Internet, Fenton launched their own web site in 2000. Fenton published a new book in 2002 titled, *Fenton Glass: Especially for QVC* to document all of the special pieces made for this home shopping network.

Within the span of only a couple of months, the Fenton family lost two valued members. Bill Fenton passed away on December 11, 2002, after a long illness. A few months later on February 3, 2003, Don Fenton died suddenly following surgery. Jon Saffell retired in 2003 and Suzi Whitaker was hired to take over the designing department. Bob Hill retired from the mould shop in 2003 and Byron Butts is now in charge.

The Lancaster Colony Company made a major decision in 2003 to sell all the moulds that they had obtained through acquisitions from Cambridge, Fostoria, Imperial, and Indiana. Some of these moulds were previously used in the Tiara home party line. For several years these moulds had languished in a warehouse at Indiana Glass. Some were in such poor condition that they won't ever be used. Bob Hill made several trips to the site to evaluate the moulds. Now these original cast iron glass moulds have found a new safe home at the Fenton Art Glass Company. Several thousand moulds were purchased in this acquisition. From the Fostoria Company, some of the identified moulds include American, Baroque, Colony, Coin, and Crown. There are several Cape Cod moulds from Imperial along with Everglade's moulds from Cambridge. Collectors should appreciate the fact that whenever Fenton reissues any of these items, they will be made in an entirely new color along with being marked with the Fenton logo. Even if Fenton never uses some of the moulds, no foreign importer will ever be able to unscrupulously reproduce these items.

Stars and Stripes collection, 2001
Top Left: #2377UZ top hat basket, 7" tall, Cranberry Opalescent with Cobalt crest, **$125**; **Top Right:** original brochure
Bottom Left: #7300F7 two piece fairy light, 4.5" tall, Cobalt, **$65**; **Bottom Center:** #7566F8 bell, 7" tall, Cobalt, **$39**; #5151F6 sitting bear, 3.5" tall, Opal Satin, **$49**; **Bottom Right:** #2376UZ top hat, 3.25" tall, Cranberry Opalescent with Cobalt crest, **$95**

The summer of 2005 brought forth the celebration of Fenton being in business for 100 years. A huge crowd of Fenton collectors descended upon Williamstown. There were lots of different activities to please everyone. Tours of the factory were constantly going on and you could view different pieces being made. Many of the family members led the various tours. Local artists were set up showing off their wares. A lively game of bingo was being played with Fenton glass as prizes. You could even decorate your own ornament or paperweight. There were several chances to sit in on a session with Dave Fetty and watch him make his unique style of glass. The annual Fenton tent sale also was going on. Our favorite activity by far was being able to be inside the glass factory among all the workers and make our own piece of glass. Each class was given a chance to make both a basket and an egg. We felt it was the chance of a lifetime. It is of course much harder to make glass than it looks. We will definitely not put any of their workers out of a job.

As exciting as the celebration was, sadly we, along with the whole collecting world lost a great friend on August 9th when Frank M. Fenton died. As a tribute to Frank, a Burmese Nautilus vase was issued as a memorial in 2006. Stacy Williams designed the decoration.

On January 2, 2007 Fenton celebrated their 100th year of glass making. Currently, Fenton is trying to survive in this turbulent market. As they look ahead to their second 100 years, the Fenton family is again looking at changes to ensure that the company is still here for the next century. One of them is dividing the company into three divisions to attract different types of customers. The main emphasis will still be their regular art glass lines, but they are expanding to have a Studio Glass line and Artware line. The Studio division will encompass the contemporary artistry of Dave Fetty along with Kelsey Murphy and Robert Bomkamp, former cameo artists at Pilgrim Glass. The Fenton Artware division will incorporate products from around the world and then accent with Fenton glass pieces that reflect a simpler and cleaner design. For now they will be using their own moulds to make the glass. In the future, they could have moulds developed and glass made over seas. But according to Scott Fenton, "Under no circumstances will they send any of their existing moulds to China, since they would never get them back".

Stop and think: Fenton Glass is here when many of the companies they once competed with are now gone. Some of these companies include Cambridge, Fostoria, Heisey, Imperial, New Martinsville, Paden City, Viking, and Westmoreland. Why are these companies gone and yet Fenton is still here? One reason is Fenton's well known ability to adapt to the ever changing needs and wants of the American consumer. Another reason is the company is still family owned and they all care about their products. A portion of Fenton Luck has also entered into many situations where being at the right place at the right time also helped.

We commend them for all their efforts and look forward to the next 100 years!

Nancy Fenton, Director of Design and George Fenton, President of Fenton Art Glass
George, son of the late Frank Fenton, grew up around the factory and did numerous different jobs. After uncle Bill stepped down as president in 1986, George assumed the position. Nancy and George were married in 1972. Nancy was hired by Fenton in 1982 and has been part of product development ever since. Their granddaughter, Audrey, was dressed up like an angel and featured in the 2005 catalog. For the Centennial Collection, Nancy chose a piece of Favrene and George, a Mosaic vase.

Centennial Collection, 2000 to 2005
Left: Early Vintage #4305QQ lamp, 13" tall, Rosalene, decoration designed by CC Hardman, Mike Fenton signature, 2004, **$280; Center:** #5460G1 epergne, 15" tall, Willow Green Opalescent, Frank Fenton signature, 2000, **$350; Right:** Manuscript Floral #4177ZH amphora vase in brass stand, 14" tall, Favrene, decoration designed by Frances Burton, Nancy Fenton signature, **$395**

Centennial Collection, 2000 to 2005
Top: Myriad #43541N vase, 6.5" tall, Mosaic, George Fenton signature, 2005, **$385**; Rainforest #8970DJ vase, 7.75" tall, Black, decoration designed by Robin Spindler, Randy Fenton signature, **$98**; Autumn Leaves #2743V8 vase, 7" tall, Coral, decoration designed by Stacy Williams, Shelley Fenton signature, 2002, **$135**; Peacock #8808KC vase, 7.5" tall, Aubergine, decoration designed by Robin Spindler, Scott Fenton signature, 2001, **$175**
Bottom: At Woodland's Edge #4259Z6 vase, 9" tall, Favrene, decoration designed by Robin Spindler, Don Fenton signature, 2003, **$260**; Elephant #5036D2, 5" tall, Cobalt, Milk Glass and Black, Tom Fenton signature, 2004, **$185**; Grape and Cable #9188FN tobacco jar, 7" tall, Favrene, Christine Fenton signature, 2002, **$150**; Nouveau Floral #5306TJ perfume, 6" tall, Pink Chiffon, decoration designed by Stacy Williams, 2001, Lynn Fenton signature, **$150**; Rose Poppy #4855WL vase, 10.25" tall, Burmese, decoration designed by Frances Burton, Bill Fenton signature, 2000, **$175**

Celebrating 95th anniversary, 2000 store display sign
Reprinted with permission from the Fenton Art Glass Company

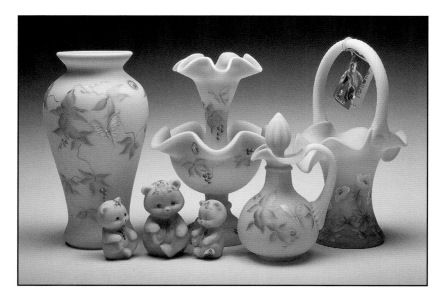

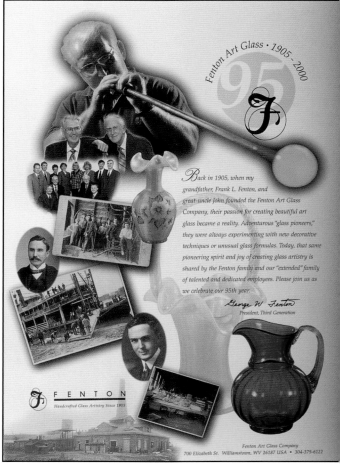

Lotus Mist, formula developed by Wayne King
Back Left: Berry and Butterfly #2955VF, vase, 9.5" tall, 2000, **$85**; **Center:** Berry and Butterfly #6509VF, epergne, 9.5" tall, 2000, **$125**; **Right:** Dancing Wildflowers #6831ZM, basket, 10" tall, Tom Fenton signature, Glass Messenger Exclusive, 2000, **$125**
Front: #5051 baby Bear, 3" tall, eyes open, Special Order for E-Group, 2001, **$30**; #5151 sitting bear, 3.75" tall, Special Order for E-Group, 2001, 2001 **$40**; #5051 baby bear, 3" tall, eyes closed, Special Order for E-Group, 2001, **$30**; Berry and Butterfly #2985VF cruet, 7" tall, 2000, **$80**

#5271 butterfly, 4.1" tall, designed by Jon Saffell, 2000
Top: Empress Rose, **$35**; **Left:** Aquamarine, **$35**;
Right: Violet, **$35**

Red Carnival, 2000 to 2004
Back: Holly #5487RC plate, 10.5" wide, Frank Fenton's 85th
birthday, 2000, **$98**
Left: Chessie #9480 basket, 9" tall, Special order for Jillian
Collection, 2003, **$150**; **Center:** Founder's #1909RN tumbler,
4.25, 2004, **$25**; **Right:** Founder's #1909RN pitcher, 7.5" tall,
2004, **$175**

Help Celebrate Frank M. Fenton's
85th Birthday
with a "birthday card shower"!!

On December 1, 2000, Frank M. Fenton will celebrate his 85th birthday. Frank began working at the Fenton Art Glass Company in the mid-1930s. After the death of their father, Frank L. Fenton, in 1948, Frank became company President and his brother Bill became Vice-President. For several decades, Frank was deeply involved in every area of Fenton glass. He was ultimately responsible for all aspects of glass production from color chemistry and product design to work scheduling and labor negotiations! Frank served as Chairman of the Board from 1978-1986 and then retired to the position of Historian.

For many years, Frank has been a great friend to glass collectors. He has given numerous talks and informative seminars at club conventions, and he has helped many clubs with convention souvenirs made by Fenton Art Glass. Dozens of books on American glass mention Frank in their "acknowledgements" sections, and he has been very generous in sharing his time and expertise with many aspiring authors and glass researchers.

You can help us celebrate Frank's birthday. We'd like to surprise him with a "birthday card shower" on the big day, Friday, December 1, 2000.

Please *do not* put Frank's name on the outside of the envelope! Send your card addressed as follows:

James Measell, Associate Historian
Fenton Art Glass Company
700 Elizabeth Street
Williamstown, WV 26187

Fenton employees will decorate the office area with the birthday cards you send. Imagine Frank's surprise when he comes to the factory on December 1, 2000!

Happy 85th Birthday for Frank Fenton, 2000 brochure
Reprinted with permission from the Fenton Art Glass Company

Scene in the factory: glass blower, Mike Sine

Tom Fenton, Vice President of Manufacturing.
Tom is the son of the late Frank Fenton and, like brother George, grew up around the factory. He oversaw the factory expansion and furnace reconstruction. Tom selected a free hand elephant for his piece in the Centennial Collection. Even though Tom recently retired, he still checks on projects at the factory.

Diamond Lattice #4808T8 epergne, 10" tall, Topaz Carnival with purple crest, 2001, **$275**

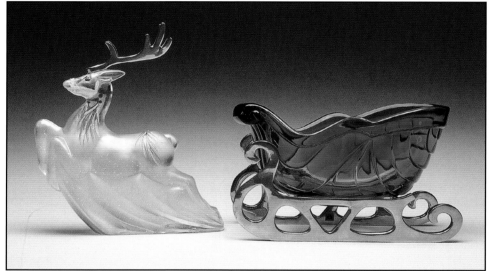

Left: Woodland Frost #5261FE reindeer, 7.5" tall, French Opalescent Iridized, 2000, **$45**; **Right:** #4695SO sleigh, 4.75" tall, Spruce Green, 2000, **$45**

Hand painted Topaz
Left: Lily Trail on Topaz Opalescent #7391BK vase, 7" tall, set on black base, 2001, **$125**; **Center:** Hydrangeas on Topaz #9550TP, fan vase, 8.75" tall, Family Signature series, Tom Fenton signature, Topaz Opalescent, 1997, **$140**; **Right:** Lemonade #1508UJ tumble up, 8.75" tall, Connoisseur collection, limited to 1950, 2002, Topaz Opalescent, **$175**

#5265 miniature rooster, 2.8" tall, designed by Jon Saffell
Top Left: Violet, 2001, **$9**; **Top Right:** Aquamarine, 2000, **$9**
Bottom Left: Blue Topaz, 2001, **$10**; Sea Mist Green, 1996, **$12**; **Bottom Right:** Empress Rose, 1999, **$10**; Chiffon Pink, 1999, **$12** (This is a diachromatic color. It is really a bubble gum like pink color under natural lighting and not the blue color it appears here under a flash.)

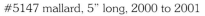

#5147 mallard, 5" long, 2000 to 2001
Top Left: Burmese, hand painted, Made for QVC, 2001, **$45**;
Top Right: Opal satin, hand painted, 2000, **$35**
Bottom Left: Willow Green Iridized, 2000, **$25**; **Bottom Center:** Burmese satin, 2001, **$28**; **Bottom Right:** Willow Green Iridized, hand painted, Made for QVC, 2000, **$35**

#5142 raccoon, 3.5" tall, 2000
Left: Rosalene, **$35**; **Center:** Opal Satin, natural painted, Made for QVC, 2000, **$48**; **Right:** Topaz Opalescent, Made for Rossos, 2000, **$30**

#5065 stylized cat, 5" tall
Top Left: Aquamarine, 1999 to 2000, **$20**;
Top Right: Empress Rose, 2000 to 2001, **$24**
Bottom Left: Amber, 2001, **$20**; **Bottom Center:** Symphony on Favrene, 2001, **$75**; **Bottom Right:** Sweet Harvest, Opal Satin, 2000, **$45**

#5365 miniature kitten, 2.75" tall, designed by Jon Saffell
Top Left: Ice Blue, 2000, **$15**; **Top Right:** Violet, 2000, **$15**
Bottom Left: Empress Rose, 2000, **$15**; **Bottom Center:**
Sea Green Satin, 1999, **$18**; **Bottom Right:** Damask Rose on
Red Carnival, 2001, **$24**

#5251 miniature sitting bear, 2.75" tall, designed by Jon Saffell
Left: Willow Green, 2001, **$12**; **Center:** Hugs for You, Violet,
2001, **$20**; **Right:** Cobalt Satin, 2000, **$12**

Fenton family today
Back Left to Right: Randy Fenton; Mike
Fenton; George Fenton; Tom Fenton;
Scott Fenton
Front Left to Right: Shelley Fenton Ash;
Christine Fenton; Nancy Fenton; Lynn
Fenton Erb
Photo reprinted with permission from the
Fenton Art Glass Company

Rick Maidens, gatherer. His job is to gather
the molten glass so it can be worked.

#5328 Little Sister, 6.8"tall,
designed by Jon Saffell
Left: Blue Topaz, 2001, **$35**;
Right: Violet Satin, hand
painted, Showcase Dealer
exclusive, 1999, **$48**

Little Sister #5328, 6.8" tall
Top Left: Apples and Leaves,
Ivory Iridized, Made for QVC,
Shelley Fenton signature, 2001,
$49; **Top Right:** Burmese satin
with purple flowers, Fenton Gift
Shop Exclusive, 2006, **$65**
Bottom Left: White flowers on
Violet Satin, Showcase Dealer
Exclusive, 1999, **$60**; **Bottom
Center:** Blue Topaz Satin, 2001,
$35; **Bottom Right:** Daisies
on Empress Rose Satin, General
Catalog, 2000, **$45**

#5257 standing rooster, 7" tall
Left: Folk Art, Black, 2001, **$125**;
Right: Opal Satin, hand painted, 2000, **$100**

Rooster, #5292, 5.25" tall, designed by Jon Safell
Left: Opal Satin, 2000, **$45**; **Center:** Black, 2001, **$45**;
Right: Opal Satin, 1998, **$45**

Jungle Cats #5065 stylized cat, 5" tall, designed by Jon Saffell,
2001
Left: Leopard, Opal Satin, **$40**; **Center:** Panther, Black, **$35**;
Right: Tiger, Opal Satin, **$40**

Folk Art #4580OM lamb box, 4.5" long, limited to sales thru 3/31,
decoration by Robin Spindler, Spring Supplement 2001, **$45**

#5267 penguin, 4.25" tall,
designed by Jon Saffell
Left: Favrene, hand painted,
QVC, 2001, **$65**; **Center:**
Crystal Iridized, 2000, **$35**;
Magnolia Holiday, Green,
2000, **$28**; **Right:** "Sunny"
Frosty Friends, Opal Satin,
2001, **$35**

Pam Dick, museum storage
Pam began at Fenton in 1978 as a decorator but went on to work in several departments. Currently she is carrying on a job Frank M. Fenton assigned to her, maintaining the museum storage area. This involves cataloging each item, along with maintaining a data base for all regular inventory including Special Orders, QVC, and glass for other companies and collector groups. Pam does presentations for different collector conventions.

Christmas Star #5070NW nativity Holy Family, French Opalescent Iridized, hand painted design by Kim Barley, designed by Jon Saffell, 2001, **$98**

#5535 Christmas tree, 6.25" tall, Spruce Green and Milk Glass slag, 2001, **$48**

Left: Steve Lamp, gatherer. His job is to gather the molten glass so it can be worked. **Right:** Ron Dick, presser. He takes the glass from the gatherer and places it into the mould so it can be pressed into the desired shape. Ron is the husband of Pam Dick.

Christmas Tree
Left: #5557C9, 3" tall, Crystal Iridized, metal teddy bear on tree, 2001, **$12**; **Center:** #5535ZB, 6.25" tall, Ruby, metal squirrel on tree, 1998, **$24**; **Right:** #5556CT, 4" tall, Spruce Green, metal teddy bear on tree, 2001, **$18**

#5279 Santa kneeling by his bag, 6.75" tall, Opal Satin, designed by Jon Saffell
Left: Americana, 2000, **$85**; **Center:** Enchantment, 1999, **$85**; **Right:** Northwoods, 2001, **$90**

Mike Fenton, Safety Director and Purchasing Manager
Mike is son of the late Frank Fenton and in 1964 joined the shipping department. After serving four years in the Navy, Mike returned to Fenton in the role of Purchasing Manager in 1971. He moved on in 1985 to also take on the job of Safety Director. Mike's daughter, Natalie, was the model for the ballerina designed by Jon Saffell.

Atlantis #5204 fairy light, 4.75" tall
Top Left: Blue Topaz, 2002, **$38**; **Top Right:** Willow Green Opalescent, 2001, **$38**
Bottom Left: Red Carnival, 2001, Tom Fenton signature, **$45**; **Bottom Right:** AY Violet, 2002, **$38**

Sunset, 2002
Left: #5255SX water nymph, 6" tall, Iridized, **$40**;
Center: #F5303S6 ginger jar, 7.25" tall, Overlay, Glass Messenger Exclusive, Mike Fenton signature, 2002, **$95**; **Right:** #F5276SX Asian goldfish, 5.25" long, Iridized, Glass Messenger Exclusive, Scott Fenton signature, **$45**

Topaz Opalescent
Top Left: September Morn #1645, 6.25" tall, bowl #846, 4" tall, Special Order for Kansas City Gala, 2002, **$98**; **Top Center:** Rib Optic #7708TC temple jar, 10" tall, Honor Collection, limited to 1950, 2004, **$125**
Bottom Left: Drapery #2077TO candleholder, 4.5" tall, upright to hold votive, Special Order for PNWFA, 2003, **$28**; Drapery #2077TO candleholder, 4.5" tall, to hold a taper candle, **$28**; **Bottom Center:** Luv Bug #5149 2.75" tall, Special Order for Westmoreland Museum Gift Shop, **$24**; Lemonade #1508UJ guest set, 7.5" tall, Connoisseur Collection, limited to 1950, 2002, **$175**

Chris Benson, Special Orders. She initially started in Hot Metal and moved on to other jobs, before being made head of Special Orders. She works with clubs, companies, and individuals to get special items made for them that are not part of Fenton's regular line.

Language of Love Anniversary, Crystal decorated, 2003
Top: #8019Z5 plate, 8.75" wide, 40th, **$18**
Bottom Left: #8088Z7 candy, 8" tall, 50th, **$20**; **Bottom Center**; #5163Z5 bird, 2.85" tall, 40th.

Opalescent Coin Dot, 2002 catalog supplement
Reprinted with permission from the Fenton Art Glass Company

Blue Burmese, formula developed by Wayne King
Top: Jacobean Floral #F5904G5 tumble up, 7" tall, Frank Fenton signature, Glass Messenger Exclusive, 2003, **$95**; **Left:** #7255 tulip vase, 10.5" tall, **$98**; **Center:** Jacobean Floral #F5293G5 flop ear bunny, 3.75" tall, Glass Messenger Exclusive, 2003, **$45**; Hibiscus on Blue Burmese #5065QZ stylized cat, 5" tall, limited to 4750, 2000, **$48**; **Right:** #CV2701P vase, 8.25" tall, Made for QVC, 1999, **$85**

Special order for Pacific NW Fenton Association
Top Left: Flop ear bunny #5293, 3.65" tall, Opal Satin with pink tulip, 2002, **$45**; **Top Right:** Baby elephant #5058, 3.5" tall, Pink satin with purple flower buds, 2003, **$45**
Bottom Left: Whale #5152, 5" long, Periwinkle Blue with blue waves, 2004, **$55**; **Bottom Center:** Fawn #5160 3.75" long, Chocolate with white spots, 2005, **$45**; **Bottom Right:** Pig #5220, 3" long, Opal satin with pink blush and spider web, 2006, **$45**

Inspirations, "Those who love the Lord Shines as the Sun", French Opalescent, decoration designed by Stacy Williams, 2003 to 2004
Top Left: #5162Q4, bunny, 3" tall, **$35**; **Top Center:** #7241Q4 rose bowl, 3.5" tall, **$30**
Bottom Left: #9474Q4 bell, 6.5" tall, **$28**; **Bottom Center:** #5233Q4 reclining bear, 2.5" tall, **$35**; #5136Q4, elephant, 3.75"tall, **$35**; **Bottom Right:** #7612Q4 basket, 9.75" tall, 2003 only, **$45**

Chessie #9480 Baskets (made from Chessie box), Special Order for Jillian Collection, 2003
Left: Ruby, 8.5" tall, sample item, **$195**;
Right: Red Carnival, 9" tall, **$125**

#5080 Santa fairy light, 4.75" tall, designed by Jon Saffell
Left: beige beard, Opal satin, 2003, **$48**;
Right: white beard, Opal satin, 2003, **$48**

Snowman fairy light, #5940, 7.25" tall, designed by Jon Saffell, Christmas Supplement
Top Left: Melton WX, 2003, **$75**; **Top Center:** Molasses X7, 2005, Opal Satin, 2005, **$85**; **Top Right:** Jingles V4 holly, 2002, **$75**
Bottom Left: Jolly #5268DA snowman, 2000 to 2001, **$30**; **Bottom Right:** Joy #5269DH snow lady, 2000 to 2001, **$30**

Jennifer Maston, Museum Curator
Jennifer came to work at Fenton in 1988
as the museum curator and is still in
the position. Her tasks include keeping
track of all the displays and maintaining
the museum. She loves to talk to the
collectors when they call the museum.
Her goal is to be of assistance and to
answer questions from collectors.

Butterfly Solstice #3244D9
vase, 8.5" tall, Ruby
and Topaz, Connoisseur
Collection, limited to 1000,
decoration designed by Stacy
Williams, 2004, **$175**

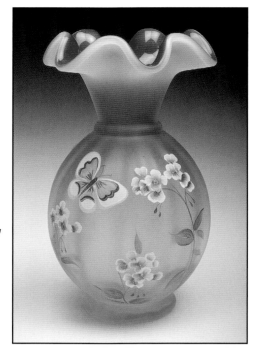

Mary Gregory on Cranberry
Top Left: #1500DI guest set, 7.5" tall,
"Breezy Day", limited to 1500, decoration
designed by Martha Reynolds, 1997, **$175**;
Top Right: #3200DQ tumble up set, 7" tall,
"Swinging", limited to 2350, 2001, **$125**
Bottom Left: #5985MH vase, 10.5" tall,
"Special Delivery", limited to 2350, 2002,
$145; #1505DW fairy light, 4.75" tall,
"Daydreaming", limited to 2350, 2002, **$75**;
Bottom Center: #7424XE rose bowl, 3.25"
tall, "Hello Friend", decoration designed by
Stacy Williams, limited to 2000, 2004, **$65**;
Bottom Right: #8001EP hurricane lamp,
10" tall, "Little Drummer Boy", limited to
1250, 2005, **$195**

Cranberry with Mary Gregory style decoration
Left: Vase #6838EE, 8" tall, "Blue Bells, Cockle
Shells," decoration designed by Stacy Williams,
limited to 1850, 2005, **$98**; **Top Center:** Fairy
Light #1505EC, 4.75" tall, "Purr-fect Pair,"
decoration designed by Stacy Williams, limited
to 1850, 2005, **$75**; **Bottom Center:** Basket
#2989Y8, 7" tall, "My First Pony," decoration
designed by Stacy Williams, limited to 2000, 2004,
$85; **Right:** Vase #1616Q2, 10" tall, "Tea Party,"
decoration designed by Martha Reynolds, limited
to 2350, 2001, **$125**

Frances Burton, Decorating Department Supervisor
Frances came to work at Fenton in 1973 and was trained under Louise Piper. Later, she trained other new decorators and became a designer. In 1991 she took over her current position. The last full Burmese line in the catalog, Let's Bee Burmese, was designed by Frances in 2003. She frequently uses ideas from her granddaughter's activities to incorporate into her designs. The 2007 Ruby Mary Gregory pitcher shows a young lady raking leaves. Other recent designs include Streamside on Blue Burmese and Paisley Mystery vase.

Inspirations, "Star Light, Star bright...," 2004 catalog
Jackson Fenton with his delightful smile is featured in this collection. He is the son of Grace and Scott Fenton.
Reprinted with permission from the Fenton Art Glass Company

Sand carved vases, decoration designed by Frances Burton
Left: Elephant Walk #2744E6 vase, 8.25" tall, Connoisseur Collection, limited to 1250, 2005, **$250**; **Right:** Mother's Love #4861DB vase, 6.25" tall, Connoisseur Collection, limited to 1500, 2006, **$225**

Periwinkle Blue, 2004
Top: Chanticleer #5077, 10.25" tall, **$650**
Center: #2752 urn, 8.25" tall, **$130;** Atlantis #5150 vase, 6.5" tall, satin finish, **$80**
Bottom: #5134 snail, 3" tall, **$30**; #9499 logo, 5" long, **$35**; #5937 paneled basket, 9.75" tall, **$65**; #9071 paneled candlestick, 8.5" tall, **$35**; Mermaid #8254 vase, 6.5" tall, satin finish, **$175**

Dave Fetty, Studio Fenton
Dave learned his glass skills at Blenko Glass. He came to work for Fenton in 1965. Through the years he has been involved in many projects. It seems ironic that Dave officially retired in 1999 but still manages to stay very busy at Fenton. He assists in designing new products and training glass workers. For 2007, Dave had taken on another role of developing the new division of Fenton called Studio Fenton. Old techniques were revived, along with learning new skills to apply to unique shapes.

Dave Fetty free hand designs, 2000 to 2005
Top: dinosaur, 8" long, Orange, **$100**
Bottom Left: fish vase, 6.75" tall, Periwinkle and Milk Glass, **$175**;
Bottom Center: #8813DO vase 7" tall, limited to 450, **$250**;
Bottom Right: vase, 7" tall, Aventurine Green with Blue Vasa Murrhina, **$125**

Hanging Hearts, Free hand, Dave Fetty designs
Top: Hat Vase, 4" tall, Ruby over Milk Glass, 2008, **$100**;
Left: Vase, 7.5" tall, Cobalt and Black over Milk Glass, 2009, **$245**;
Right: Pitcher, 8.25" tall, Cobalt over Milk Glass, 2010, **$98**

Free hand, Made by Dave Fetty
Top: Mushroom, Hanging Heart, 3.5" tall, 4.5" wide, Ruby and Milk Glass, 2006, **$115**
Bottom Left: Hat vase, Mosaic and Black, 4.5" tall, 5.5" wide, Made for Kansas City Gala, 2007, **$98**; **Bottom Right:** Pumpkin, Hanging Heart, 5" tall, 6" wide, Orange Slice with Black, 2011, **$125**

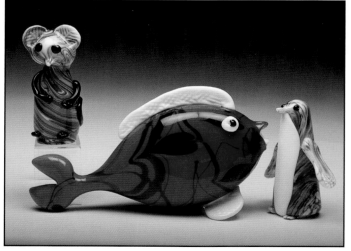

Free hand animals by Dave Fetty, 2008
Left: Mouse, 4" tall, **$95**; **Center:** Fish, 4.25" tall, 8.25" long, **$165**; **Right:** Penguin, 4" tall, **$95**

Suzi Whitaker, Designer
Suzi had previously worked in graphic design and advertising. She came to work at Fenton in 2003 and worked part time with Jon Saffell. After he retired in 2004, Suzi took over his job full time. Suzi loves working with clay to develop her ideas. Recent creations at Fenton include bunny box, cat ring holder, dancing lady urn, dragon, lamb, purse box and song bird

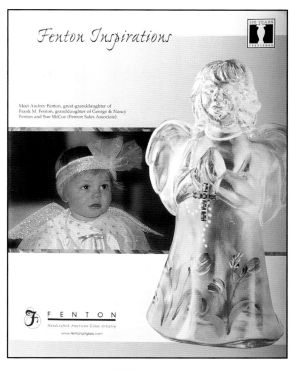

Fenton Inspirations, 2005 catalog
Shown on this page is the adorable Audrey Fenton, dressed up like an angel. She is the granddaughter of Nancy and George Fenton
Reprinted with permission from the Fenton Art Glass Company

Tour group at factory. This group of collectors gets to see the many steps involved during the making of glass.

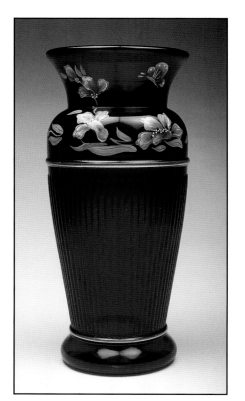

Adam's Rib vase #6656, 9.5" tall, Landmark Collection, pillar shape, hand painted white flowers, Cobalt, George Fenton signature, limited to 5000, 2006, **$85**

True Blue on Milk Glass, 2005
Top Center: #6833FV basket, 8.5" tall, $79
Left: #6667FV pitcher, 8" tall, **$99**;
Bottom Center: #9667FV bell, 7" tall, **$36**;
Right: #6656FV vase, 9.5" tall, **$79**

Centennial Exclusives, 2005
Left: #5177 alley cat, 10.5" tall, Orange, Special Order for Fenton Art Glass Collectors of America, **$195**; **Center:** Panel and Ball #4388 nut dish, 6.25" wide, Mandarin, **$40**; **Right:** #5291 scaredy cat, 4.4" tall, Orange, Glass Messenger enrollment gift, **$65**

Centennial glass making school, 2005
Left: Ribbed #4228 basket, 7.75" tall, Amber; **Right:** Hanging Heart egg, 4.75" tall, Violet with Milk Glass
Note: At the 2005 Centennial celebration, you could sign up to attend the glass making session. Above are the two pieces we made.

Back Row: Alley #5177 cats, 10.5" tall, Special Order for Carolyn Grable
Left: calico, 2005, **$195**; black & white, 2005, **$195**; **Center:** tye dye, 2005, **$175**; **Right:** Siamese, 2005, **$225**
Front Row: Happy #5277 cats, 6" tall, Special Order for Fenton Art Glass Collectors of America
Left: calico, 2006, **$75**; **Center:** Burmese, 2005, **$95**; #DS508P2 mouse, 3" tall, 2005, Special Order for National Fenton Glass Society, 2005, **$35**; **Right:** Black and White, 2006, **$85**

Sleeping Kitten, #5064, 3" long
Top Left: Whispering Wings on Lotus Mist, 2004, **$39**;
Top Center: Precious, Frosty Friends, Opal Satin, 2004, **$35**;
Top Right: brown tabby, Special Order, 2005, **$65**
Bottom Left: PJ Babies, Opal Satin, 2005, **$30**;
Bottom Center: Star Light, Cobalt, 2004, **$30**; Rosalene with hearts, Made for QVC, **$40**; **Bottom Right:** Blue Hydrangeas Black, 2005, **$30**

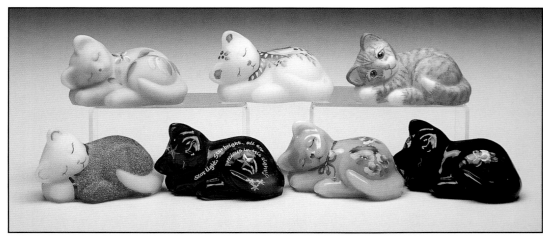

Shelley Fenton Ash, Graphics Manager and QVC Coordinator
Shelley is the youngest daughter of the late Bill Fenton. She first
appeared in Fenton catalogs at the young age of 3 1/2. During high
school and college summers, she worked as a tour guide. She enjoys
designing the company catalogs, supplements, and brochures.
Shelley also develops new products for the QVC program.

Blue Rueven collection, Special Order for
McRitchies, limited edition of 30, 2005
Top Left: #5074 grooming cat, 4.5" tall,
satin, **$40**; **Top Right:** #5151 sitting
bear, 3.75" tall, gloss, **$45**
Bottom Left: #5058 baby elephant,
3.5"tall, satin, **$40**; **Bottom Center:**
#5064 sleeping cat, 3.25" long, satin,
$35; **Bottom Right:** #5151 sitting
bear, 3.75" tall, satin, **$45**

Mosaic, Fenton Gift Shop, 2005
Left: #5151 sitting bear, 3.5" tall, **$200**;
Right: #5168 owl, 3" tall, **$200**

Kitten with ball, #5044, 3" long, designed by Suzi Whitaker
Top Left: hand painted Burmese, 2005, **$38**; **Top Right:**
Chocolate, Scott Fenton signature, 2005, **$35**
Bottom Left: Cranberry Blossom, Amethyst Carnival, Shelley
Fenton signature, 2006, **$30**; **Bottom Right:** Black, 2005, **$28**

Aqua Opalescent Marigold, 2005
Left: Atlantis #5364 bell, 6.75" tall, **$45**;
Center: #96534P rose bowl, 4.5" tall, **$35**;
Right: Plume #59564P fan vase, 8" tall, **$60**

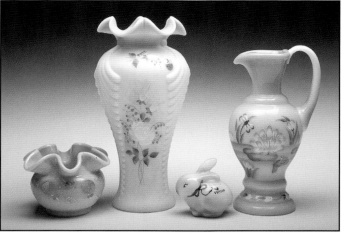

Rosalene, 2000s
Left: rose bowl #7546, 3.75" tall, decorated with balloons, Special Order for PNWFA Convention, table display gift, limited to 18, 2005, **$50**; **Center:** Faith Bouquet #9507 vase, 11" tall, Special Order for Mary Jachim, limited to 55, 2003, **$145**; bunny #5162, 3.35" tall, Fenton Tent sale, 2005, **$45**; **Right:** Tranquil Pond #2968D7 pitcher, 9.25" tall, Connoisseur Collection, limited to 1950, 2003, **$125**

Top Left: Hobby Horse #5135, 2.75" tall, Pearlized French Opalescent, celebrating Jackson's (Scott Fenton's son) first birthday 10-2-03, **$24**; **Top Right:** Sitting Clown #5111CW, "Fool in Love," 4.5" tall, Pearlized Opal, 1991, **$45**
Bottom Left: Hobby Horse #5135, Black, 2.75" tall, **$24**;
Bottom Right: Sitting Clown #5111NL, 4.5" tall, Hand painted Opal Satin, 1985, **$48**

Hats on stands, 4.5" wide, designed by Suzi Whitaker, 2004 to 2006
Top Left: #5385ZY hand painted Opal, **$49**; #5385 Amber, **$30**; **Top Right:** #5385XZ Burmese, **$65**
Bottom Left: #5385T7 Red, 4.5", **$49**;
Bottom Center: #53859J Red with purple feather & pearls, **$39**; #5385XJ Black, **$49**;
Bottom Right: #5385MZ Red with 2 purple feather, **$49**

A scene in the factory: blower, Steve Lamp and presser, Don Buchanan

Perfume Grouping
Left: Heart Optic #2760U7, 5" tall, Ruby Opalescent, 2009, **$60**; **Center:** Hobnail, Boxtle #C3386, (combination perfume and powder box), 7" tall, Willow Green Iridized, Made for QVC Museum Collection, 2002, **$98**; **Right:** Honeycomb #5332RN, Red Carnival, 7" tall, limited to 135, 2009, **$75**

Atlantis #5150 vase, 6.5" tall
Left: Periwinkle Carnival, 2004, **$60**; **Center:** Chocolate, 2005, **$75**; **Right:** Plum Opalescent, 2000, **$95**

Petite Bell #7665, 4.5" tall, Turquoise, 100th decoration, 2005, **$24**

Butterfly Minuet on Turquoise, decoration designed by Frances Burton, 2005 to 2006
Top Center: #5980EF fairy light, 5.5" tall, **$69**
Bottom Left: #6335EF basket, 10" tall, **$89**; **Center:** #4694EF bell, 6" tall, **$40**; **Right:** #8155EF vase, 7.5" tall, **$89**

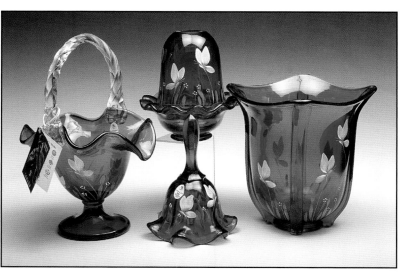

Amberina Stretch, 2003 to 2005
Top Left: #1168RL vase, 5.75" tall, Diamond Optic, 2004, **$48**; **Top Right:** #8329, tulip vase, 7" tall, hand painted, special award at PNWFA convention, 2006, **$65**
Bottom Left: #5951RL vase, 8.5" tall, 2003, **$95**; **Bottom Center:** #6501RL epergne, 9" tall, Nancy Fenton signature, 2004, **$150**; **Bottom Right:** #2753RL vase, 8.75" tall, 2004, **$98**

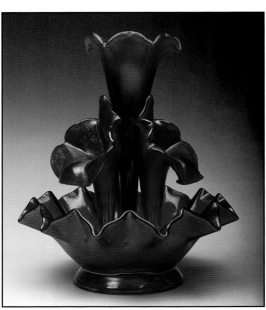

Four Horn Epergne #7601RL, 13" tall, 11.5" wide, Red Amberina Stretch, single crimp, 2003, **$295**

Sunflower #5437YZ vase, 8.75" tall, Plated Amberina, Connoisseur Collection, family signatures, limited to 1500, decoration designed by Stacy Williams, 2006 supplement, **$199**

Top Center: Star Bright #9035SQ paneled basket, 7.25" tall, Ruby, 2002, **$75**
Bottom Left: Mary Gregory #1649 vase, 10.5" tall, Nancy Fenton signature, Ruby, **$295**; Star Bright #3292SQ vase, 9" tall, Ruby, 2004, **$99**; **Bottom Center:** Star Bright #1774SQ bell, 6.25" tall, Ruby, 2002, **$55**; **Bottom Right:** #7380SQ candy, 9.5" tall, 2005, **$99**

Robin Spindler, Designer
Robin came to work at Fenton as a decorator in 1979. Her given name is Judith Kay but she goes by Robin. She signs her pieces JK Spindler which led to the confusion that Robin was another decorator. Recent designs include: Freedom Soars, Meadow Berry on Madras Pink, Mother's Day vase, Floral Cameo on Blue Burmese, Persian Tent on Indigo Blue and Shootin Marbles scene on Aubergine.

Christine Fenton, daughter of the late Bill Fenton. She spent high school and college summers working at the company. Following college graduation she spent seven years at Union Carbide before coming to work full time at Fenton in 1975. She is the Personnel Manager of the Fenton Gift Shop. One of her favorite items is the tobacco jar that she stores treats in for her cats and dogs.

Lynn Fenton Erb, Assistant to the President
Lynn was the first of the fourth generation members to join the company. She came to work at Fenton in 1994 as part of the sales department. She was an active participant in the new company publication, Glass Messenger. Lynn moved on to gain experience in manufacturing and continuous quality. Currently working with engineering and management support, Lynn is always looking to learn more about the company operations. She is also overseeing the responsibility of historical archives, a project that was dear to her grandfather, Frank.

Freedom Soars #8801ZR vase, 9.5" tall, Favrene, Connoisseur Collection, limited to 950, decoration designed by Robin Spindler, 2006, **$595**

Burmese, 2000s
Top Left: Hummingbird #2994QH vase, 8" tall, Connoisseur Collection, limited to 2500, 2002, **$145**; Floral Filigree #4358ER basket, 8.25" tall, Showcase Dealer Exclusive, Scott Fenton signature, 2005, **$125**; **Top Center:** Nautilus #5062BT vase, 7.75" tall, Frank Fenton memorial, limited to 1950, family signatures, 2006, **$250**; **Top Right:** Let's Bee Burmese #6853QR vase, 8.75" tall, limited to 2500, 2003, **$80**; Regal Peacock #8559SE vase, 10" tall, Connoisseur Collection, family signatures, limited to 1950, 2004, **$225**

Bottom Left: Let's Bee Burmese #5293QR flop ear bunny, 3.75" tall, limited to 3500, 2003, **$38**; Patches #5233 reclining bear, 3.75" long, Made for National Fenton Glass Society, 2005, **$45**; **Bottom Center:** Hibiscus #CV476N2 fairy light, 5.5" tall, Museum Collection, Made for QVC, 2002, **$115**; **Bottom Right:** Peaches #F5021HJ pig, 4" tall, Glass Messenger Exclusive, wood base, Shelley Fenton signature, 2005, **$45**

Randy Fenton, Fenton Gift Shop President and Treasurer
Randy is the son of the late Bill Fenton. He worked in the gift shop while in high school and college. With a degree in business management he first went to work with his brother Don in sales. Several years later, Randy went to work in the gift shop.

Coral Bells #4680Q9 rooster box, 8.5" long, Burmese satin, decoration designed by Robin Spindler, Spring supplement 2006, **$125**

Chocolate Glass
Top: Oval logo #9499CK, 5" wide, 3" tall, Made for FAGCA, 1982, **$38**
Left: Cactus covered jar #3488CK, 6.25" tall, 4.5" wide, 2005, **$49**;
Right: Rooster on nest #4680CK, 6.5" tall, 9" long, 2005, **$60**

Chocolate, 2006
Top Left: #4930CK bunny box, 5.25" tall, **$34**; **Top Right:** #5292CK rooster, 5" tall, **$37**
Bottom Left: #5258CK, owl, 5.75" tall, **$95**; **Center:** #5098CK bunny box, 4" tall, **$39**; **Right:** September Morn in Blackberry bowl, 7.25" tall, Special Order for FAGCA, **$65**

Burmese roosters
Left: #5292, 5.5" tall, rose buds, 2005, **$35**; **Center:** Coral Bells #5257Q9, 8.5" tall, limited to 950, George Fenton signature, Spring Supplement 2006, **$140**; **Right:** Coral Bells #5084Q9, 2.75" tall, Spring Supplement 2006, **$65**

#10926 pickle castors, 13.5" tall, Special Order for Rossos, 2006
Left: Daisy and Fern, insert 4.85" tall, Topaz Opalescent, **$98**;
Center: Honeycomb, insert 4.85" tall, Cranberry Opalescent, **$98**; Daisy and Fern, insert 4.85" tall, Blue Opalescent, **$88**;
Right: Fern, insert 4.85" tall, Lavender Opalescent, **$150**

Wayne King, Chemist
Wayne was hired by Fenton
in 1971 to first assist with
mixing and research. He later
became a lab technician.
In 1973 he became the
supervisor of mixing. He
designs new colors to match
today's decorating accents.
The special colors of Blue
Burmese, Lotus Mist, and
Rosemilk were designed by
Wayne.

Bee Wilfong, quality control
selector. This job involves
checking items for any
damage or imperfections as
they come off the lehr.

Halloween
Top Left: Webster #5258ZB owl, 5.75" tall, Black, 2004,
$55; **Top Center:** Boo Boo #5278YK ghost, 5.5" tall,
Scott Fenton signature, Opal, 2004, **$48**; **Top Right:**
Bull's Eye #5085KY dog, 4" tall, Opal Satin, 2006, **$45**
Bottom Left: Goldie #5284PJ witch, 6.5" tall, Autumn
Gold satin, 2005, **$48**; **Bottom Center:** Black Magic
#5291ZB scaredy cat, 4.4" tall, Black, 2004, **$30**; Lil
Punkin #5151QL bear, Opal satin, 2006, **$38** **Bottom
Right:** Skelly #5278YB skeleton ghost, 5.5" tall, Black,
2004, **$40**

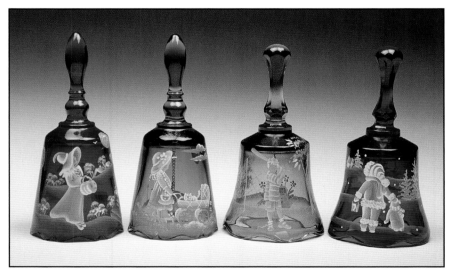

Aubergine, 2006, formula developed by Wayne King
Top Left: Vision #5980JN fairy light, 6" tall, Family
Signature series, George Fenton signature, **$70**;
Top Right: Vision #5469JN vase, 8" tall, **$65**
Bottom: Verlys #9873WL bird vase, 12.5" long,
limited to 1250, **$185**

Four Seasons bells, Mary Gregory style, 2006
Left: #7463F3, "Trick or Treat" Fall, 6.5" tall, Ruby, **$49**;
Center: #7463F1, "Kitty Ride" Spring, 6.5" tall, Emerald Green,
$45; #7668FX, "Batter Up" Summer, Violet, **$45**;
Right: #7668FR, "Bubba's Walk" Winter, Cobalt, **$45**

Scott Fenton, National Sales Manager with wife, Grace and son, Jack.
Scott is the son of Tom Fenton and grandson of the late Frank Fenton. He is the second of the fourth generation family members to come to work full time for the company. While growing up he spent holidays and summers working at the factory. His current job keeps him plenty busy traveling back and forth across the country attending retailer gift shows and signing events. His wife, Grace recently came to work at Fenton in sales. His son, Jack was featured in the 2004 catalog as part of the Inspirations line. Hanging on the wall behind them is a picture of Scott's grandfather, Frank.

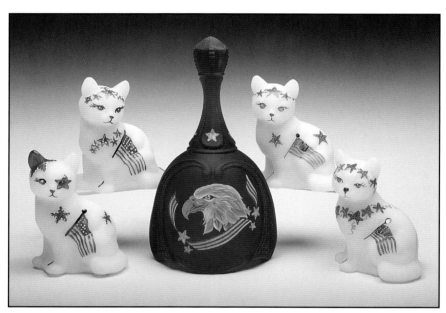

Patriotic, Fenton Gift Shop Exclusives
Top Left: #5165 sitting cat, Independence Day, July 2006, **$65**; Top Right; #5165 sitting cat, Presidents Day, February 2007, **$65**
Center: Americana Eagle #7566 bell, 6.75" tall, Cobalt Satin, limited to 25, 2007, **$95**
Bottom Left: #5165 sitting cat, Memorial Day, May 2006, **$65**;
Bottom Right: #5165 sitting cat, Labor Day, September 2006, **$65**

Patriotic, Fairy Light #7300, 4.5" tall, 3.25" wide, Ruby top hand painted with a flag and God Bless America, bottom piece, is plain Milk Glass, two piece, 2000, **$65**

Bridesmaid #5228, 7" tall, 2000s
Top Left: Splendor, Pink Chiffon (Note: this is actually a bubble gum pink color but it changes color when photographed), 2001, **$78**; **Top Right:** Christmas, Opal Satin with red frit, 2006, **$90**
Bottom Left: Periwinkle, 2004, **$48**; **Bottom Center:** Chocolate CK, 2005, **$48**; **Bottom Right:** Turquoise, Centennial Exclusive, 2005, **$65**

Pat Hill, Selector
Pat came to work for Fenton in 1991 in both the selecting and packing departments. In 1992 she went full time as a Selector. This job involves checking for defects in items as they come off the lehr. A selector is trained to evaluate each piece as first quality, a second or cullet. The items deemed to be cullet are discarded and broken in a barrel for recycling. This broken glass can be used in pots to facilitate the melting of new glass or sold to marble factories.

Bob Hill, Mould Shop Supervisor. Bob began his work in the glass industry at Wheaton Glass. He was hired at Fenton in 1967. Bob was in charge of keeping current moulds in top form along with having any new moulds made. He retired in 2003.

Spring Supplement, 2007
Top: #5361FP cat ring tree box, 4.5" tall, Opal Satin, **$50**
Bottom Left: #5098XA bunny box, 4" tall, Burmese, **$69**;
Right: #4683XA bunny box, 5.5" tall, Burmese, **$140**

Horizon collection, Burmese, 2007
Left: Vivid Poppies #4199MJ pitcher, 8.5" tall, **$165**;
Right: Floral Breeze #4194JV vase, 13.25" tall, **$199**

Spring supplement, 2007
Back: #5739IP basket, 9.25" tall, Plum Opalescent Carnival, sales limited to June 15, **$99**
Front Left: #51697H girl duckling, 3.5" tall, Opal satin, Spring animal collection, **$35**; **Right:** #5169YJ boy duckling, 3.5" tall, Opal satin, Spring animal collection, **$35**

Stacy Williams, Designer
Stacy started at Fenton in 1993 as a decorator and moved up to designer in 2000. Designs for 2007 included Asian Art on Aubergine, Ginkgo Leaves on Lotus Mist, Climbing Clematis on Madras Pink, Spring Sunshine on Burmese and Vision on Aubergine. On many of the Mary Gregory scenes she designed, she utilized children and frequently an image of her dog. She has been honored with an award from the Society of Glass and Ceramic Decorators.

Aubergine, formula developed by Wayne King, Vision on Aubergine decoration, designed by Stacy Williams, 2006
Left: Fan vase #A300040, 12.5" tall, **$98**;
Right: Petal Lamp #4244JN, 18.75" tall, **$175**

Mary Gregory, Aubergine, Spring supplement 2007
Left: Little Mommy #8966D7 pitcher, 6" tall, limited to 1850, designed by Stacy Williams, **$135**; **Right:** Hold Still #7688BD vase, 6" tall, limited to 1850, designed by Stacy Williams, **$77**

Spring Supplement, 2007
Top Left: #5074P6 grooming cat, 4.5" tall, Madras Pink, **$38**; **Top Right:** #50216A pig, 4" tall, Milk Glass, **$32**
Bottom Left: #50635M hippo, 3.25" tall, Aubergine, **$32**;
Bottom Center: #5757DJ horse, 3.25" tall, Black, **$45**; **Bottom Right:** #5296ND butterfly, 3.25" tall, Fern Green, **$39**

2007 catalog
Left: #5066PU hummingbird, 4" tall, Natural Animals, 2007, **$39**; **Center:** #6892H1 Ring pitcher, 8.75" tall, Madras Pink with Black handle, 2007, **$125**; **Top Right:** #5366Y9 lamb, 2.75" tall, Spring Animals, 2007, **$35**; **Bottom Right:** #5293HI lop ear bunny, 3.5" tall, Spring Animals, 2007, **$38**

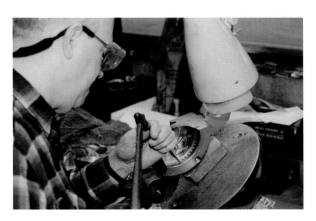

Alan Van Dyke, new mould shop carver

#5063 hippo, 3.25" tall, designed by Suzi Whitaker
Top Left: Autumn Gold, 2006, **$22**; **Top Right:** Rosemilk, 2005, **$22**
Bottom Left: Paradise, Black, 2006, **$32**; **Bottom Center:** Black, 2006, **$24**; **Bottom Right:** Violet, 2006, **$24**

A scene in the factory: Tom Ingram, finisher and Mike Sine, blower

Natural Animals, 2007
Top Left: elephant #5136FH, 4" tall, **$37**; **Top Right:** grooming cat #5074AZ, 4.5" tall, **$37**
Bottom Left: song bird #5363E1, 3" tall, **$39**; **Bottom Center:** frog #5274CG, 2.5" tall, **$37**; **Bottom Right:** Hummingbird # 5066PU, 4.5" tall, **$39**

Kim Barley, Designer
Kim came to work at Fenton as a decorator in 1979. Later, she also trained other decorators. Now in the position of Designer she has taken personal interests and applied them to the glass. New for 2007 is Sail Away in Indigo Blue, Tranquil Sea and Cherry Blossoms on Indigo and Penguins on Ebony. She designed the very cute animals as part of the Flower Power, Beach Babies, and Exotic Butterflies collections, also for 2007.

Artware Fenton, 2007 catalog supplement
This new imported pottery line is accented with Fenton glass.
Reprinted with permission from the Fenton Art Glass Company

Opal satin, hand painted, 2007
Top: pig #5220VT, 2.75" tall, Beach Babies collection, designed by Kim Barley, **$35**
Bottom Left: angel #5014QQ, 6.5" tall, **$59**;
Bottom Center: hippo #5063VP, 3.25" tall, Beach Babies collection, designed by Kim Barley, **$35**; mouse #5148YC, 3" tall, Beach Babies collection, designed by Kim Barley, **$35**; **Bottom Right:** angel #5014QR, 6.5" tall, **$59**

Animals, 2007
Top Right: dinosaur #5056AM, 3.5" tall, Amber, **$20**
Bottom Left: Stylin Stella #5148BU mouse, 3" tall, Opal satin, Designer Figurine collection, designed by Kim Barley, limited to 2500, **$40**; **Bottom Center:** Francine #5226BF fox, 4.5" tall, Aubergine, Designer Figurine collection, designed by Frances Burton, limited to 2500, **$40**; Duffy #5056BL dinosaur, 3.5" tall, Designer Figurine collection, designed by Stacy Williams, limited to 2500, **$40**; **Bottom Right:** dinosaur #5056KF, 3.5" tall, Aubergine, **$20**

Press Shop Group
Back- Left to Right: Tim Reynolds; James Boyd; Dan Sampson; Shawn Snyder; Stoney Greathouse; Charles Porter; Steve Lockhart; Donald Lancaster
Front: Butch Wright

Sculptured Ice one piece fairy light, 6" tall, Violet Opalescent, Special Order for Pacific NW Fenton Association, 2005
Left: #DS9534R, gloss, limited to 119, **$125**;
Right: #DS9534RCJ satin, limited to 67, **$95**

Dancing Lady, designed by Suzi Whitaker, Favrene, 2005
Left: 8180FN covered urn, 9.75" tall, family signatures, **$175**; **Right:** whimsey vase, 6.75" tall, **$275**

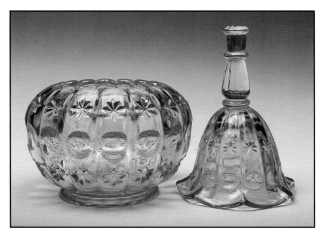

Priscilla #1890
Left: Rose Bowl #56-8, 3.25" tall, 4" wide, Blue, Made for LG Wright, 1963 to 1966, **$28; Right:** Bell #5966SY, 4.75" tall, 3" wide, Blue Topaz, 2002, **$20**
Note: This shows the comparison of the two different blue colors done in Priscilla that were created almost forty years apart. They are similar, yet different tints.

Irish Treasures, Milk Glass with green shamrocks and Swarovski crystals, decoration designed by Robin Spindler
Top Left: #5163JB bird, 2.75" tall, 2005, **$40; Top Right:** #5151JB bear, 3.5" tall, 2004, **$40**
Bottom Left: #5034JB angel, 6" tall, 2005, **$32; Bottom Center:** #5091JB lamb, 2.65" tall, 2005, **$30**; #5064JB sleeping cat, 3.25" long, 2004, **$35; Bottom Right:** #4258JB vase, 4.25" tall, 2005, **$35**

Dancing Lady vases, shaped from #8180 urn, made for Kansas City Gala
Left: Fan vase, 7.25" tall, Ruby satin with gold accent, limited to 75, 2007, **$85; Center:** Vase, 7" tall, Sky Blue, 2009, **$50**;
Right: Vase, Rosalene, 6.75" tall, limited to 49, 2008, **$75**

Vase #C1643E5, 7.5" tall, Iridized Gold Overlay, Made for QVC, 2001, **$75 for vase only**
Note: This is a Progressive set to show the various steps on how the vase is made, **$500 for set**

Baby Elephant #5058, 3" tall
Top: Purple Roses, Opal Satin, Made for eGroup, 2004, **$35**
Bottom Left: Red overalls, Burmese, Museum Collection, 2005, **$40**; **Bottom Right:** Circus blanket, Lotus Mist, 2006, **$40**

Blue Burmese
Left: Christmas tree #5563, 7" tall, 2006, **$49**; **Top Left:** Hippo #5063, 3" tall, Purple Roses, 2003, **$45**; **Bottom Left:** Grooming cat #5074, 4" tall, Purple Roses, 2003, **$40**; **Center:** Flame lamp, 8.25" tall, Made for FAGCA, 2004, **$100**; **Right:** Doll #5228, 6.75" tall, Gift Shop Exclusive, 2007, **$125**

Fairy Lights, Hobnail
Left: #C11677V Cobalt Carnival with Milk Glass crest, 8.75" tall, three piece, footed, Made for QVC, 2001, **$85**; **Center:** #3608RU, Ruby, 4.25" tall, two piece, 1972 to 1984, **$24**; **Right:** #1167, Milk Glass with Silver Crest, 6.75" tall, three piece, 1995 to 1996, **$60**

Peacock vases #8257, Made for QVC
Left: Iridized Willow Green decorated C8257G1, 2000, **$95**; **Right:** #8257 Chocolate decorated, 7.75" tall, 2007, **$125**

Ricky Collins, glass worker carrying glass to the lehr.

Bridesmaid Doll #5228, 7" tall
Top Row- Made for QVC
Left to Right: Pink buds on Apple Green Iridized, 2004, **$85**; Charleton on Opal Satin, 2009, **$75**; Plum Opalescent Iridized, 2006, **$75**
Bottom Row- Made for General catalog
Left to Right: Violets on Rosalene, 2002, **$85**; Christmas on Opal Satin, 2006, **$90**; Roses on Opal gloss, limited edition of 2500, on music box, 1996, **$125**; Romance on Crystal Iridized, 1998, **$85**

Bridesmaid Doll, #5228, 7" tall
Top Left: Raspberries on Key Lime, Gift Shop Exclusive, VIP event, 2009, **$115**;
Top Right: Red Hearts and Roses on Opal Iridized, decorated by Louise Plues (former Westmoreland designer and decorator), 1992, **$125**
Bottom Left: Almost Heaven, Blue Slag, 1989, **$150**; **Center:** Castle on Chocolate (Gift Shop Exclusive 2005), decorated for Marcee Becker by Gail Mullins, 2008, **$125**; **Bottom:** Purple Tiger Lilies on Blue Burmese, decorated by Marilyn Wagner, 2008, **$145**

Tribute to Sharon Bragg
Left: Doll #5228, 6.75" tall, 4.25" wide, Milk Glass, floral decoration with gold trim, special order for Fenton Dollers, 2009, **$125**; **Center:** Fawn #5160, 3.75" tall, 3.75" long, Violets on Opal Satin, special order for Fenton Fanatics, 2008, **$45**; **Right:** Doll #5228, 6.75" tall, 4.25" wide, Milk Glass, floral decoration with yellow trim, special order for Fenton Dollers, 2009, **$125**
Note: Sharon was a longtime Fenton collector, dealer, researcher, and a friend to all. She passed away in 2008. Sharon set up the animal data base on the Fenton Fanatics web site.

Bridesmaid Doll #5228, 7" tall, Special Orders
Top Left: Sunflowers on Opal Satin, made for Classic Glass, Pennsylvania, 2004, **$110**; **Top Center:** Tye Dye, Opal Satin, made for Carolyn's Collectibles, limited edition of 100, **$125**; **Top Right:** Pansies on Opal Satin, made for B & B Shop, limited edition of 100, 2007, **$115**
Bottom Left to Right: Chickens on Orange Slice, featured artist of Sue Bryan, limited edition of 15, 2011, **$145**; Forget-me-Knot on Topaz Iridized, made for Joyce Collela, limited edition of 100, 2001, **$125**; Bronze look on Opal Satin, made for Bronze Look, limited edition of 85, 2010, **$125**; White flowers on Violet, made for Jillian Collection, 2004, **$125**; Valentine on Ruby Satin, made for Fenton Collectibles, limited edition of 30, 2010, **$145**

Lady Figurines
Left: Ellie #C533893, 6.75" tall, 4.25" wide, 4" long, Patriotic design on Opal Satin, QVC 2009, named for the daughter of Shelley Fenton, designed by Suzi Whitaker, **$49**; **Center:** Little Sister #5328, 6.8" tall, 3.25" wide, 3" long, Burmese, Fenton Gift Shop, 2007, **$60**; Bridesmaid #5228, 6.75" tall, 4.25" wide, Lagoon Blue, 2009, **$69**; **Right:** Southern Belle #5141BG, 7.75" tall, 5" wide, 4" long, limited edition of 2000, Burmese, 1997, **$90**

Kelsey Murphy, Cameo artist. Kelsey and her partner, Robert Bomkamp were cameo artists at Pilgrim Glass. After Pilgrim closed they formed their own glass studio called Studios of Heaven. In 2007 they were hired to be designers for Fenton's new Studio Glass line. Kelsey has created some spectacular cameo pieces out of Fenton glass.

Kelsey Murphy design
Left: Falls Gift To Spring vase #8812XX, 10.5" tall, Ruby, 2009, **$495**; **Right:** Holly, Temple jar #7488, 6" tall, 4" wide, limited to 350, 2009, **$275**
Front: Bird #5163HB, 2.75" tall, 2.5" wide, 4" long, Green Carnival, limited to 500, 2009, **$95**

Kelsey Murphy design
Left: Panda vase #34142Z, 4.75" tall, 5.5" wide, Milk Glass over Black, 2009, **$450**; **Right:** Panda, Bell, 7.75" tall, 4" wide, 2009, made from Fenton Burmese cullet at Ron Hinkle Studio, **$350**

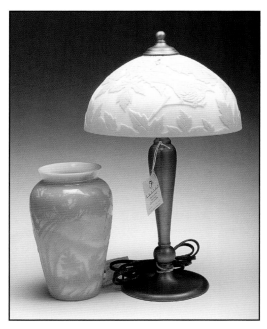

Burmese sand carved, Kelsey Murphy collection, 2007
Left: #7661H2 vase, 8.75" tall, limited to 375, **$595**;
Right: #4350H7 lamp, 17" tall, limited to 100, **$975**

Kelsey Murphy design
Left: Burmese vase, 6" tall, 6.5" wide, Greek goddess, sample vase for PNWFA convention auction, 2008, **$500**;
Right: Ruby vase, Roses, 5" tall, 6" wide, sample vase for PNWFA convention auction, 2009, **$450**

Frank Workman, artist.
Frank came to work at Fenton in
1996. He has worked closely with
Dave Fetty to learn all the various
techniques to free hand designs.
Some of his favorites are Hanging
Hearts, geometric patterns, and
threading.

Bird House, Free hand,
10.25" tall, 6" wide,
Mosaic, designed by
Frank Workman, sample,
2007, **$195**

Burmese
Left: Ginger Jar #5057SS, Horse and foal decoration, 7" tall,
three family signatures—Shelley, Nancy & Lynn—limited to 1950,
2008, **$195**; **Center:** Lamp #6200HW, 16.5" tall, Burmese
Memories, Connoisseur Collection, limited to 950, 2009, **$295**;
Right: Free hand vase, 6" tall, limited edition of 500, Dave Fetty,
2009, **$145**

PNWFA convention
Left: Dinosaur #5056, 3.5" tall, 3.75" long, Orange over Opal
Satin, 2008, **$48**; **Center:** Mushroom, free hand, 3.25" tall, 2"
wide, made from Fenton Rosalene cullet at Jack Loranger's studio,
2009, **$35**; **Right:** Fox #5226, 4.5" tall, 3.5" long, sold by Fenton
as Pink Foxglove flowers on Opal Satin (however it looks like Lotus
Mist color), 2011, **$59**

PNWFA convention, decorations designed by Anne van
Bemmelen
Left: Tulip vase, 7" tall, White lilies with hummingbird, Ruby
Amberina Stretch, 2006, **$75**; **Center:** Vase #4558, 6" tall,
Ocean with trees on mountain, Aubergine, 2007, **$69**; **Right:**
Vase #5983, 7" tall, Giraffe, Indigo Blue, 2008, **$45**

PNWFA subscription animals
Top: Gold Finch #5163, 2.75" tall, 2.5" wide, 4" long, Yellow on
Opal Satin, limited to 433, 2009, **$35**
Center: Girl Hippo #5063, 3.25" tall, 2.5" wide, 2.25" long,
Gray on Opal Satin, limited to 200, 2007, **$35**; Boy Skunk
#5251, 2.75" tall, 1.75" wide, 2.5" long, Black, limited to 172,
2008, **$35**; Horse #5757, 3.25" tall, 2.25" wide, 4" long, Brown
on Opal Satin, limited to 160, 2010, **$45**
Bottom: Boy Hippo #5063, 3.25" tall, 2.5" wide, 2.25" long,
Gray on Opal Satin, limited to 200, 2007, **$35**; Girl Skunk
#5251, 2.75" tall, 1.75" wide, 2.5" long, Black, limited to 172,
2008, **$35**; Horse #5757, 3.25" tall, 2.25" wide, 4" long, Black
on Opal Satin, limited to 150, 2010, **$45**

Chessie box vase (made from the bottom) #9480, 8" tall, 4.5" wide, Black, Sample Decorations for Debbie and Randy Coe, 2007, **$145 each**
Top Left: Crimped top; **Top Right:** Crimped in
Bottom Left: Flared out and crimped;
Bottom Right: Flared

Chessie Box #9480, 8" tall, 4.5" wide, Black Satin, Sample decorations for Debbie and Randy Coe, designed by Stacy Williams, 2009, **$145**

Chessie Box #9480, 8" tall, 4.5" wide, 2007
Left: Black gloss with hand painted white kitten, special order for Pacific NW Fenton Association, **$100**; **Right:** Opal Satin hand painted Siamese cat with blue blanket, limited to 76, special order for Debbie and Randy Coe, **$150**

Chessie Box #9480, 8" tall, 4.5" wide, Chameleon Green, Sample decorations for Debbie and Randy Coe, designed by Stacy Williams, 2009, **$125**

2010 TO 2012
STRUGGLES AND DISAPPOINTMENTS

As we were finishing work on this updated edition, the dreaded disclosure came that Fenton was going to cease making glass. All of us Fenton collectors had hoped that Fenton would be able to see it through this economic slump. On July 6, 2011, came the following announcement by George Fenton:

(Williamstown, W. Va., July 6, 2011). The Fenton Art Glass Company announced today that it would wind down production of its collectible and giftware glass products. The company has faced financial challenges since its restructuring in 2007, and recent developments combined to force the shutdown of its traditional glassmaking business.

"The market for our pressed and blown glassware has diminished," company President George Fenton said. "We cannot sustain the overhead costs. Our employees have worked hard and efficiently, so this is a very sad day for us. Shortly, we will begin the process of shutting down our main furnace. Remaining employees will be finishing existing glassware from the company's inventory that will be available through the Fenton Gift Shop as well as the company's web site and Fenton dealers across the country.

"As a part of winding down the traditional business, Fenton Art Glass is exploring the sales of one or more product lines.

"We know that our many customers and friends will have questions," Fenton said. "Our web site www. fentonartglass.com will be updated regularly beginning the week of July 11.

"Inquiries regarding sales of equipment and other assets should be directed to Fenton Art Glass at assetinfo@fentonartglass.com

"Management at the Fenton Gift Shop is evaluating the impact of the termination of traditional glassmaking at Fenton Art Glass. 'The Fenton Gift Shop is in discussions with Fenton Art Glass, the glass manufacturing company, to provide customers with a wide range of samples and special decorations as well as final quantities of limited edition pieces,' said Randall Fenton, President of the Fenton Gift Shop. The annual Tent Sale in Williamstown starts July 8, and the Fenton Gift Shop and the outlet store in Flatwoods, West Virginia, remain open."

Natural Birds, 2010, **$35 each**
Top: Cardinal #5041OZ, 3.25" tall, 2.25" wide, 4" long
Center: Gold Finch #5115C6, 2.75" tall, 2" wide, 3.75" long; Blue Jay #5041C2, 3.25" tall, 2.25" wide, 4" long
Bottom: Bunting #5238CD, 3" tall, 2.5" wide, 4.5" long; Wren #5163C9, 2.75" tall, 2.5" wide, 4" long; Tanager #5363CG, 3" tall, 2.5" wide, 3.75" long

Natural Birds, 2011, **$35 each**
Top: Yellow Warbler #5363AV, 3" tall, 2.5" wide, 3.75" long
Center: Baltimore Oriole #5238AN, 3" tall, 2.5" wide, 4.5" long; Hummingbird–Golden Tailed Sapphire #5066F4, 4.25" tall, 3" wide, 3" long
Bottom: Pine Grosbeck #5115TT, 2.75" tall, 2" wide, 3.75" long; Cedar Waxwing #5041T2, 3.25" tall, 2.25" wide, 4" long

After the announcement was made, Fenton concentrated on liquidating their remaining glassware. Fall and holiday orders were decorated for dealers with supplies on hand. These were sent out as they were completed. Fenton began decorating many of their blanks to have one of a kind samples for their November auction and VIP night. Their new bead production, which was started in the spring, was expanded to now offer over 100 different examples. It was hoped this new line would be able to generate enough income to keep a dozen or so employees working. Other new opportunities are being looked at to keep the company going.

Dealers were offered the opportunity to purchase any blanks to be decorated as a special order for themselves. We discovered there were remaining blanks of Chessie boxes in Opal Satin and Bridesmaid dolls in Opal Satin and Black Gloss. We purchased all of these blanks to be decorated at Fenton. Michelle Kibbe designed our decorations and they were decorated by remaining Fenton decorators. In the Black Bridesmaid dolls we had three styles done: a Witch; Autumn Leaves; and Pumpkin Harvest. In the Opal Satin we had four styles done: Mary and her lamb; Goldilocks and baby bear; Red Riding Hood with wolf; and a Christmas elf. For the Chessie boxes, we had three styles done. One was a Siamese cat with yellow blanket and black train in the background. The second one was a yellow tabby with a green blanket and black train in the background. The last one was a yellow tabby surrounded by yellow daffodils. All of these were the last items made and decorated at Fenton as a special order.

VIP night was held on November 12 at the Fenton Gift Shop. Normally around 250 attend this annual event. This year, being the last one, over 500 people attended. In the morning was a 400 lot auction conducted by Randy Clark for the Fenton Art Glass Company. There were vintage items, along with contemporary and new sample decorated items. Starting at 4pm was the special VIP event. Timed entrance to the back of the gift shop allowed you to choose only one item from a large selection of sample items to purchase. While you waited your turn, you had the opportunity to shop in the gift shop with a 30% discount on all of your purchases. A special lottery was held for the chance to purchase three gift shop specials: Patriotic Alley Cat; Buttercup Alley Cat and Bridesmaid Doll with a red cardinal painted on them. Fenton provided dinner and dessert to all their attendees, along with a complimentary copy of Mike Carwile's new book on Carnival Glass. It was both fun and sad to be part of this bittersweet event. Many friends were seen and new ones met during this time.

What becomes of Fenton employees and family members remains to be seen. Several questions have emerged. How long will the gift shop be able to stay open? As we were finishing work on this edition, we learned that the Gift Shop would remain open until at least July 2012. What will become of all the Fenton moulds? What is going to happen to the glass in the museum? What will become of all the archival material? To the last three questions, we have not been furnished with this information. Two more auctions are scheduled for April and July 2012 to raise additional funds to pay down their debt. More questions will emerge that will need to be answered as decisions are made by Fenton family members. Several of the decorators will be setting up their own studios to decorate Fenton glass. Possibly some of the glass workers can be involved in other glass operations. Retraining sessions loom ahead for many people as they transform their lives into lives without glass making at Fenton. Williamstown and the state of West Virginia have definitely lost a valuable resource and will never be the same again. We wish everyone well as they make new adjustments in their lives.

As this book was going to press, we have gotten some updated information. An auction of Fenton assets was sold to the Fenton Gift Shop. At this time it looks like Fenton may survive and we look forward to possibly being able to buy new Fenton glass again.

Decorator Group
Top Row: Left to Right:
Donna Robinson; Sue Jackson; Charlotte Smith; Jeanne Cutshaw; Dane Frederick; Michelle Kibbe
Bottom Row: Left to Right:
Kim Barley; Pam Lauderman; Debra Cutshaw; Sharon Waters

Scott Fenton, son of Tom Fenton; formerly National Sales Manager. Scott has now left the company to return to his previous profession as a tennis instructor.

Bridesmaid Dolls, #5228, 7" tall, 4.25" wide
Left to Right: Black with candy corns, sample for PNWFA convention auction, 2011, **$145**; Log Cabin on Burmese, limited to 75, Gift Shop Exclusive, 2011, **$125**; Orange Slice QQ, Fall catalog 2010, **$75**; Lavender Satin, Gift Shop Exclusive, 2011, **$85**

Natural Cats, Opal Satin, 2011, **$35 each**
Top: Brown Tabby #5165GC, 3.75" tall, 2.75" wide; Siamese #5039GX, 4.25" tall, 2.5" wide
Left: Gray Tabby #5074FP, 4" tall, 2" wide; **Center:** Calico #5318FE, 3" tall, 1.75" wide; **Right:** Black and White #5243GL, 3.75" tall, 1.75" wide

Michelle Kibbe, Decorating Designer.
She came to work at Fenton in 1993 as a decorator.
Michelle has learned various techniques on a variety of
shapes. She really likes floral decorations. The challenge of
special designs on the Connoisseur and limited edition items
enabled Michelle to gain experience on painting styles. She
was promoted to Decorating Designer in 2007.

Bridesmaid Dolls, #5228, 7" tall, 4.5" wide, special
order for Debbie and Randy Coe, Fall 2011
Top Left to Right: Opal – Red Riding Hood with wolf,
limited to 36, **$99**; Goldilocks and baby bear, limited to
38, **$99**; Mary and Her Lamb, limited to 33, **$99**
Bottom Left to Right: Black Gloss – Pumpkin
Harvest, limited to 24, **$109**; Autumn Leaves, limited
to 24, **$109**; Witch, limited to 12, **$125**; Christmas Elf,
limited to 34, **$99**

#9480 Chessie Boxes, 8" tall, 4.5" wide, Black train in
background, special order for Debbie and Randy Coe,
Fall 2011, **$125 each**
Top: # K9480HPK Brown and gray Tabby with
Daffodils, limited to 22
Bottom Left: Yellow Tabby, limited to 46;
Bottom Right: Siamese, limited to 46

Sue McCue, office and accounting

Cindy Carpenter, Cameo carver

Left: Cameo Vase with Glass Workers at Fenton: Artists – Dave Fetty & Frank Workman; Decorators – Carol Griffith & Alice Farley; Cameo carver – Cindy Carpenter, Ruby and Opal, designed by Kelsey Murphy and Bob Bamkamp, carved by Cindy Carpenter, 9.5" tall, 2011, **$1950**; **Center:** Sitting bear, #5151, free hand with Hanging Hearts, Pink, 3.5" tall, signed by Dave Fetty, 2011, **$150**; **Right:** Hanging Heart vase, free hand, Orange Spice with Black, 10" tall, signed by Dave Fetty, 2011, **$350**

Birds by Birdhouse vase #9866, 8" tall, shape designed by Jon Saffell, Lotus Mist, sample for PNWFA convention auction, 2011, **$125**

Jena Lane Blair, bead maker;
Truda Mendenhall, bead decorator

Glass Beads with Sterling Core, .38" wide, designed by Jena Lane Blair,
decoration by Truda Mendenhall, 2011, **$35 each**
Left: Milk Glass with Violet in Snow decoration;
Right: Rosalene with Mystic Butterfly decoration

Howard Seufer,
former Fenton
employee. He is a
terrific photographer
who has captured
so many wonderful
images for us.

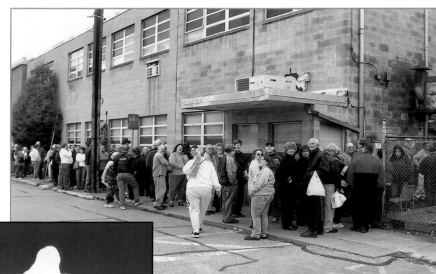

Group of collectors waiting to get inside the
Fenton Gift Shop during 2011 VIP night

VIP Night Lottery Items
Left: Patriotic Alley Cat #Z5177YJHP, Opal
Satin, 11" tall, 4.5" wide, limited to 56,
$98; **Center:** Bridesmaid doll, #Z5228HP,
Buttercup Satin with hand painted Cardinal,
7" tall, 4.5" wide, limited to 86, **$95**; **Right:**
Cardinal Alley Cat #Z5177YJHP, Buttercup
Satin, 11" tall, 4.5" wide, limited to 100, **$150**

Collector Information

No matter what pattern or color you collect, we encourage you to belong to an organization that works to preserve the history of the American glass making industry. All of the collector groups listed below provide information by publishing an educational newsletter, doing study guides, reprinting of company catalogs, doing seminars, holding a convention, having a museum and/or presenting other educational activities.

Coes Mercantile
P. O. Box 173
Hillsboro, OR 97123
Phone contact: 503-640-9122
$25/year   4 full color newsletters featuring Fenton and other glass
Email: coesmercantile@yahoo.com
Web site: www.coesmercantile.com

Fenton Art Glass Collectors of America
P. O. Box 384, Williamstown, WV 26187
Phone contact: 304-375-6196
$20/year   6 newsletters "Butterfly Net"
Email: kkenworthy@foth.com
Web site: www.collectoronline.com/club-FAGCA.html
Info: Convention in August

National Fenton Glass Society
P. O. Box 4008, Marietta, OH 45750
Phone contact: 740-374-3345
$35/year   6 newsletters "Fenton Flyer"
Email: www.nfgs@ee.net
Web site: www.fentonglasssociety.org
Info: Convention in August

West Virginia Museum of American Glass
P. O. Box 574, Weston, WV 26452
Phone contact: 304-269-5006
$25/year   4 newsletters "All About Glass"
Email: tfelt@ma.rr.com or glassmuse1@frontier.com
Web site: http.//magwv.com/
Info: Convention in October

Web Sites

Fenton Art Glass Company: www.fentonartglass.com
Fenton Forum: www.forum.fentonartglass.com
Fenton Fanatics: www.fentonfan.com
Berry Patch Gifts (Joe Berry) assumed sponsorship in January 2011 but a large number of people continue to provide updates.

Chat Groups

All of these groups are by invitation only. Any newcomer needs to be recommended by a member.

fenton_friendly_folks@yahoogroups.com Discussion of General Fenton items
fenton-glass@yahoogroups.com Discussion of General Fenton items
fentoncritters@yahoogroups.com Discussion of Fenton animals
fenton-dolls@yahoogroups.com Discussion of Fenton lady figurines
cameoglass@yahoogroups.com Discussion of Fenton Cameo glass

Bibliography

Books

Coe, Debbie and Randy. *Elegant Glass: Early, Depression and Beyond.* Atglen, Pennsylvania: Schiffer Publishing, 2007

Coe, Debbie and Randy. *Fenton Burmese Glass.* Atglen, Pennsylvania: Schiffer Publishing, 2004

Coe, Debbie and Randy. *Fenton Glass Baskets Acanthus to Hummingbird.* Atglen, Pennsylvania: Schiffer Publishing, 2005.

Coe, Debbie and Randy. *Fenton Glass Baskets Innovation to Wistaria.* Atglen, Pennsylvania: Schiffer Publishing, 2005.

Edwards, Bill and Mike Carwile. *Standard Encyclopedia of Carnival Glass.* Paducah, Kentucky: Collector Books, 2000.

Edwards, Bill and Mike Carwile. *Standard Encyclopedia of Opalescent Glass.* Paducah, Kentucky: Collector Books, 1999.

Felt, Tom and Elaine & Rich Stoer. *Glass Candlestick Book Volume 1.* Paducah, Kentucky: Collector Books, 2003.

Felt, Tom and Elaine & Rich Stoer. *Glass Candlestick Book Volume 3.* Paducah, Kentucky: Collector Books, 2005.

Fenton Art Glass Collectors of America. *Glass made for Fenton Art Glass Collectors of America From 1978 to 2002.* Marietta, Ohio: Richardson Printing Corp., 2003.

Fenton Art Glass Company. *Fenton: Hand Crafted Glass Artistry.* Marietta, Ohio: Richardson Printing Corporation.

Griffith, Shirley. *Pictorial Review of Fenton's White Hobnail Milk Glass.* Warren, Ohio: Shirley Griffith, 1994.

Heacock, Bill. *Fenton Glass The First Twenty-Five Years.* Marietta, Ohio: Richardson Printing Corp, 1978.

Heacock, Bill. *Fenton Glass The Second Twenty-Five Years.* Marietta, Ohio: O-Val Advertising Corporation, 1980.

Heacock, Bill. *Fenton Glass The Third Twenty-Five Years.* Marietta, Ohio: O-Val Advertising Corporation, 1989.

Heacock, Bill, with James Measell and Berry Wiggins. Harry Northwood, *The Early Years 1881-1900.* Marietta, Ohio: Antique Publications, 1991.

Heacock, Bill, with James Measell and Berry Wiggins. Harry Northwood, *The Wheeling Years 1901-1925.* Marietta, Ohio: Antique Publications, 1990.

Heacock, Bill and William Gamble. *Encyclopedia of Victorian Colored Pattern Glass Book 9 Cranberry Opalescent from A to Z.* Marietta, Ohio: Antique Publications, 1987.

Hixson, Myra Coe. *Glass Elephants.* Atglen, Pennsylvania: Schiffer Publishing, 2004.

Measell, James. *Fenton Glass The 1980s Decade.* Marietta, Ohio: The Glass Press, 1996.

Measell, James. *Fenton Glass The 1990s Decade.* Marietta, Ohio: The Glass Press, 2000.

Measell, James. *Fenton Glass Especially for QVC.* Williamstown, West Virginia: Richardson Printing, 2002.

Measell, James, and W.C. Roetteis. *L.G. Wright Glass Company.* Marietta, Ohio: Glass Press, 1997.

McRitchie, Tara Coe. *Fenton Glass Cats and Dogs.* Atglen, Pennsylvania: Schiffer Publishing, 2002.

Moran, Mark. *Warman's Fenton Glass.* Iola, Wisconsin: KP Books, 2004.

Mordini, Tom and Sharon. *Carnival Glass Auction Prices Guide.* Freeport, Illinois: Tom and Sharon Mordini, 2006.

Rice, Ferill J. *Caught in the Butterfly Net.* Williamstown, West Virginia: Fenton Art Glass Collectors of America, 1991.

Smith, Thomas. *Early Fenton Rarities 1907 to 1938.* Atglen, Pennsylvania: Schiffer Publishing, 2005.

Teal, Sr., Ron. *Tiara Exclusives.* Marietta, Ohio: Glass Press, 2000.

Thistlewood, Glen and Stephen. *The Art of Carnival Glass.* Atglen, Pennsylvania: Schiffer Publishing, 2004.

Thistlewood, Glen and Stephen. *A Century of Carnival Glass.* Atglen, Pennsylvania: Schiffer Publishing, 2001.

Thistlewood, Glen and Stephen. *Carnival Glass, The Magic and Mystery.* Atglen, Pennsylvania: Schiffer Publishing, 1998.

Walk, John. *Fenton Glass A to Z.* Atglen, Pennsylvania: Schiffer Publishing, 2004.

Walk, John. *Big Book of Fenton Glass 1940 to 1970.* Atglen, Pennsylvania: Schiffer Publishing, 1999

Walk, John. *Big Book of Milk Glass.* Atglen, Pennsylvania: Schiffer Publishing, 2002

Walk, John. *Fenton Glass Compendium 1940-1970.* Atglen, Pennsylvania: Schiffer Publishing, 2001.

Walk, John. *Fenton Glass Compendium 1970-1985.* Atglen, Pennsylvania: Schiffer Publishing, 2001.

Walk, John. *Fenton Glass Compendium 1985-2001.* Atglen, Pennsylvania: Schiffer Publishing, 2003.

Walk, John. *Fenton Rarities 1940-1985.* Atglen, Pennsylvania: Schiffer Publishing, 2002.

Walk, John. *Fenton Special Orders 1940-1980.* Atglen, Pennsylvania: Schiffer Publishing, 2003.

Walk, John. *Fenton Special Orders 1980-Present.* Atglen, Pennsylvania: Schiffer Publishing, 2003.

West Virginia Museum of American Glass. *Black Glass Encyclopedia.* Atglen, Pennsylvania: Schiffer Publishing, 2005.

West Virginia Museum of American Glass. *L.G. Wright Glass.* Atglen, Pennsylvania: Schiffer Publishing, 2003.

Whitmyer, Margaret and Kenn. *Fenton Art Glass Company 1907 to 1939.* Paducah, Kentucky: Collector Books, 2003.

Whitmyer, Margaret and Kenn. *Fenton Art Glass Company 1939 to 1980.* Paducah, Kentucky: Collector Books, 1999.

Whitmyer, Margaret and Kenn. *Fenton Art Glass Colors and Hand Decorated Patterns 1939 to 1980.* Paducah, Kentucky: Collector Books, 2005.

Whitmyer, Margaret and Kenn. *Fenton Art Glass Hobnail Pattern.* Paducah, Kentucky: Collector Books, 2006.

Catalogs

Fenton Art Glass Company. Company Catalogs. Williamstown, West Virginia: Fenton Art Glass Company, 1950 to 2011.

Wright, L. G. Glass Company. Company Catalogs. New Martinsville, West Virginia: L. G. Wright Glass Company, 1960s to 1970s.

Rosso, Phil and Helen. Company Catalogs. Port Vue, Pennsylvania: Wholesale Glass Dealers, 1990s to 2011.

Tiara Exclusives. Tiara Exclusive Catalogs. Dunkirk, Indiana: Lancaster Colony, 1982 to 1992.

Periodicals

All About Glass: 2003- 2011.

Butterfly Net: 1985- 2006.

Fenton Flyer: 1995- 2011.

Fenton Nor'Wester: 1995- 2011.

Glass Collectors Digest: 1987- 1997.

Glass Messenger: 1996- 2007.

Glass Review: 1975- 1991.

Glory Hole: 1990- 2002.

Personal Correspondence

Erb, Lynn Fenton, Email to author, Fenton Art Glass Company, 2007

Fenton, George & Nancy. Email and telephone conversation to authors, Fenton Art Glass Company, 2007 and 2011

Fenton, Mike. Email to author, Fenton Art Glass Company, 2007

Fenton, Scott. Email to author, Fenton Art Glass Company, 2007

Seufer, Howard. Email to author, Fenton Art Glass Company, 2007, 2010, 2011

Walk, John. Email & telephone conversation to author, Fenton books author, 2007 and 2011

Index